IN A QUIET PLACE

DAILY DEVOTIONS WITH
Jill & Stuart Briscoe

In a Quiet Place

Harold Shaw Publishers
Wheaton, Illinois

Devotions on June 24 and October 29 are taken from *What Works When Life Doesn't* by Stuart Briscoe (Wheaton, IL: Victor, 1976). Devotions on October 8-10 are taken from *Dry Bones* by Stuart Briscoe (Wheaton, IL: Victor, 1977). Devotions on October 12-16 are taken from *Starlight* by Jill Briscoe (Wheaton, IL: Victor). Devotions on November 15-25 are taken from *Hearing God's Voice Above the Noise* by Stuart Briscoe (Wheaton, IL: Victor, 1991). Devotions on November 26 and December 30-31 are taken from *It Had to Be a Monday* by Jill Briscoe (Wheaton, IL: Tyndale House, 1995). Used by permission.

All Scripture quotations, unless otherwise indicated, are taken from the HOLY BIBLE, NEW INTERNATIONAL VERSION®. NIV®. Copyright © 1973, 1978, 1984 by International Bible Society. Used by permission of Zondervan Publishing House. All rights reserved.

The compact disc *In a Quiet Place*, © 1997 by Harold Shaw Publishers, features selections from *The Journey* © 1994 by Simeon Wood and John Gerighty, and is included by special arrangement with Eagle Publishing. All rights reserved. No part of this CD may be reproduced in any form without written permission from Eagle Publishing, 59 Woodbridge Road, Guildford, Surrey, GU1 4RF, U.K.

Many thanks to Vinita Hampton Wright for her expertise in compiling this work. Copy editors: Robert Bittner, Mary Horner Collins, Miriam Mindemin. Cover and inside design by David LaPlaca.

ISBN 0-87788-065-4

Library of Congress Cataloging-in-Publication Data

Briscoe, Jill.
    In a quiet place : daily devotions with Jill and Stuart Briscoe.
      p. cm.
    ISBN 0-87788-065-4 (hardcover)
    1. Devotional calendars.   I. Briscoe, D. Stuart.   II. Title.
    BV4810.B73 1997
    242'.2—dc21   97-15985
                                              CIP

---

03 02 01 00 99 98 97

10 9 8 7 6 5 4 3 2 1

January

January 1—Not Perfect, But Growing

Scripture reading: Titus 2:7-8

People don't just hear what we say; they watch what we do, which is rather unnerving. That's exactly what the apostle Paul says to Titus: "In everything set them an example by doing what is good." In other words, teach the truth and also model it in your life.

Jill was talking to another woman in ministry one day about this whole business of people's expectations. They discussed the pressure of trying to be role models knowing their own weaknesses and frailties, failures and fallenness—stuff we all cope with. The other woman said something very helpful: "We are called to be models, Jill. But we're not called to be models of perfection. We're called to be models of growth."

Perfection is what people expect of you, and that's tough. Generally, they don't expect it of themselves; they expect it of other people. It's an unrealistic expectation. But growth is always possible. It is not an unreasonable expectation that, through all kinds of circumstances and situations, we will learn more about ourselves, about our Lord, and about how we can depend more on his Spirit for help. This is an example we can set consistently.

Prayer

Dear Lord, please deliver me from the unrealistic expectations of others and the undue pressure of perfection I place on myself. Never let me settle for anything less than steady growth into Christ's likeness, in whose name I pray. Amen.

January 2—Today Is Enough

Scripture reading: Matthew 6:25-34

Jesus' lesson here is so simple: Don't worry about what hasn't happened yet. But we do borrow trouble and stress from miles down the road. Will we become ill? Will someone we love die? Will our relationships stay healthy and happy? Will we keep our job? Will we be able to afford clothes for the next season? Our lists go on and on.

Sometimes heavy burdens can teach us a lot about taking worry a day at a time. Chronic pain or illness, for example. After a point, we simply can't carry any more than what one day, or one hour, holds. We might say to ourselves, *Today the pain is not too bad, and I'm grateful. Today will be a good day. I will greet friends, work on work, cook a little, laugh a lot, watch my favorite basketball team on TV. I will plan for the next ten hours ONLY—but carefully—trying to pack the precious moments with right things to do.*

We can learn this day-at-a-time attitude even before we are forced to embrace it by overwhelming things. Today is going to be quite achievable. Tomorrow may not be like this. But, hallelujah, "then" is not "now," and I don't need to live it yet. And I'm glad!

Prayer

Today, Lord, today I need you, look to you, draw my strength and solace from you. Today is all I have. Teach me that worry about tomorrow empties today of its strength. Today, Lord, touch me, bless me, mend me. Amen.

January 3—Handling Change

Scripture reading: Psalm 32:8-11

Having survived years of frequent change remarkably well, I must admit I have found some benefits. Change can be a tremendous incentive for spiritual growth. Changes bring new life experiences with opportunities to discover and use new personal skills. Change challenges us. Even anxiety—possibly the most difficult aspect of change—has its good points, because every anxious thought gives an opportunity to trust God in a new way. With change we have a new start, a clean page, an opportunity to try again. That hope renews us. It's a chance to do it right this time.

Most people like to do things as they have always been done. Our favorite text is "As it was in the beginning, is now and ever shall be, world without end, Amen." I think that more difficulties show up in churches when you try to institute change than for any other reason. I heard about a church that terminated their pastor because he tried to change things. The incoming pastor took note of this and, when he wanted to change the piano from the left side of the sanctuary to the right side, wisely decided to move it an inch a month!

I don't know if there was any truth in that story, but I do know that you have to take people at the pace they are willing to go. If we can see that change can *change us* as we institute it, maybe those big changes will come more easily.

Prayer

When change challenges my comfort zone, Lord, help me to turn to you. Help me to allow uncomfortable changes to change me into your image. Amen.

January 4—"Lazarus, Come Out!"

Scripture reading: John 11:17-27, 38-44

In the lovely story of Jesus and Lazarus, we see a perfect illustration of how spiritual life is made available to a person who is spiritually dead.

Jesus said the reason he came into the world was that he might give life "more abundant." Here we find Jesus, himself the "resurrection and the life," outside his friend's tomb, weeping. What a moment, full of dramatic possibilities! Jesus took the initiative and cried with a loud voice, "Lazarus, come out!" As the loud, clear voice of the Lord penetrated his deadness, Lazarus had to react against or respond to the authoritative command. Lazarus responded to the call, and "the dead man came out."

What a picture of what can happen to spiritually dead people today. The place of your spiritual deadness is your daily existence. Your physical body is the tomb of your spiritual death. Jesus, who died for you, rose again, and now lives in the power of an endless life, is calling to you personally. He wants you to admit to being spiritually dead in your sin.

If you can understand what Christ is saying to you, you can either respond to his offer to live or reject his call and remain in your deadness. Come out! Commit your life to him in order that the power of his resurrection might be released in you through his Holy Spirit.

Prayer

Lord, if there had not been power to obey conveyed in the call you extended, the dead man could not have come forth. Thank you that with every command you issue, you grant the power to obey. Amen.

January 5—What's In a Name?

Scripture reading: Exodus 3:1-15; 20:7

Proverbs says a good name is to be desired more than riches. But what's in a name? "When I tell somebody my name," Frederick Buechner observes, "I have given him a hold over me that he didn't have before. If he calls it out, I stop, look, and listen whether I want to or not." A name is a powerful thing, representing the reputation and character of the person who bears it. This was especially true in Old Testament times.

When God gave his name to Moses, he took the initiative to reveal something more about himself than had previously been known. In effect, he was saying, "I'm knowable. I want to introduce myself to you." In giving us his name, God gives us an understanding of himself that we did not have before. We can never know all of who God is, but we have a glimpse of his true character and being through his name. We must be careful to cherish and honor what it represents.

Prayer

Dear Lord, how could I ever have known that you are a good God, a holy God, a kind God, if you had not taken the initiative and introduced yourself through your name? Thank you for telling me who you are and how I can get to know you better. Amen.

January 6—Circles of Friendship

Scripture reading: Matthew 10:1-4; 17:1-8

Jesus never apologized for his friendships, and that often got him into trouble, even among his closest friends, the twelve disciples. He always picked three of his disciples out of the crowd and didn't explain why. One friend, John, was the disciple "whom he loved." He made friends with people on the fringe of society. He treated even the crowds of followers with compassion. Jesus modeled friendship because he knew that we all needed it, too.

One day as I thought about Jesus' friendships, I sat down at my kitchen table and drew some circles within each other. The outside circle was the space representing the multitudes and Jesus' acquaintances. The next circle was for the Twelve, the next smaller circle for the three disciples, and the circle in the center for his one special friend. I prayed, asking the Lord which individuals in my life belonged in those concentric circles.

As I wrote names in those circles that day, I finally quit feeling guilty about having friends and about not spending as much time with my "seventy" as I spent with my "twelve." This freed me to pursue friendships, to meet many needs, and to be a better and less stressed minister to others.

Prayer

Lord, friends bring light and joy into our lives. They expand our ability to be better spouses, mentors, and encouragers. When I can't find a good friend, help me to show myself friendly to others, and remind me that you are the best friend of all. Amen.

January 7—Spiritual Shopping

Scripture reading: Galatians 5:22-25

On rare occasions I go grocery shopping with Jill, and I love to see the variety of colors and shapes and smells in the produce section. I watch customers pick up the plums and squeeze them. They lift grapes up to the light, polish apples, inspect oranges, look at the bottom of the little green baskets of strawberries. Then they make their choices.

It is not uncommon for Christians to treat the fruit of the Spirit in the same way, shopping around for one or two. Some people are very loving and squeeze love for all they can get out of it. Others are joyful to a fault and spend much time polishing their jokes and their teeth. Faithful people take everything seriously and carefully hold their motives up to the light, and the self-controlled peer under the baskets of their actions, looking carefully for any signs of overripeness.

Sometimes Christians concentrate on the fruit that comes easily to them, without bothering with other aspects of the fruit of the Spirit. So a really loving person is not self-controlled, or the joyful one is not at all gentle. Christian maturity develops as we cultivate *all* the fruit of the Spirit.

Prayer

In all the changing scenes of life you give opportunities for reactions of various kinds. Sometimes love is called for, other times patience. But always your Spirit, Lord, empowers me for an appropriate response. Keep me balanced, Lord, and deliver me from picky reactions. Amen.

January 8—Behavior and Belief

Scripture reading: Matthew 7:16; James 2:14-26

James explored the link between behavior and belief in his epistle, under the headings of "faith" and "works." He insisted that faith without works is dead, reminding us not only that belief behaves but also that correct belief behaves properly. The Lord Jesus made a similar point when he explained that people could be known by their fruits in much the same way that trees and plants can be identified by their produce.

The fruit of the Spirit is most definitely the result of inner workings of the blessed Holy Spirit, without which no such thing as Spirit life would be possible. But there is also a human factor. The Spirit life is a product of both Spirit activity and human response. It comes from our following God's commands to love, be patient, kind, and self-controlled, but it also requires our reliance on God's power, through the Spirit, to make it possible.

Prayer

Lord, if living in the Spirit means responding to your inner working, please help me recognize your Spirit's gracious prompting and persuading, and then grant me the desire and the will to do what he says. Amen.

January 9—Truth and Lies

Scripture reading: Exodus 20:16; Ephesians 4:20-25

Not wanting to insult a fellow member of Parliament, Winston Churchill once accused him, not of lying, but of "perpetrating a terminological inexactitude." We dress up lying in many ways: we excuse it, or we philosophize about it. But a lie is still a lie. And lies—in their many forms—undermine principles that hold a society together.

This commandment in Exodus expresses a positive concern in negative terms. The forbidding of giving false testimony against your neighbor expresses God's desire for his people to love and examine the truth. Although we might think of this verse in terms of testimony in a court of law, the Scriptures make it clear that God by no means limits it to that context. He wants all of our relationships to be characterized by truth and righteousness.

Prayer

Surely, Lord, you desire truth in the inner parts of my life, and if truth is not inside, lies will appear outside. So keep me true, Lord, and then I will do what is right and speak what is true. Amen.

January 10—True Peace

Scripture reading: Romans 5:1-8; 12:16-21

We usually define peace in negative terms such as the absence of tension or living without hostility. When we regard peace only as the absence of conflict or tension, we may feel that the way to peace is by manipulating our circumstances to eliminate stress.

Augustine of Hippo captured a more biblical view in his definition of peace when he called it "the tranquility of order." For the Christian, there are three applications of the experience of peace. We have "peace with God," or spiritual order; "peace on earth," or relational order; and "the peace of God," or psychological order. True peace is that overall sense of well-being that comes from knowing that ultimately our lives are in God's control.

Prayer

Lord, I've tried to get rid of tension, but try as I will, I can't avoid conflict. I'm encouraged to know that the peace you give does not mean the absence of tension or hostility, but rather the inner sense of tranquility in the midst of trouble that comes from knowing you are in control. Thank you, Lord.

January 11—Faith and Faithfulness

Scripture reading: Lamentations 3:19-24;
Matthew 7:24-27

Faithfulness is an integral part of human existence, so important that without it society would disintegrate. Every morning of our lives demands an eye-opening act of faith that rushes us into a series of trusting actions and dependent attitudes. We breathe air we cannot see (most of the time), eat food we don't examine, keep appointments with people we trust to be there, and board planes we trust will stay in the air. Truly we live by faith because we were created to operate in the environment of dependence as surely as fish were made for water.

But faith requires *faithfulness* or it will produce only disaster. Trust a leading pain reliever and get cyanide, trust a banker and get a crook, trust a husband and get an alcoholic, and you will understand the importance of faithfulness and the disaster of faithlessness. One of life's greatest treasures is the knowledge that with God, there is no false advertising, no deceptive business practices, and no broken contracts. He is utterly faithful. Upon this we can build lives set upon a rock; without this we have only sinking sand.

Prayer

Great is your faithfulness, O God, my Father, and shaky at times is mine. Each time I trust you to be who you say you are, remind me to be trustworthy and keep my promises too. Amen.

January 12—Is Meekness Weakness?

Scripture reading: Matthew 5:5; 11:28-30

Robert Ringer wrote a book years ago called *Looking Out for No. 1,* which became a best seller. This was a surprise to me, because most people I have met could probably have written it and hardly needed to read it. Against our culture's emphasis on being aggressive, standing up for your rights, and speaking out, Jesus' teaching that "the meek shall inherit the earth" looks impractical and naive.

The word *meekness* suffers because it rhymes with *weakness,* and the two have become synonymous in people's minds. But we see from Jesus' life that being meek is not being weak, and it usually doesn't come naturally. This kind of meekness requires a great strength of character and the willingness to rely on God when it would be easier to force our own way on a situation or person. Like every other aspect of Spirit life, meekness, also called gentleness, is possible through obedience to and dependence on the Spirit of Christ, who himself was gentle and humble in heart.

Prayer

You are a gentle giant of a God who holds the little tiny baby in his hands without crushing him. Your mighty strength is under control. On the other hand, I use all my powers to get my own way. Gentle me down, Lord. Amen.

January 13—The Mystery Solved

Scripture reading: Colossians 2:2-4; 1 Peter 1:12

There's something tantalizing about a secret. Do you remember the childhood taunt—in that awful singsong voice—"I know something you don't know!" Many cults use the lure of secrets to charm the unwary into their web of lies. "We know the hidden way to God," they whisper. "Join us and learn the secret. Nobody else can help you."

Something just like that was going on in Paul's time. In those days "mystery religions" were sprouting up all over. Paul borrows that little word *mystery* and uses it for his own purposes. When he writes about a mystery, he's not talking about an Agatha Christie-style mystery. What he's saying is, "Look, do you really want to understand how the universe is put together? Do you really want to know the mystery of God? Then come to Christ. Christ is the mystery of God; Christ is the one who unveils God. Commit yourself to Christ, and you'll begin to understand who God really is."

Would getting a clearer vision of God meet a desperate need in your life? You needn't join some secretive, select clique to do so. The Christ you need to know was crucified publicly, was resurrected in power, was written about in the Gospels, and is available to anyone who calls upon him. The mystery of God has been openly revealed in Jesus.

Prayer

Heavenly Father, thank you for the beauty and the simplicity of the fact that all your mystery is summed up in Christ. Please help me to come to know him better. Amen.

January 14—Being Available

Scripture reading: Matthew 14:13-21

I'm a scheduled sort of person. Efficiency is one of my gifts. But sometimes, with my personality type, it is very hard to be flexible and available for people. Over the years I've constantly had to remind myself that people matter more than schedules.

We see this in the life of Jesus. When he heard about John the Baptist's brutal death by King Herod, he was devastated. John was a dear friend—actually, one of Jesus' relatives. Jesus decided to get away for a while. It's hard to bear private grief publicly. So Jesus said to the disciples, "Come on. Let's go to the other side of the lake."

Desperately exhausted and looking forward to their mini-vacation, they get into the boat, and what happens? A crowd of five thousand people make the trip around the water and meet them as they land! Can't you imagine whoever's rowing saying, "Let's turn around, Master, and go back the other way. They'll never have the strength to run all the way around again." And Jesus says, "No. They needn't go away. We'll feed them." Now that's availability!

And then Jesus does what he originally intended to do: climbs the mountain and spends time with God. Jesus got his minimum time alone when he was looking for maximum time. That happens sometimes when you are available.

Prayer

Lord, help me to maximize the minimum time I get to spend with you. When I'm interrupted by others, help me to attend to their immediate needs, even when I'm struggling with pain of my own. Make me like you. Amen.

January 15—What Is the Kingdom of God?

Scripture reading: John 3:1-12

Nicodemus was confused. He and Jesus were using the same term, *kingdom of God*, but thinking of totally different things. In effect, the Lord was saying, "Nicodemus, I want you to understand that there is something worse than being unable to *see* the kingdom of God, and that is being unable to *enter* it."

Nicodemus the politician may have been thinking primarily in terms of a political kingdom, with a king sitting on a throne in Jerusalem. Was he thinking of the Romans who had conquered his beloved country and now controlled it? Was he interested in ousting them from the land? Little wonder, then, that he was having difficulty understanding why it was necessary to be "born again" to get into *that* kind of kingdom!

Nicodemus the theologian did understand that there would be a spiritual component to God's kingdom. He believed that when God's king reigned in Jerusalem, then God would be reigning in the world. But Jesus was talking about a kingdom that exists inside the person—the kingdom that comes when God makes that person into someone new and spiritually alive. God's kingdom extends to the universe and beyond, of course. But if we are to be part of it, we must be like children. In fact, we must be born again.

Prayer

What a thrill to know, Lord, that in my new birth I have entered into your kingdom that will span the universe and last forever, and which I can be part of right now, right here. Praise the Lord. Amen.

January 16—A Priceless Gift

Scripture reading: Luke 9:23-26

Occasionally you hear people talking about the cost of becoming a Christian; then in the next breath they will tell you that salvation is free! "Eternal life is a gift, but there is a price to pay," they exclaim. How it can be a gift and also require payment, I haven't been able to discover. But we know what they mean. They are pointing out, quite rightly, that accepting the gift of eternal life affects all a person says and does and that some requirements are hard and therefore are regarded as part of the price that has to be paid for following Christ.

I think a better way of looking at it would be to realize that there is a price, but it has been completely paid—by Christ. Having paid the price of our ransom from sin with his death on the cross, Christ rose again to offer us life through a relationship with him. Eternal life is based absolutely on him. If there is no relationship, there is no eternal life.

Obviously, if eternal life is based on a relationship to him, then he is perfectly entitled to state the terms of the relationship. His terms are quite straightforward: He is Lord, and therefore eternal life is a relationship that involves acknowledging his lordship. That isn't the cost so much as it is purely an elementary aspect of the relationship.

Prayer

Teach me more of your saving lordship, dear Jesus, that by my careful consistent demeanor people may recognize I honor a lordly Savior. Amen.

January 17—In God's Image

Scripture reading: John 14:9; Colossians 1:15

When Paul says that Christ is "the image of the invisible God," he means that Christ came to give us a visible expression of the God we can't see. "Anyone who has seen me has seen the Father," Jesus told his disciples. But he does more than show us who God is; he also reflects what we were intended to be.

One of the enigmatic characteristics of human beings is how we can possess traits that are so opposed to one another. We are incredibly creative. We can do such magnificent and brilliant things. At the same time, however, we humans are capable of inexplicable cruelty and hostility. We pervert and pollute the most precious and beautiful things. How can these two impulses coexist? How can we be so creative and yet so destructive? I submit that the only adequate theory sees humans as having a marred vestige of the divine image.

But then Christ came into the world and demonstrated to us how far we have fallen from God's image. If we ever want to know how we're doing as human beings, we mustn't compare ourselves with ourselves. Instead we must measure ourselves against Jesus, the image of the invisible God—the sort of person each of us was intended to be in the first place.

Prayer

Thank you, Father, for sending Christ into the world to show us what you are like, and how we ought to be. Through your Spirit, produce in me attitudes and actions that reflect your image and bring you glory. Amen.

January 18—Costs of Commitment

Scripture reading: Luke 22:39-46

When death seems far away—someone else's
   nightmare,
When the day dawns, lending its light to
   despondence,
   or when we celebrate life rather than endure
      suffering,
   commitment stands guard—
   knowing the day brings its own snares.

When you're having fun, commitment can be a
   real nuisance,
   calling your actions into debate
   reminding you of past promises—
   shaming you into His arms!

Commitment is really love in disguise—
   intent on blessing you—always.
Commitment—
   is Christ on a cross,
   refusing the gift of vinegar—
   accepting the gift of our sin as His own.

I want to be like Him—
   committed!

Prayer

You struggled and endured, Lord. Toughen me up. Help
me to stick to tasks and see them through—like you did.
Amen.

January 19—Modern Idols

Scripture reading: Exodus 20:4-6; Jeremiah 10:1-16

The children of Israel faced pressure to pay homage to local, manmade deities. Idolatry is not so clear-cut in our Western society today. It's easy for Christians to feel superior to religions that use images or articles as objects of worship. We don't bow down to any images, so we relax, thinking that here's at least *one* commandment we can easily keep.

But idols can take nonreligious forms too, and we face pressures to replace the intangible reality of God with more tangible things. Money, status, our families, our careers—these things vie with God for our allegiance. Herbert Schlossberg said in his book *Idols for Destruction,* "Anyone with a hierarchy of values has placed something at its apex, and whatever that is, is the God he serves."

Prayer

The dearest idol I have known,
Whate'er that idol be,
Help me to tear it from thy throne,
And worship only thee. Amen.
(William Cowper)

January 20—Jesus, the "Stone"

Scripture reading: 1 Peter 2:4-10

Today God's elect people are the church. We are the chosen of God by virtue of our relationship with his Son, Jesus Christ. Using the metaphor of a building, Peter shows how Christ is the cornerstone of the church (vs. 6), the capstone (vs. 7), and the stumbling stone (vs. 8).

A *cornerstone* is the base upon which everything is built; the foundation. A *capstone* is the locking stone that makes everything hold together. A *stumbling stone* is that over which people trip if they don't treat it properly. This is what Christ was chosen to be. He was chosen to be the foundation of everything that God is doing for humanity. He was chosen to be the piece that makes everything in God's dealings with us make sense and hold together. He is the foundation and the basis of everything God wants to do, if people will respond. But if they won't respond, Jesus will be the one against whom they will bang their shins and skin their knees and bump their noses, spiritually speaking. They will stumble over him and find him an offense.

Prayer

So many around me stumble over you, Lord, for they are blind to your glory and oblivious to your grace. Open their eyes that they may see you as the Rock of our salvation. Amen.

January 21—The Cutting Edge

Scripture reading: 2 Kings 6:1-7

How easy it is to lose the cutting edge of our Christian life—even when we are living in a Christian environment. There was a young man in a school for believers who did just that. The principal of the school was Elijah, and enrollment was so healthy that expansion was planned. All the students set to work to help. This particular young man had borrowed an axe (a very precious implement in those days) and set about felling trees to clear a plot of ground by a river. He went to his task with great enthusiasm, but suddenly the axe head flew off the handle and fell into the river. He definitely lost his "cutting edge" and wasn't of much help until it was recovered.

I have found my life ineffective for many reasons. I love to work for the Lord, but I can become so absorbed in it that the Lord comes last on my agenda. Time with God fades into the background. Prayers grow sporadic. Lack of trust soon translates into lack of power. Our cutting edge is a gift from God. And we receive gifts when we are in his presence. The devotional time you spend with the Lord not only sustains you through trials and triumphs but also makes the difference between your being effective or ineffective.

Whenever you become conscious that you are "blunt," ask yourself, "Where did I lose my edge?"

Prayer

Lord, I lose my cutting edge so often! Make me sensitive to the times my "faith-edge" falls into some river of sin or selfishness. Trouble me—then restore me to usefulness. Amen.

January 22—Avoiding Controversy

Scripture reading: 2 Timothy 2:22-26; Titus 3:9

"Avoid foolish controversies and genealogies." When Paul wrote this advice to Timothy and Titus, he knew there were certain teachers who would take some of the genealogies of the Old Testament and decide they weren't complete enough. So they began to fill in the cracks—or what they thought were cracks—with all kinds of myths. As a result, they would produce the most fanciful ideas imaginable; then they would spend all their time discussing and debating the particulars.

I don't know if you have noticed this, but in the church of Jesus Christ, it is easy to get interested in an *emphasis,* that is, overstressing and exaggerating a biblical truth. Remember that any teaching that is emphasized more than its actual corresponding emphasis in Scripture is the breeding ground for a heresy. Perhaps one of the most chronic ills of the contemporary church in North America today is "fad-ism." We're not into endless genealogies; rather, not satisfied with what Scripture says, we fill in what we feel it *should* have said to fit cultural fads, and build up and emphasize the whole thing. As a result, we begin to muddy the waters. This kind of a situation, coupled with foolish controversies, can be ecclesiastical dynamite. It can be the beginning of a division in the church.

Prayer

Lord, there are some aspects of truth that I find appealing and others that appear appalling. Please help me to be as balanced as truth, and protect me from pet emphases that will make me a petty person. Amen.

January 23—Reasonable Expectations

Scripture reading: 1 Timothy 3:1-13

The apostle Paul maps out some general qualifications of a person who would be a leader in the church. "An elder must be blameless." That doesn't mean he has to be perfect, because it would rather narrow our choices, wouldn't it?

This list of qualifications is not all that special; they can reasonably be expected of anyone who professes to be a follower of Jesus Christ.

I heard about a secular business-management seminar in which a debate was going on about the qualifications for managers. One gentleman, listening to all the qualifications being spelled out, took out a New Testament, turned to Titus 1 and 1 Timothy 3, and pointed out to the leader of the seminar that they were paying an awful lot of money to hear from him what they could have gotten for nothing from the Bible. The interesting thing is that businesses today are looking for leaders who have basically the qualifications spelled out here in this passage of Scripture.

This does not mean that we take lightly these qualifications. What it does mean is that elders are people whose lives show the characteristics of spiritual maturity that can reasonably be expected of anyone who is serious about the Lord.

Prayer

Lord, we expect a lot from our leaders, but perhaps we who are led settle for too little. Raise my sights, Lord. Help me aim higher and give me the great joy of hitting the target. Amen.

January 24—The Privilege of Hospitality

Scripture reading: 1 Timothy 3:2; Titus 1:8

In Scripture, hospitality is not a gift but a command. And incidentally, it didn't have much to do with women in the beginning. In these two passages it is the men who are commanded to be hospitable. The word actually means "the love of strangers." Strangers would often come into the local church or assembly, and a leader would make a beeline for them and take them home. Hospitality involves what you do with the people who come into your home.

Hostessing is the ability to make the environment such that the stranger feels welcome—to make it comfortable, pleasant, and as attractive as you can with what you've got. The idea is to make it a place people want to come to. That's the gift of hostessing, and you know as well as I do that some people have it and some people don't.

I do not have this hostessing gift in large measure, so what I do is make friends with someone who does! And these "hostess friends" teach me the ropes. You can develop and improve the skills you do have. All this is not in the interest of earning a reputation for the tastiest dessert or the most attractive home, however. What we should always be about is *hospitality*—taking people into our midst in Jesus' name to show them Jesus' love.

Prayer

Lord, sometimes I don't want to share my home with anybody. Remind me that my home is yours and that you have every right to send who you want for a meal, an overnight, or even a vacation. Help me to catch the privilege of caring for your friends. Amen.

January 25—People of Resource

Scripture reading: 2 Corinthians 12:7-10

While traveling in Africa and visiting missionaries, I noted with amusement a poster with the following notice:

> We the unwilling led by the unknowing are doing the impossible for the ungrateful. We have done so much for so long with so little, we are now qualified to do anything with nothing!

I wonder if you can relate to that. Yet the greatest resource God has is people, and people have the Holy Spirit. Other priceless helps given to us mortals are prayer, fellowship, the promises of God from the Word of God, and faith. Add it all up and you have some pure spiritual resources to draw on that can empower you to do anything that needs doing.

How do we know? Jesus said so. He said that with faith (not earth movers) we could move mountains. Paul said so, too. He even went so far as to say, "When I am weak, then I am strong"! What's more, our "nothingness" gives God a chance to fill us with his "somethingness" and blow the devil away! Little is much when God is in it.

Prayer

Lord, thank you that sometimes you take away my props so I will depend on you and not on things. When mountains need removing in my life, it's hard not to call in the bulldozers. Teach me first to ask you for the faith that says, "Jesus is in charge—he will show me my part." Amen.

January 26—Assurance, Not Arrogance

Scripture reading: Titus 1:1-4; 1 John 5:13

People who are identified with the living God are people who are characterized by hope. That hope is an overwhelming confidence, and it relates to eternal life. They believe the Scriptures: "I write these things . . . so that you may know that you have eternal life."

I remember talking to someone who said, "Do you mean to stand there and tell me that you think you have eternal life?"

"Yes," I replied. "And I don't think it, I know it."

"I think you're arrogant."

I said, "I can understand that."

"Nobody can know that they have eternal life," he claimed.

So I said, "Now I think you're arrogant. Because you presume to know better than the Word of God. The Word of God says that these things are written that you may *know* that you have eternal life. Who's arrogant? Somebody who believes the Word of God or somebody who knows better than the Word does?"

It is not arrogance to put your trust in Christ, to come humbly before God, to admit that you can't save yourself, and to say, "God, for Christ's sake, forgive me and give me what I don't deserve." That's not arrogance. That's common sense. And when we do this, we have the assurance of eternal life promised to us by a God who cannot lie.

Prayer

Make me confident in you, Lord, not cocky. Give me assurance, dear Lord, not arrogance. Let me humbly hear your words of promise and calmly walk through life today. Amen.

January 27—Tired of the Lord's Work

Scripture reading: 1 Kings 19:1-9

Have you ever felt like a pooped prophet? Perhaps you have been diligently serving the Lord, but just doing too much of everything—running in circles until eventually you've met yourself coming back. Suddenly it all overwhelms you. If this is the case, watch out! You could end up flat on your face under a broom tree, just like Elijah.

It is one thing to be tired *in* the work of the Lord; it is quite another to be tired *of* the work itself. When Elijah said, "I've had it, Lord," he meant it! He was tired of all of it. It's interesting to see how the Lord dealt with Elijah. First, he let Elijah sleep. Then he sent an angel to feed the prophet. Then he instructed Elijah to rest some more and to eat some more. Then Elijah went to the mountain of the Lord.

When we're worn out from the Lord's work, it's time to seek rest, nourishment, and time alone on God's mountain. Now, maybe that mountain is in your own home, on a day you set everything aside and sit and listen for God's voice. Maybe there's another place you can go for thinking and resting. But be assured that God will nourish and strengthen you—if you'll give him the chance.

Prayer

Lord, sometimes like Elijah, the journey gets too much for me. Meet me on the way as you met your servant. Nourish my soul, touch my body, mend my mind, rejuvenate my spirit. I'm listening for your still small voice. Help me to do what you tell me to do. Amen.

January 28—Keeping the Sabbath

Scripture reading: Exodus 20:8-11; Mark 2:23-27

Keeping the Sabbath. In today's driven, entertainment-saturated society this sounds like an impossible, old-fashioned idea. If we think about it at all, we usually operate on the basis of what we want to do with our leisure time or we simply follow the tradition in which we were raised. That's a far cry from thinking the issues through and coming to a conclusion before the Lord as to what we ought to do on a Sabbath day.

After bringing the Israelites out of slavery, God instituted a Sabbath day for them. Obviously our circumstances are different from theirs. They were runaway slaves from Egypt, a nomadic people wandering in the desert. Their work day was quite different from ours. But regardless of the situation, God recognized the human need to rest and regain perspective. We can demonstrate our relationship to God by the choices we make about how we do our work and, maybe more important, by what we do when we are not working.

Prayer

Lord, I know I must "beware the barrenness of a busy life," but life is so demanding and time is so fleeting. If I am to take time to take in, I must cut back to go forward. I'll start by checking on my attitude toward your prescribed Sabbath. Amen.

January 29—Come, Follow Me

Scripture reading: Matthew 19:16-30

God is not remotely interested in a snap decision to follow him that doesn't develop into an attitude of life. Jesus called the rich young ruler to follow him. This means that he instructed the young candidate for eternal life to be prepared to go where God led him. New avenues and possibilities were to be explored. Fresh areas of life and adventure were to be opened up as Jesus directed; the man had to be ready for anything.

The young man's lined face betrayed the battle raging in his heart. He was torn. He knew what he wanted and how he could get it. He knew all he needed to know. But knowing wasn't enough. Now he had to *do* what he *knew*. The decision was all his and only his. Not a soul could help him. Not even Jesus could do a thing for him. God is able to do all things, but he will not break his own rules. And one of his rules is that he allows us the right to choose. Therefore, the young man had the right to choose. Slowly he turned away. His shoulders hunched; his feet dragged in the dust. He decided in that moment to walk away from eternal life.

If you have not yet made your choice, you need to do so without delay. Like the rich young ruler, you have the responsibility to choose rightly. If you came running to Jesus today, what do you think he might challenge you to change or give up?

Prayer

It's hard, Lord, when my choices involve spiritual and material things. My mind gets messed up with what really matters. I am so earthbound. Open my eyes to spiritual realities and help me to make right eternal choices. Amen.

January 30—A New Dimension

Scripture reading: John 3:6-8

When a baby is born, it is suddenly conscious of a new world. At first it almost appears to regret having arrived. But the new baby can see and hear, and very soon he or she begins to know and understand. There is also such a thing as spiritual seeing and hearing. A born-again person can see and understand, often in a remarkable way, the deep things of God. They become real to that person. Truths that were once dark now become crystal clear. A dull Bible becomes a blazing book.

One of the most exciting aspects of being born anew of God's Spirit is learning to experience the world in this new way—through the Spirit. Even ordinary life is no longer ordinary, because there is a whole new dimension to it. The Christian is aware of things going on in the world that are not necessarily perceived through the five physical senses. And, with time, the Christian develops spiritual senses that supply information no less real than what he receives through sight or hearing.

Prayer

Lord, help me to make sure I have experienced this "second" birth. Spirit of God, regenerate me, bring me to life, help me to grow. Make me a healthy, whole person, and may my discovery of this "new world" delight my spiritual senses. Amen.

January 31—True Reality

Scripture reading: Colossians 2:6-10

Colossians 2:9 ought to be so heavily underlined in your Bible that it comes right through to the leather binding. It is so important. If you forget that in Christ is found all the fullness of deity in bodily form, you will have a shallow view of his reality. If you have a shallow view of the reality of Christ, your relationship with him will suffer—and the essence of your life is relationship with Christ.

All that makes God God is invested in the Lord Jesus Christ. All truth, life, and righteousness emanate from the very being, nature, and essence of God and are found in Christ. But that's not usually where people today look. When men and women search for truth, life, and righteousness today, where do they look? All over the place. Paul brings us back to square one and says, "No, don't wander from Christ in your search for reality."

This is the basis of our faith. Never let yourself be diverted from it! Deceivers will try to deflect your attention from Christ. They will pervert the gospel and oppose the lordship of Christ. But remember that all reality is found in him—the One with whom we have a living relationship.

Prayer

Lord, we talk about "virtual reality" today, but what a contradiction in terms! No wonder we're confused. We need to turn our eyes upon Jesus and see in him all that is really real. Help us not to be distracted. Amen.

February

February 1—Blessings through Children

Scripture reading: Genesis 29:26-35; Matthew 19:13-14

"The Lord saw that Leah was not loved," the Scripture says. But the Lord did more than that; he acted on Leah's behalf. Leah did not have the love of her husband, at least not the kind of love every wife wants—to be cherished and loved romantically. Sometimes we don't get the love we're looking for (or in Leah's case, scheming for). Even though she had been foolish and deceitful, God gave her children to alleviate her misery.

When you are living with daily rejection, God can reveal himself to you in many ways, not the least of which is through children. Whether you have your own children or not, the love of a child is special. Even though it's not the same as romantic love, it can touch us deeply and give us the incentive to keep going and to enjoy life.

Jesus loved children too. Their simple faith is the essence of the kingdom of God. Has the Lord sent you love through a child? Take some time to reflect on what children have given you.

Prayer

Thank you for children in my life, Lord—for the kids in my Sunday school class, the kids on the block, my nieces and nephews, or my own kids and grandkids. Thank you for their sweet trust and dependence. May I ever cherish, nourish, and reciprocate their gift of love. Amen.

February 2—The Door to Mercy

Scripture reading: John 5:1-4; 10:7-10

The pool of Bethesda was a place of healing and mercy for suffering people. The name *Bethesda* means "the House of Mercy." What a vivid picture of the church as well—the place where Christians come to know the difference between justice and mercy.

There are many people who feel that their lives are up to standard, and they trust that God will treat them fairly and with justice in the Day of Judgment. But the Bible teaches that the justice of God toward sinners is certain condemnation and eternal separation from God's presence for those who fail to keep his law. Justice means that God metes out to people what they deserve.

Mercy is exactly the opposite. The mercy of God deals with a person in a way he or she doesn't deserve. Mercy means that God recognizes our guilt, forgives it for Christ's sake, and then gives us what we *don't* deserve— new life and rich blessing, the certainty of heaven, and the presence of his Holy Spirit. Only sinners who repent and claim the effectiveness of Christ's atoning death come into the place called the "House of Mercy."

There is a further interesting point about Bethesda. You arrived there by means of the Sheep Gate. This reminds us of the Lord Jesus, who said, "I am the gate for the sheep." Jesus is not only the Good Shepherd who knows and cares for the sheep, he is also the entrance to all the blessings in the House of Mercy.

Prayer

Lord, let me never forget I'm living in your House of Mercy. Keep ever before me the truth that you are the door to all life and blessing. Amen.

February 3—Do You Want to Be Whole?

Scripture reading: John 5:5-7

I'm sure that this crippled man had been asked many questions during his thirty-eight years of seeking healing by the pool of Bethesda. But the question the Lord asked him was a revelation in itself: "Do you really want to be healed and made fit?"

It is possible to lose the desire or will to get well after a long illness. Helplessness often leads to hopelessness, and this may be what the Lord had in mind to reveal to the man. Or there is the problem of responsibility. As an invalid, the man had friends who carried him and cared for him. A man in that condition is in danger of becoming a parasite. His thoughts might have been, *If I get better, I will no longer be able to let them do everything for me. I might have responsibilities of my own. I don't know if I want to be burdened with responsibility.*

This is the message to spiritually crippled, invalid saints: "Do you really want to be made powerful and dynamic through the power of God in your life? Or would you much prefer to be able to stay in an unusable condition so there won't be any risk of having to give up something for the sake of God's plans? Has your evangelical niche become so comfortable that you would not be willing to have the Lord ruffle the waters and disturb your stagnant calm? Christian, are you really willing to be made whole?"

Prayer

Lord, I do have a deep desire for a tranquil, untroubled life. But if I stay there, I may miss the growing that difficulties alone make possible. Renew my desire not to stay shallow. Amen.

February 4—Get Up and Walk!

Scripture reading: John 5:8-13

The command Jesus gave to the crippled man seems ludicrous. If the man could have walked, he would not have lain there for thirty-eight years. What was the point of telling him to do something that everyone knew he couldn't do? Had the Lord taken leave of his senses? No, there is a great lesson here for us all.

The Lord never gives a command that we ourselves can fulfill. But he also never commands us to do anything that he himself cannot perform. Jesus makes available to us all the power of his ability when he commands, so that it is possible for us to access his power at the moment of his command. Then we can obey and do what, for us, is otherwise impossible. This is good news for defeated people, lying dormant at Bethesda.

The man had a decision to make. Obviously he knew that the Lord was capable; the onus was on him to act upon what he knew. The challenge rested squarely on his emaciated shoulders. He decided that he wanted to be different. He chose to allow the Lord to work in his life. He grabbed his bedroll and stepped out. The person who allows the Lord to take away his or her invalid status always expects something to happen and is never disappointed.

Prayer

Lord, I have been so aware of my incapacities that I have become heedless of your commands. I need to recognize that you never command without enabling, so help me focus on your empowering rather than my impotence. Amen.

February 5—Life after Healing

Scripture reading: John 5:14-15

Jesus gave complete physical healing to the man at Bethesda, but he doesn't always do so. One such case is Joni Eareckson, who was paralyzed from the neck down after a diving accident. God did not heal her body. But Joni accepted her life as from God's hand, and he did a far greater healing. He cleansed her spirit of the pride, bitterness, anger, and self-pity that could have destroyed her. And in their place he gave love, joy, hope, and faith. He also gave her an ability to communicate powerfully those same qualities to thousands of people in a most remarkable ministry.

Will you accept the Lord's challenge? Will you let him heal your spirit and give you new life, even if you have some physical problem he doesn't heal? If Christ were to come to you today and "make you well," what do you think his next words to you would be? What would he tell you to do?

Prayer

Lord, our past prepares us for the present day of opportunity. Help me to use my joys and sorrows to help others. May my "permitted past" be a healing place for many. Amen.

February 6—Salvaging Mistakes

Scripture reading: Joel 2:23-27

Suppose you discover that you have made a big mistake. You didn't assess the situation, you decided too soon, or you railroaded through what you wanted, and now here you are. What do you do now?

First of all, God is quite used to handling our mistakes. He has been dealing with blind, deaf, dumb, impatient, and rebellious people for a long time—some whose stories of failure are spread out for us in the Scriptures. So if you have made a mistake, it may cost you something, but God *will* provide a way of redemption. He is an old hand at salvaging! As the prophet Joel declares, God can even "repay you for the years the locusts have eaten."

You may have to stay in the situation for a while if a certain commitment has been made. Or you may need to get out now if the Holy Spirit is really sounding the alarm for you to move. Each situation is different. But the important thing is to follow those two general principles: communicate with God, and seek help from godly counselors.

With God, even in your mistakes there is potential to learn, to grow, and to move on. If you're married and perhaps made the mistake together, don't waste time and energy blaming one another. Love each other, and get through the rough periods to the next part of the journey. Whatever you do, give yourself a little time to heal and regroup.

Prayer

Lord, so many people have experienced damaging locusts in their lives, nibbling away at their relationships until there's nothing left. You will restore—somehow, someway, sometime, somewhere. Help me to rest in this promise. Amen.

February 7—Attuned to Divine Revelation

Scripture reading: Galatians 1:11-12

The church of Jesus Christ must constantly be reminded that fundamental to church life is sound doctrine—preaching the gospel of our Lord Jesus Christ. It is a God-given revelation. This is what sets the church apart from the rest of society.

Society does not operate on the basis of God's revelations, but on the basis of human speculation. Christians are tuned in to sound doctrine, to divine revelation. Non-Christians couldn't care less about it. They do whatever they feel they should do, or whatever society allows. Therefore, one of the fundamental distinctives of the Christian and the church is the high regard in which sound doctrine is held, because it comes from divine revelation.

Are you living attuned to human thinking or in tune with God's revealed truth?

Prayer

Lord, there is no shortage of advice in our world, but there is a marked lack of truth. People freely offer their opinions, but they are so often bankrupt of wisdom. Help me to zero in again on your divine revelation and treat with suspicion the human speculation that floods my eyes and fills my ears. Amen.

February 8—Dealing with Opposition

Scripture reading: 2 Timothy 2:25-26; Titus 1:10-16

The responsibility of a church leader when trouble arises is, first of all, to deal with the people who are doing the damage. Paul charges Titus to do two things in this situation: silence the troublemakers and rebuke them sharply.

Now leaders know that if they carry out these instructions, they will be criticized. Yet the Bible tells us to, literally, "put a muzzle on" people who are teaching wrong doctrine. Such people should be taken out of positions where they have opportunity to propagate what is in opposition to the Christian gospel.

You have to rebuke them to point out the error. You have to silence them to protect those who are affected by what they are saying. But it doesn't mean you kick them out and say, "Get lost." By no means. Call them on the trouble, and then take every opportunity to patiently teach them, in hope that they might come to a knowledge of the truth.

Prayer

Lord, when things get difficult at church, it is sometimes easy to rebuke and never restore, or even easier to do nothing and let wrong triumph. How I need your wisdom, patience, courage, and love, dear Lord. Grant this for the sake of Christ and his church. Amen.

February 9—Weary of the Battle

Scripture reading: 2 Samuel 11:1-5

David was somewhere near fifty and was tired of fighting the battles of the Lord. You can almost hear him saying, "I've done my bit; let others do it now—younger and stronger ones like Joab." You could hardly blame David. He had been a warrior for many years, and his battle record was quite impressive. But today was different. King David was weary of the struggle and suddenly fed up with all of it. So he stayed home during the time of year when kings went to war.

David lived in a beautiful palace, with all the comforts a king would command. Who could blame David for enjoying all the rich things he'd been given? I'm sure he knew his palace must never become an end in itself, but maybe he was unaware that his lovely environment had become a snare to him. This time, when he stayed home, the beauty of Bathsheba became a snare also. David's sin of adultery later led to the sin of murdering Bathsheba's husband. David's heart was a lot cleaner when he lived in caves on the run, hunted by Saul, than when he lived safe and secure in his castle! Isn't this often the case?

Are you tired of fighting the Lord's battles? Press on. You are not alone in the fight.

Prayer

Lord, it's not how we begin the Christian life that matters, but how we finish it. This story is a stern warning to me to never let my spiritual disciplines stay in bed in the morning! Lord, help me guard my heart and mind all the days of my life. Amen.

February 10—True Repentance

Scripture reading: 2 Samuel 12:7-10; Psalm 51

Through the prophet Nathan, God confronted David about his sin. David responded with repentance. He knew he was wrong, and that he must turn back to God.

When the Spirit of God forgives us, that is only the beginning; it's the start of spiritual renewal. What do we mean by renewal? It's not a psychological catharsis that lasts a few hours or days. Renewal is a process. And David sang about this in his magnificent psalm.

When true repentance and renewal have taken place, there is a new sense of God's presence (Ps. 51:11). God is "close," nearer than breathing. We are searingly aware that "he is." Then there is the "joy of [our] salvation" to contend with (51:12). Yes, to contend with! We find ourselves surprised by joy as we wake on a Monday morning and discover ourselves running hand in hand with happiness through dark valleys filled with obstacles.

What is more, David prayed for a willing spirit to sustain him, to keep him keeping on. He wanted that sustaining ability to enjoy the Lord and his work as he began to share again what God had done for him. Repentance and renewal are far more than saying, "I'm sorry." They bear results: God will give you a willing spirit, an evangelist's heart, and a new world view.

Prayer

Lord, what a prize! Repentence brings the grand reward of your company, compassion and cleansing. Teach me to live in a constant mode of being sorry for sin. Then help me to share my joy with others. Amen.

February 11—Wonderfully Supreme

Scripture reading: Colossians 1:16-20

What do we make of this statement that Jesus is head of creation and head of the church? What should that really mean to our lives? First, we can't say, "Well, one part of my life is sacred and the rest of it is secular." Jesus refuses to give us that option. He is head of both the sacred and the secular, if it were even possible to make those distinctions. When living under the lordship of Christ, every aspect of our lives becomes sacred. He is head of the natural realm as well as head of our spiritual experiences, and there is no sacred/secular dichotomy.

Second, if Christ is supreme, he is absolutely sufficient. He created the world and keeps it going. We worship the Creator of all things, the One who upholds everything by the word of his power. Therefore, he can work in our lives, too. Do we believe that? Too often we think, *He can handle the universe, but not me. The universe must bow to him, but I don't need to bow myself.* What foolishness! Jesus is all-powerful and all-sufficient. How much better to acknowledge that fact with humility and joy!

Third, Jesus is the unifying and unique factor of all existence. There is nothing we can add to him. Nothing. Therefore, we shouldn't even try. He is the King of kings and Lord of lords, and everything we have—everything—belongs ultimately to him.

Prayer

Lord, the more I look into your Word, the more clearly I see the beauty and majesty of the Lord Jesus. My heart is warmed, my vision enlarged, my life enriched. Thank you, Lord. Amen.

February 12—Overloaded

Scripture reading: Matthew 11:28-30

Most boats have water lines. A water line is drawn on the outside by the maker of the craft to indicate how deep in the water the boat should be sitting. If the boat sits low, over the water line, then there is too much weight in the boat, and it's going to sink. On the other hand, if it's sitting high above the water line, it will be "unfulfilled." Think of yourself as a little boat.

Most boats have some kind of flag on the tops of their masts. Right now maybe all that is showing of your boat is a little white flag. You've sunk way below the water line. Even while you are reading this book, you may be so overloaded that you are sinking. Or maybe this isn't the case at all. You are perhaps floating high above the water line. You're unfulfilled; you're carrying hardly anything that you've been created to carry.

Jesus says, "Come unto me all you who are overladen and I will give you rest (or balance). Yoked to me, close to me, I'll show you the burdens you are meant to bear" (Matt. 11:28, my paraphrase). Let Christ set your water line.

Prayer

Lord, when I'm sinking because I'm overloaded, please help me. Reorganize my cargo. Balance me. Then set me off sailing in your will once again. Amen.

February 13—In Process

Scripture reading: Colossians 3:9-14

Growing into our new self requires time. We need to understand this about ourselves and about each other. Do you know why? When we understand that we're imperfect and incomplete and that we don't have it all together, it's amazing how tolerant we can become of each other. If we expect everybody to be perfect, to have it all together, and if we suggest we've already arrived, then there's no room for making mistakes and every excuse for being hard, harsh, unrelenting, and unforgiving.

On the other hand, if we know that we are people in process, then forgiveness, tolerance, and openness are in order. If it were not for this, it would be nonsense for Paul in verses 12-13 to talk about compassion, kindness, humility, gentleness, patience, bearing with each other, and forgiving one another. Because we are people in process, we can respond to each other in gentleness and compassion. We should respect the struggle we're all going through. We should respect the aspirations we have but don't always achieve. We should remember that God is still working on us.

If you are a believer, you are a person in process. As is every Christian you know. Do yourself a favor and treat others as the incomplete, maturing saints they are. Remember, God isn't finished with any of us yet.

Prayer

Lord, if you held all our mistakes and imperfections against us, who could stand? Help me offer grace to others in process, just as you offer it to me. Amen.

February 14—The Essence of Love

Scripture reading: 1 John 4:7-8

Love is the essence of God's being. There is nothing about God that is not an expression of love. Whatever we do, we must not exclude God from our definition of love, because to do that would automatically make it an inadequate definition. The Bible states without apology: "God is love." If we want to have any understanding of love at all, we must understand that it has its roots, its origins, and its clearest demonstration *in God himself.* There is no way that anybody can understand love adequately without being able to some degree to understand God.

The mistake we often make is in trying so hard to understand *ourselves* without understanding God. We think that if we study human nature long enough, learn enough about genetics and psychology and social dynamics, that we will in fact discover the key to loving. But if we look only to ourselves, we are horribly limited. If we are to discover the true meaning of love, we must discover God, our Creator, and the One who loves us.

Prayer

If you are truly love, dear Lord, then all your actions are loving and all your divine permissions spring from a loving concern. To believe this liberates me from fear, for you are in control of circumstances, and your strong hand is gentle. I rest in you. Amen.

February 15—The Gift of Sacrifice

Scripture reading: 1 Samuel 1:21-28

What joys and what tests faced Hannah. She had promised the Lord she would not keep her baby, if there ever *was* a baby. Can those of you who have borne children imagine giving them up? Surely Hannah must have been tempted to renege on her promise once Samuel was born. To keep the little one until he was three or even four and then give him up must have been sheer torture. Yet Hannah had promised God the child should serve him, and she kept her word. Taking little Samuel to the temple as soon as he was weaned, she left him there with Eli the priest. Samuel became a godly leader, judge, and prophet for the nation of Israel.

"What a waste," I overheard one woman say to another, on hearing that a brilliant young doctor had resigned his job to go to the mission field. "He said he promised God if he got through medical school, he would offer himself for full-time Christian service," she said with obvious disapproval. "Surely God would understand if he stayed here." The other woman agreed. "Look at his poor wife and child—what about them?"

But like Hannah, you can't present your Samuel to God without sacrifice.

Prayer

May my ongoing commitment to my children and other young people in my life be to help them serve you, whatever the cost to myself. Amen.

February 16—Wrestling with God

Scripture reading: Genesis 32:22-28

Let's spend a moment looking at Jacob, sitting alone in the dark. His thoughts troubled him. As he looked into the future, he was afraid. There didn't seem to be much hope for him. He had no one to blame but himself, but that didn't make him any less afraid. As he looked back over his life, he was ashamed. He knew that he had squandered his advantages and abused his blessings.

People have a habit of becoming reflective when they are left alone in the stillness. They can become almost melancholy when they sit down and think. That is why they don't like to be left alone with their thoughts. They switch on a radio the moment they enter a room or drive off in their car. The television is indispensable when they have an idle moment. If neither is available and friendly company is not at hand, they stick their head in a book. But they hate to be left alone with their thoughts, because their thoughts often trouble them.

Jacob was alone and in this frame of mind when God met him. An unexpected visitor arrived. We are not told how the interview started, but we do know that it developed into a wrestling match. Jacob confronted his fears, struggled "with God and with men," and overcame.

Prayer

Lord, I admit there are times when I fill my life with noise and activity because being quiet and alone with you leads me to confront the issues I'd rather not wrestle with. Be patient and persistent with me Lord, until I deal with the things that matter most. Amen.

February 17—The Value of the Past

Scripture reading: Exodus 2:1-10

It disturbs me that today so many seem prone to denigrate their past. I recognize that many people have had difficult and traumatic childhoods. Wounds have been inflicted that may take years to heal, and even then scars remain. Yet I can't help thinking about Moses. He would have had plenty of opportunity to tell us how he was affected by the knowledge that his mother had thrown him to the crocodiles in the Nile! Maybe he would have had a hard time understanding or forgiving her for that—or for his feelings of hostility toward Pharaoh for trying to take his life in the first place, just because he was a baby boy!

I have heard some people blame their non-Christian background, a parent's drinking problem, lack of Christian teaching, or wild friends for much of their behavior in the present, and I can understand how tempting it is to do that. I didn't have a Christian background or godly friends myself. Things were pretty secular all my young life, and I saw my share of people self-destructing or being taken by unscrupulous people. But as I look back, I see this as my own personal preparation that fortified me and prepared me for a delivering ministry now. Even my secular school gave me many useful skills that I use for the Lord today.

Prayer

Lord, show me I am fully responsible for my response to you and others whatever my past has been like. Show me how I can become a "wounded healer." Use me, Lord, as a blessing. Amen.

February 18—No Longer Alienated

Scripture reading: Colossians 1:21-23

The Bible teaches that people were made by God for God and that the only way we can truly live is in relationship to God. But we are born alienated from him, and there is an enormous hole in our lives without him. St. Augustine described it as a God-shaped vacuum inside each of us that can only be filled and satisfied with God himself.

These holes express themselves in different ways. Some people are blatantly antagonistic to God. Some of us deny his existence or live brazenly opposed to everything he said. Others disregard him as irrelevant. Some of us live inexpressibly evil lives. Others might say, "I am a decent, law-abiding citizen."

The problem with that evaluation is that human and cultural standards of decency and morality are such that it is quite possible to be a law-abiding citizen and still be considered evil in God's eyes. We need to measure our behavior against what God has said in his Word. Christians quite readily say, "I remember when I was alienated from God. I am not proud of the kind of person I was then, but I am so glad that Jesus came into my life and set me on a new course."

Can you make that kind of declaration? If you can, then I'd like to encourage you to continue growing in the faith you've embraced. It only gets better. And if you can't, there's no time like the present to get started with God.

Prayer

Lord, please help me to remember that when I long for fulfillment, I am really longing for you, and that when I feel alienated from you, you can deal with whatever stands between us. Amen.

February 19—Don't Live Foolishly

Scripture reading: Titus 3:3-8

When we talk about someone being foolish today, we mean something different from what writers meant in biblical times. In their day, "foolish" referred to a person who was devoid of knowledge about and sensitivity toward God. Proverbs reminds us that "the fear of the LORD is the beginning of knowledge" (1:7). In other words, the knowledge of the Lord is the fundamental basis of all real knowledge.

The apostle Paul is saying this to Titus: You and I at one time were fools, darkened in our understanding about life. We didn't understand that all things are created; we didn't know that all things are upheld by God's mighty power; we had no sense of purpose. We understood a lot of things, but we didn't know God. And in that lack of knowledge of God—or foolishness—we were darkened in every area of our experience.

Many of us can look back to the time when God turned on the lights in our lives and things began to make sense. When the light of his kindness and love shone into the darkness of our lives, we realized how utterly dark it had been. When we remember how foolish and lost we were before God saved us, how easy it is to rejoice and be grateful—and to strive to live in a way that honors him.

Prayer

Lord, in the same way that you said at Creation, "Let there be light," you spoke to my darkened heart and shone into it the knowledge of yourself. Thank you! Now I need daily to walk in the light that comes from knowing you. Amen.

February 20—Gentle Rebuke for Martha

Scripture reading: Luke 10:38-41

I came to the conclusion years ago that some Christians are Marthas by nature and some are Marys. The Marthas are practical: they love to serve. The Marys are the mystical dreamers: they love to pray. No one is purely one or the other, of course, because of the way our personalities are designed, but most of us tend to lean toward one or the other.

Those of us with Martha natures usually overdo until we are done in. We are bound to get irritable, unhappy, and exhausted if we insist on doing things without any reference to Christ. No matter how much we love doing our work, we have no right to love doing it if he wants us to be doing something else!

However, also notice the Lord's tender treatment of his harassed hostess. "Martha, Martha," he began, using her name twice to soften his rebuke. And he acknowledged her work on his behalf. Jesus realized that Martha undoubtedly believed she was serving him exactly as he wished to be served. She was working for him just as hard as she knew how, and the Lord wanted her to know he had indeed noticed and appreciated all her thoughtful plans. But he also wanted her to see things clearly for what they were.

Prayer

Father, if I become distracted by the work of the Lord from the *Lord* of the work, rebuke me. Then call me to sit at your feet and look in your face, and remake me. Amen.

February 21—Faith in the Right Thing

Scripture reading: Romans 4:17-25

During early winter in Wisconsin, where we live, some people exercise phenomenal faith. They believe that lake water, when it is frozen, turns into ice. They believe that the ice is thick and will bear their weight. They believe it so much that they drive out on large half-frozen lakes in their cars, sleds, and snowmobiles, and drown—by faith. Absolutely nothing is wrong with their faith, but the *object* of their faith is totally unworthy of such trust. Conversely and ironically, very minimal faith in deep-winter thick ice will keep you as secure as if you're standing on reinforced concrete. The thing that determines the validity of our faith is the object of our faith.

In whom did Abraham believe? He believed in God against all the odds. Abraham believed two things about God: that he brings life out of deadness, and that he speaks into existence things that did not exist. Abraham had absolute confidence in his God, and that was the essence of his secure faith: confidence in a person.

Prayer

Lord, if my faith is only as valid as its object, help me to operate on the basis of total confidence in you, rather than a naive dependence on something else unworthy of my trust. I need to know you better, Lord. Amen.

February 22—Are You Coordinated?

Scripture reading: Ephesians 1:22-23

I once had the privilege of attending a soccer game in Brazil. As it happened, this soccer game was the Brazilian equivalent of America's Super Bowl. The teams were evenly matched; neither could get an advantage over the other. Near the end of the game there was still no score.

Suddenly the center forward came right down the middle with a phenomenal burst of speed. He gauged his run until his head intersected with the ball, a fabulous piece of judgment. He came between two defenders, brought the ball down on his chest, held his arms out to keep from touching it, and with his chest brought the ball down onto his left knee. He flipped it up onto his right foot, took it around a man, and hit it on the half volley with his left foot. It went straight into the top corner of the net, winning the game!

Why do I explain all that to you? Because it demonstrates just how wonderfully coordinated the human body is. The apostle Paul says that Jesus Christ controls and coordinates members of the church—the body of Christ—and holds the church together, just like a head controls a body. Christ is the head of the church, and the key to making it a phenomenal team is to allow the Lord Jesus to direct our coordinating moves and shots.

Prayer

Lord, please help me as I struggle to submit to your coordination in my church experience. Show me my place, reveal my gifts, and help me to encourage my sisters and brothers to do the same so that the body of Christ works together. Amen.

February 23—What's Your Nineveh?

Scripture reading: Jonah 1–2

It's hard to know just when Jonah's nightmare really started. Perhaps it began with his disobedience. God had told him to preach to the city of Nineveh, a pompous enemy of Israel. Well, that was asking a bit too much. Instead of obeying, he boarded a ship bound for Tarshish exactly in the opposite direction. Even though Jonah was God's man of the moment, this was the moment he chose not to be the man God called him to be.

It's easy to criticize Jonah, but he represents the whole heart of humanity that is at war with God. We humans don't like God's presence or his programs. We want to go our own way and plan our own lives. Yet somehow we imagine that God's people always love him easily and delight in the things he asks them to do.

I suppose most of us have some kind of a "Nineveh" experience in our lives—something that is difficult or overwhelming or unreasonable to us. For some it is a responsibility God has given to us, or a vocation he has called us to follow. For others, it is a challenge to grapple with, or a relationship that needs to be mended. For still others, it is a serious illness. When God tells us to go and do something about our Nineveh, we can confront the challenge or run away from it. And it saves us and God an awful lot of trouble if we do what we are told!

Prayer

Lord, help me to be big enough spiritually to quickly "go to Nineveh" when the call comes. May I come to the place in my walk with you when I easily delight in your commands, however difficult. Amen.

February 24—Obeying a Step at a Time

Scripture reading: Jonah 3—4

In the course of my work I met a young man one day who was greatly in need. He was a wild teenager—a Ninevite, if you like. I won his confidence, and he took me to meet his other street friends. I knew God wanted me to explain the gospel to them, but I didn't want to. Like Jonah, I much preferred the "Israelites"—the churched kids I taught in Sunday school.

But then God sent a whale of a circumstance into my life to turn me around. This young man got into trouble and was arrested. He gave my name as his friend, and I ended up at the police station! Shaken by this event, I decided I'd better get involved. I didn't have a clue where to start, so I simply got on a bus and went to where the Ninevites lived—downtown. I hung out in their town and became their "prophet." I caught Ninevitis! I discovered that these teens hadn't rejected Christ; they just hadn't had a chance to receive him. As God worked with me and with them, I realized I was full of joy and excitement, full of purpose and plans, full of peace—full of God!

Disobedience empties your life, but obedience fills it to overflowing. Start with the one thing you can do. The things you can't do will wait for another day. One obedience lends strength and builds you up for the next.

Prayer

Lord, show me the first step in the plan that links me to your purposes in this world. Count me in; I'm ready. Amen.

February 25—Dangerous or Defeated?

Scripture reading: 1 Corinthians 2:14—3:3

I believe there are only three kinds of people in God's economy—the dead, the defeated, and the dangerous. The Bible talks about *natural* people who are spiritually dead, *carnal* people who are spiritually defeated, and the *spiritually minded* who are dangerous.

You may feel you aren't quite defeated, but you know you aren't causing the devil any loss of sleep. Sorry, if you aren't dangerous, you are defeated. You might say, "We can't all be dangerous in the forefront of the battle." I can't think why. You live among people, don't you? They need a glimpse of reality, don't they? The risen Lord lives in you by his Spirit, doesn't he? The promises of God apply to you, don't they? Then don't make excuses. If you aren't dangerous with all these opportunities, then you are defeated.

Remember the words of the Lord to the people who witnessed Lazarus come out of the tomb, powerful words that make the defeated dangerous—"Take off the grave clothes and let him go" (John 11:44).

Prayer

Lord, I sometimes pose little threat to Satan's empire because my life is too often bound up with trivialities and fettered with the mundane. Take off my bindings, Lord, and make me spiritually dangerous for your sake. Amen.

February 26—A Thimbleful of God

Scripture reading: Exodus 33:12-23; 34:6-8

Moses saw God's glory in a unique way, but he could not possibly take in all of God's face and live. Imagine trying to pour the whole ocean into a thimble. You can put the thimble in the ocean and scoop up enough water to understand the characteristics of the ocean, but there's no way you can include the whole ocean in a thimble.

In the same way, finite minds cannot comprehend an infinite God. But if an infinite God pours his ocean-ness into our little thimble-ness, then we can understand something of who he is by revelation, still recognizing that we can never understand his infinite being.

That's what Scripture is all about—the infinite God revealing himself to finite people. God takes the initiative so that we might grasp something of who he is—something we could never understand apart from his revealing it to us.

Prayer

Lord, because I cannot totally understand you does not mean that I cannot get to know you at all. Show me your glory. I want to know you better, so here's my thimble, Lord. Amen.

February 27—Gifts and Roles

Scripture reading: Ephesians 4:7-13

God knows us far better than we know ourselves or each other. He is not nearly as concerned with roles as we are, but he is concerned with the gifts he gave to us. He is disappointed when we let those gifts go to waste.

What are your gifts? Does it give you real joy to be with people all the time, listening to their stories, taking on big emotional cargo? If so, then that's the kind of vessel you were made to be, able to carry a lot of those kinds of burdens. Or you may be built to handle completely different kinds of tasks and ministries.

Ask yourself two very important questions: (1) "What gifts and talents do I have?" and (2) "Do they fit my role?" If you don't know what your gifts are or if your gifts don't fit your present role, it's time to talk it out with God and with the people who are closest to you.

Prayer

Every Christian is gifted by the Holy Spirit, Lord; you've told us so. Help me to get busy serving you and meeting needs. Help me to recognize my gifts that surface as I begin to forget myself and serve others. Amen.

February 28—All God's Fullness

Scripture reading: John 1:14; Colossians 1:19-20

Notice Paul's emphasis on God's fullness (which is spiritual) residing in Christ's body (which is physical). These two facts existing side by side refute the Gnostic heresy, which taught that spiritual is good and physical is bad and that the two could never mix any more than good and evil could mix. Here, Paul is insisting that God's Spirit is found in Christ, as man, in bodily form.

This emphasis on the physical reminds us of the Incarnation, the Crucifixion, the Resurrection, and the Ascension:

> In the Incarnation, this wonderful God came to be with us.
> In the Crucifixion, this wonderful God chose to die for us.
> In the Resurrection, this wonderful God gave us life.
> In the Ascension, this wonderful God gave us hope and access to the Father.

When we think of all God's fullness in bodily form, we rejoice that this wonderful God—in whom truth and righteousness and reality and life are to be found—lived among us, died for us, and now constantly prays for us.

Prayer

Thank you, Father, that by coming in Christ you not only showed me how to live out truth and righteousness, but you also came to be with me and give me life, hope, and access to yourself. Amen.

February 29—Clear Vision

Scripture reading: Luke 7:24-28

John the Baptist was a prophet. In Jesus' day a prophet was also called a seer. A seer looks past the immediate to the ultimate. He or she has been given the perspective of God himself and is able to see the meaning behind events. A seer has a vision for possibilities. He or she can see through a situation and envision how it can glorify God. A seer can look past people's exterior to discover what is really making them tick. A prophet is a person of clear vision.

Unfortunately, in the fast pace of our modern day we often do not realize the ultimate consequences of what we do. All we are interested in is an immediate solution to a present problem. We see the outside; God knows the inside. We know the "now"; God understands the "then." We react to life's "what"; God sees the "why." We need to develop the ability to see past the immediate to the ultimate. We need this not just for ourselves, but also to be able to help other people see the eternal consequences of their actions.

Prayer

Lord, I know I need to see things differently. Lead me to see things more clearly as I catch your vision and understand your heart. Amen.

March

March 1—Playing with Sin

Scripture reading: Luke 15:11-20

Sin is an odd thing. When you begin playing around with it, you never suspect that it will end up playing with you. But sin does that, of course.

Like the circus owner who bought a baby snake and began to play with it. The snake was so small that he could easily have ground it to death with the heel of his shoe. As the snake grew, the man trained it to wrap itself around his body—a wonderful trick and act of courage. Then one day, when it was fully grown, the snake crushed the man to death. Sin will do that if you insist on playing with it long enough. Ask the Prodigal Son.

But we do have a choice. The young man realized he didn't have to continue playing with sin; he didn't have to sit in the pigsty. We can do something about our empty condition. We can go home to the Father.

Prayer

Lord, I want to be really honest. I am guilty of finding sin alluring and amusing. I have been naively confident that I could handle it rather than it manhandle me. I was wrong. I'm sorry. Give me a better perspective on sin. Amen.

March 2—Beginning the Journey

Scripture reading: Luke 15:20-24

When I was fourteen years old and hadn't a serious thought in my empty little head, I remember looking at a Bible on a bookshelf and struggling with myself.

"Read it," insisted a little voice inside.

"What for?" I argued. "I don't need it."

"You don't even know what's inside," said the voice, "so how can you know you don't need it! Go on, take it down off the shelf and open it up."

"No," I answered stubbornly.

The funny thing was that I suddenly wanted to pick it up, but then something held me back. I never did obey that still, small voice, but I do believe at that initial moment of spiritual awakening in my young heart, the Father turned to the angels, pointed me out, and said, "She's coming home!"

I didn't arrive until five years later, when I realized that the Father of love runs down the road of repentance and meets us at the Cross. He does not make us crawl home, because his Son already crawled to Calvary for us, carrying our cross on his back! It's such a powerful picture, it leaves me breathless. God's grace is an amazing thing. God's truth tells us the truth about ourselves, but his grace forgives us for the truth he reveals!

Has your journey begun yet?

Prayer

Lord, when I sense your Spirit saying, "Read my Word," help me not to resist. Your Word is life! Thank you, Lord. Amen.

March 3—Garments of Grace

Scripture reading: Luke 15:25-31

A woman I met at a conference told me how she was sexually abused as a small child by her father. She grew up, overcame the emotional damage that had been done, and eventually married a missionary. Years later, she received a letter from her father telling her he had become a Christian. He realized he had sinned dreadfully against her and was writing to ask for her pardon.

Feelings she didn't know were there suddenly surfaced. *It wasn't fair! He should pay for what he had done,* she thought bitterly. She was sure her home church was busy killing the fattened calf for him and that she would be invited to the party! She was angry, resentful, and determined that, like the elder brother, she "would not go in."

Then she had a dream. She saw her father standing on an empty stage, and above him God was holding a white robe of righteousness. She was wearing one just like it. As the robe descended toward her father, she cried out, "No! It isn't fair! What about me?" Then she realized that they were the same in God's sight. It had cost his Son's life to provide both those robes. As she began to see her father clothed with the garments of grace, she was able to begin to rejoice.

Prayer

Lord, some people I love have been treated so abominably that it's hard to cope. Help them know your healing grace. Teach me how deep my need is for forgiveness too. Amen.

March 4—Stephen's Example

Scripture reading: Acts 6:5-15

There are three aspects of Stephen's life that are of value to us. First, his character was irreproachable. There is no substitute for a life of consistency and conviction. Dangerous Christians are those who live out their faith in the eyes of others in such a way that people know by watching them exactly what they believe and what difference it makes to their behavior.

It wasn't only Stephen's character that made an impression, however. His actions were also irrefutable. Who he *was* constituted a challenge, but what he *did* also caused the devil problems. The sorts of things this pen-pushing deacon did are described for us in Scripture as "great wonders and miracles."

There is one other thing about this dangerous man that I would like to mention. Stephen's life didn't take him to the top of any popularity poll on earth, but the Lord Jesus himself stood to welcome him as he made his way to heaven (Acts 6:55-60). Who cares about fickle popularity polls when the acclamation of heaven is a possibility? Better to live briefly and dangerously for God than to live a long and easy life for yourself. It is infinitely richer to be God's person on earth, seeing God at work, making inroads into enemy territory, than to be saved but defeated.

Prayer

Lord, Scripture says you stood to welcome Stephen into heaven. I don't expect that, but I would like to be irreproachable and to live with conviction. Work in me by your Spirit as you did in Stephen. Amen.

March 5—A Reasonable Faith

Scripture reading: 1 Peter 3:15-16

If we're to have a solid Christian belief in God, we will utilize both reason and revelation. And then we can speak with compelling effect to our contemporary world.

Can you say "I believe in God"? If so, you should be willing to answer the question "Why?" And if you affirm that you believe in God, then you would be open to answering inquiries such as "What's he like? Tell me about him." That's how Christian belief should be relating to the world. We arrive at conclusions concerning God, and we understand the evidence our reasoning is based on.

But there's a lot more to believing in God than arriving at a conclusion. We believe because of what God has revealed to us in his Word. And we must trust that others will believe, partly from reasoning (and from our thought-out explanations), but also from God's revelation. We can only argue a position so much. At a certain point, we proclaim what God has revealed and allow that revelation to do its work in others.

Prayer

Lord, you gave us reason, expecting us to use it, and revelation, requiring us to embrace it. Deliver me from arrogant assumptions that deny your truth, and forbid that I should lazily "believe" without careful thought. Amen.

March 6—Planless, Not Purposeless

Scripture reading: Mark 6:30-44

There will be times when you arrive somewhere for a much needed break, and you will be met by what feels like five thousand people, all demanding your attention. The Bible says that Jesus was moved with compassion when he saw the multitude and was able to put aside his own personal problems in order to meet others' needs. Jesus believed that people mattered more than his own personal plans.

In a way, Jesus led a planless life. Not a purposeless life, but a planless one. He allowed his heavenly Father to change his schedule as he wished. He probably did have something in mind each day about what he planned to do. Perhaps he wanted to go from Jerusalem to Jericho on a ministry tour. Maybe he hoped to spend time with family or friends. Perhaps he planned to retreat for a day of prayer with his disciples. But when he was interrupted by the multitude, he didn't slam the door in their faces or react in anger or resentment. He fit them into his plans.

Prayer

Lord, help me to lead a "planless life." Fill in my schedule with your appointments and give me a sense of excitement and anticipation every new day. Show me, Lord, how to grow compassion for others in my cold, hard heart. Amen.

March 7—Love Is a Command

Scripture reading: John 13:31-35

The Master held himself before the disciples as an example to emulate: "As I have loved you, so you must love one another." But the challenge is so great and the consequences so far-reaching, that there is always a tendency for us to treat such a statement with benign neglect, as if to say tacitly, "It is truly a wonderful concept, and the world would be a better place if it worked. But it won't work. It's just too much!" I offer two responses to this reaction.

First, Jesus did not ask us to consider a possible approach to see if we thought it was practical. He said, "A new *command* I give you: Love one another" (John 13:34, italics added). A commandment is not a suggestion!

Second, this teaching was given about the time Jesus introduced the disciples to the ministry of the Holy Spirit. Among other things, they were going to learn that loving as the Master loved required obedience to his command when they did not feel like being obedient; plus it meant dependence upon the Holy Spirit to work in them continually, because they would always find themselves inadequate. It is only through obedience and dependence that the capacity to love as commanded becomes even a remote possibility.

Prayer

How many times do I need to be reminded to "trust and obey, for there's no other way"? When I fail to trust, I show only my own inadequacy. When I cease to obey, I demonstrate my own willfulness, and neither can produce your likeness in me. It's trust and obey all the way. Amen.

March 8—The Meaning of Victory

Scripture reading: 1 John 5:1-5

During World War II, I lived close to one of Britain's biggest shipbuilding yards where the largest aircraft carriers were built. When the ships were first started, the enemy ignored them. As the aircraft carriers came nearer and nearer to completion, German reconnaissance aircraft began to appear with increasing regularity. Then one night, when we were all expecting it, Germany bombed the almost completed ship. As night followed night, the attacks increased in intensity. The longer the men worked on the ship, the more dangerous she became. The more dangerous she became, the more violent the attacks. I am glad to say that every ship escaped fully complete and fully operative.

The more dangerous you become through ever increasing spiritual fullness, the more you can expect attack from the enemy. As the attacks increase, so should your dependence upon the Holy Spirit. I get worried when I hear people talking in glib language about victory in the Christian life. They seem to think that victory means vacation. But victory presupposes *battle*. Other Christians are so busy concentrating on their battles that they never *win* one through the power of the Spirit of God. There will be no victory without a battle, but there need be no battle that ends in defeat.

Prayer

Lord, my turmoil and spiritual battles are no surprise to you. When I bear your name and identify with your cause, your enemy becomes mine. But your power is mine too. Enable me to live and triumph. Amen.

March 9—My Father and Your Father

Scripture reading: John 14:6-14; Romans 8:15

In the Old Testament, God as Father is related to his identity as Creator. When we move into the New Testament, the idea of God being Father is related to the Lord Jesus. About a hundred times in John's gospel alone, Jesus talked about the Father. He used a very interesting word for "Father": the Aramaic word *Abba*. When a little baby starts to stammer something in the English language, one of the first words he will probably say is "Dada." The Aramaic equivalent of "Dada" is *Abba*. When Jesus began to use this deeply intimate, wonderfully personal word to describe God, it was scandalous. People were offended that he could talk about God in such an intimate, familiar way. And yet, repeatedly, he did it.

He then added to the controversy by saying, "I and the Father are one. The Father is in me, and I in the Father" (John 10:30, 38). He was speaking of the intimacy and affinity that he as the Son had with the Father. And later in John 20:17, he says, "I am returning to my Father and your Father, to my God and your God." Clearly Jesus was linking his well-defined sense of intimacy with God the Father with the intimacy his disciples would enjoy with God. He was introducing them to a sense of the Father's loving care, intimate interest, and concern.

Prayer

My loving heavenly Father, see me, hear me, forgive me. I am waiting here as your child, expecting your Father love. Amen.

March 10—Adopted into the Family

Scripture reading: Galatians 4:1-7

How do we become children of the heavenly Father? In part, we become part of God's family through adoption. Adoption means that the Sovereign God reaches out and chooses us to be his children.

I remember staying with a delightful family in New England on one occasion. They had two daughters who didn't look at all alike. One of them looked very much like her father, and the other girl looked totally different. As we talked, it suddenly dawned on me why the other girl looked so different. She told me quite openly, "My sister is the natural child of my parents, but I was adopted."

Because we were getting along very well I said, "I've always wanted to ask somebody who's adopted this question: Do you feel different from your sister?"

"Yes, of course I feel different."

"In what way?" I asked.

She said, "Oh, they just had her, but they chose me."

Now there's the emphasis of adoption. When we become children of the Father through adoption, it is because he *chose* us to be his children. That's belonging!

Prayer

Lord, thank you for choosing to choose me! Your initiative takes my breath away and makes my heart smile. I praise you, Lord, for my spiritual adoption. Amen.

March 11—Like Father, Like Child

Scripture reading: 2 Peter 1:3-4

God chooses us and thereby adopts us as children. But he doesn't stop there. We also become God's children through regeneration. We are actually born again by the Spirit of God. In the same way that a human father transmits life to his children, so our heavenly Father imparts his life to us. And through Christ's ministry to us in the person of the Holy Spirit, Peter says here that we actually partake of God's divine nature, similar to how we share something of a human parent's nature. We're born again of the Spirit of God.

Because we have the Holy Spirit, we are able to relate intimately to God. We can grow to know and to understand more about our heavenly Father through his Spirit. We have an affinity with God as his children. And though he is holy and transcendent, he is near and dear. We have access to him, and he hears our every prayer.

Prayer

Lord, thank you that I am reborn and can share your nature. What a joy it is when the Holy Spirit affirms that I am your child and draws me near. Amen.

March 12—Hospitality House

Scripture reading: Romans 12:13; 1 Peter 4:9-10

Years ago I learned what Christian hospitality was all about. At the time we lived in a tiny house and didn't have much money for entertaining. Yet as we got involved in youth work, I discovered that the young people we were working with were very eager to come into our home, whereas they were extremely uncomfortable in a church. They were not interested in the color of the drapes or the way a meal was served, but they loved being included in our family. They loved just "hanging around," whether I was ironing, or bathing the baby, or sewing buttons on a child's coat.

One of the boys gave me a clue as to the attraction when one day he remarked rather wistfully, "Jesus lives in this 'ere house. Wish he lived in mine!" That was it then. They had come because of Jesus—not because of me!

Prayer

Lord, make my home a haven where your presence is so real that others beat a pathway here, to meet you, know you, and grow to love you. Amen.

March 13—God's Steadfast Love

Scripture reading: Hosea 2:19-20, 23

Thomas Aquinas said, "Creation sprang from God's love of giving." Enoch walked with God, knowing the personal love of God. So did Noah. So did Abraham, through whom God's redemptive love for humankind was revealed and from whom a nation called Israel came into being. One hundred and seventy-one times in the Old Testament we read about God's "steadfast love" for his people. Psalm 136 talks about his steadfast love enduring forever.

This passage in Hosea describes love that would take back a wife who had been unfaithful. In fact, the prophet Hosea had just such a wife; he ended up buying her back and bringing her home to be his wife again. God used this painful situation to illustrate the nature of his kind of love for us. Because God's love is steadfast, he has committed himself totally and eternally to being concerned with our well-being, regardless of our condition or our reaction.

Prayer

Lord, we live in uncertain days, unsure, uneasy, unable so often to cope with the unknown. There are fewer and fewer rock-solid certainties. It is in the environment and circumstance that the sheer steadfastness of your love holds us steady and keeps us strong. May it show, dear Lord, in our steady, steadfast love to others. Amen.

March 14—The Cross That Liberates

Scripture reading: Colossians 2:13-15

I can still visualize one of the happiest days of my life. I was standing on parade in my Royal Marine uniform. The officer announced, "David Stuart Briscoe, you are now temporarily dismissed from His Majesty's Royal Marines and may, if you wish, seek civilian employment." I was free!

Now we had all served under a tough regimental sergeant major. Whenever we saw him coming, our backs would spring up straight, and we'd swing our arms to the shoulder, thumb on top, heels dug in. That's what you did when the RSM showed up. The day I was released, I saw the RSM walking toward me. My back straightened and I began to march. Then a little voice inside me said:

You died to him.

What? But he's not dead!

That's right, but you have no further obligation to him, and he has no further authority over you. So if you'd like, you can go on marching around like that. But why continue in subjection to that to which you died?

So my back relaxed and I scuffed my heels as I walked past the sergeant. He couldn't do a thing. And that's what the cross of Christ means for you and me. His death canceled out the sin that enslaves us. Because he conquered evil, we are released from the power it once held over us. Why go on in bondage to it? We're free!

Prayer

Lord, I'm painfully aware that sin isn't dead in my life. But I see now that I don't have to be obligated to it. Etch this deeply in my heart and give me the desire to live only obligated to you, the One who makes me free. Amen.

March 15—True Authority

Scripture reading: Matthew 9:1-8

One day I saw a young policeman, full of authority and oozing with self-importance, try to arrest a large drunken man. The drunken man was too strong for him and without any effort at all deposited the young policeman in the gutter—authority and all.

An older policeman came to his rescue. There was a calm authority about him, but there was power, too. With a swift twist of his hips and a grip like iron, he whipped the legs of the drunken man from under him. Then he pulled his jacket over his head, fastening his arms round his neck, and dragged him like a sack of potatoes unceremoniously to the police station. The young policeman, crestfallen, followed at a respectful distance. Both officers of the law had equal authority, but only one had the power to match his authority.

This is the position of strength for a Christian. We have the authority of heaven behind us and the dynamic of heaven within us. When we recognize our rightful authority, we are confident and don't have to go around trying to prove ourselves. Our authority in Christ is obvious. If we have the corresponding power, we are a force to be reckoned with.

Prayer

Lord, all too often I stand in my own strength and show nothing but my own weakness. Let me live as if I stand in heaven's true authority, indwelt by the Spirit's power. Amen.

March 16—Hell Is Being without Hope

Scripture reading: Jude 11-13

Jude 12 captures the idea of hell with graphic word pictures. Lost souls are like "clouds without rain," he says, "autumn trees without fruit—twice dead!" To die once physically and be eternally uprooted from all that is dear and familiar, and then to die again eternally is like riding "wild waves of the sea." Hell is being beyond the chance to have Jesus calm the tumultuous sea of fear and dread in our tossing soul.

But it is the last picture in Jude that catches my attention. Jude says lost souls are, in effect, "orbitless." They are caught in a hellish circuit that does not go anywhere. Lost and godless people are like "wandering stars for whom the blackest darkness has been reserved forever." Such orbitless stars are out of control, with no hope of belonging or having purpose or usefulness.

Jesus used reference to fire—*Gehenna*—to describe hell (Matt. 18:9). Gehenna was a valley south of Jerusalem where human beings were once sacrificed and corpses burned, lending itself to a very graphic picture of a fire that is never quenched. Jude urges those who know God to snatch godless people from the fire.

Prayer

We all feel a need to belong, Lord. What "hell" to find ourselves belonging to no one and going nowhere for ever. Save us, Savior. Amen.

March 17—Palace Training

Scripture reading: Exodus 3:11-12; Acts 7:20-22

Moses was feeling pretty inadequate for the task. But it was not as if he had no preparation for what God was asking him to do. From the moment Pharaoh's daughter lifted him out of the river and into her arms, Moses was destined for the throne. He had the best education available. This was his palace training—although God intended that training for something infinitely more important. God saw to it that Moses had the tools to do the jobs of managing and leading God's people.

Just think of it: Moses learned to be an author in the palace—a skill he would certainly need if he were to write a large chunk of the world's best-selling book. He learned to be a general—a knowledge he would draw upon to fight Pharaoh, the Canaanites, and all the guerrilla groups that would attack his people in their desert wanderings. He was schooled in governing skills—a competency that he would use as Israel's judge and leader. Above all, he would need spiritual knowledge and discernment, which Pharaoh could not provide, but which God made available through Moses' own family during his vital infant years.

Everything in our past that goes into making us God's man or God's woman is our "palace training." We may not be living with Pharaoh or have the privilege of private tutelage, but whatever our upbringing, it is God's way of getting us ready for the job he has in mind.

Prayer

Lord, thank you that no experiences in my life are ever wasted. Show me how I can serve you with the "palace training" I have been given. Amen.

March 18—Cleaning Up

Scripture reading: Colossians 3:7-10

When Jack Eckerd, owner of the Eckerd Drug chain, became a Christian, he knew his life would never be the same. His employees discovered the same thing a short time later.

Eckerd once walked into one of his stores and spied some soft-core porno magazines for sale. His newly awakened conscience blared an alert, and he ordered his chief of operations to remove the offensive publications from all his stores.

"But, Mr. Eckerd," the man said, "you don't know how much money those magazines bring in!" The magazines did earn a substantial profit. "Take 'em out," Eckerd repeated. "That's an order."

Eckerd understood that when he came to Christ, he took off his old life, as if it were an old garment, and threw it away. When you asked to be forgiven of your sins, it is unthinkable that you intended to continue in them. You have taken off the old life like a dirty garment, stepped into the shower, and been cleansed by Christ. Then you were dressed splendidly in a new wardrobe—in Christ's righteousness. Don't put your dirty old gear on top of it!

You are a new person. If that's true, then you need to clean up your personal and social life. Whatever is holding you down, put it where it belongs and begin to live in Christ.

Prayer

Father, please help me get rid of the old stuff that is left behind, and keep renewing me to bring me closer to your image. Amen.

March 19—Go beyond the Daily Grind

Scripture reading: Acts 5:17-42

The apostles lived in exciting, groundbreaking times for the early church. Their lives were filled with power, and their approach to suffering was to rejoice to have been worthy of suffering for Christ.

We too live in exciting days with great victories to be won. Will you settle for anything other than the fullness of the grace of God in your life that will make you able to handle all that comes your way? Are you interested in anything less than the dynamic of the Spirit of God in your life that will give the evil one plenty of headaches?

Just like the apostles, you have the authority of heaven behind you, the Spirit of God within you, and the plan of God before you. Released with all this power and authority, you will be dangerous to the enemy, for God plans to deal him a body blow through you. The Lord intends to win victories through you. Are you content to trudge through life never a victor? Or are you ready to live expectantly, existing beyond the daily grind and engulfed in God's adventures for you?

Prayer

By nature I'm timid and retiring, committed to avoiding unpleasantness and discomfort. But I realize that discipleship pushes me to risk's edge. I'm willing to go, Lord, but only because you're there. Amen.

March 20—Working Together

Scripture reading: Psalm 133; Ecclesiastes 4:9-12

One day I was talking to a friend who was starting a new ministry, and this is what he told me: "I am looking for ten committed men."

I said, "Why ten committed men?"

"I'm looking for ten committed men who will commit one-tenth of their salary to my ministry, which will then enable me to live among them at the level they live."

I calculated and figured that if they did that, he'd be slightly ahead, because they'd be living on 90 percent and he'd be living on 100 percent. But I didn't point that out to him. Mathematically he needed a slight adjustment, but what a powerful thought all the same.

Ten people gathering around another person and saying, "We are partners in this ministry, and you can count on us. We will share realistically with you. We can count on you to minister; you can count on us to be your partners." Think of the possibilities! That's the communion of saints—devoted to the fellowship, sharing in partnership.

Prayer

Lord, too often "fellowship" means little more than socializing with friends. You want to see a sharing of lives. Make me a person who will dare to care enough to share. Amen.

March 21—"I've Had It Up to Here, Lord"

Scripture reading: Numbers 11:4-15

I heard a wonderful tale about a well-known evangelist who had traveled extensively in Africa. He loved the country and the travel, and he wanted his wife to love it too. She, however, hated heat, bugs, and unfamiliar places. The evangelist thought that if only he could get his wife to Victoria Falls, where she could see the magnificent view, with the great statue of David Livingstone, she would fall in love with the land just as he had. So he persuaded her to go with him on his next ministry tour.

The trip was a disaster. It was steaming hot, the biggest bugs ever seen seemed to make a beeline for his wife, and she was thoroughly miserable! When they eventually rounded the bend and she could view the statue and the falls, he said to her, "Well, dear, there he is, David Livingstone, gazing over his beloved Africa. What do you think he is thinking?" She looked at the frowning statue and replied, "I think he's saying, 'I've had it up to here with Africa!'"

By the time Moses had led the people of Israel to the middle of the wilderness, he had had it "up to here" with the desert, with Israel's complaining, and even with the Lord himself. He began to complain bitterly to God. Can you identify with Moses? Is the burden of your work too heavy for you? Are you wondering, "Why me, Lord?" So often there are just too few hands to do so much work.

Prayer

Lord, when I've had it with your people, give me patience. Remind me how patient you are with me. Give me insights into the reasons people behave the way they do. Make me a good leader and a good example. Amen.

March 22—Our Need for Support

Scripture reading: Numbers 11:16-17

Some of Moses' problems stemmed not from the people but from himself, for he was not finding it easy to delegate responsibility. Some of the heavy burdens that we complain to God about are largely our own fault. The "people work" that grinds us to a halt can be shared, but we won't let go of it and share it. I have found that frustrated leaders who are not finding an outlet for their gifts will begin to complain bitterly themselves.

All leaders of God's people must spend time at the Tent of Meeting—in God's presence. They need to be renewed and filled by his Spirit so they won't be running on empty. The people Moses had been called to lead were crushing him with their problems. Probably the seventy elders began to listen to some of these problems so that Moses wouldn't have to carry the people's burdens alone.

An elder in one church we know proposed that the elders, instead of the pastor, be available to listen to anyone's complaints. It wasn't long before these elders were overwhelmed by the extent of the complaints they received! As a result, a committee was formed to create an ongoing support system for their pastor.

Prayer

Lord, there is help to be found if I look around. Somehow it seems so much easier to do things myself than to delegate. Teach me that ministry is a blessing to all who engage in it, and I shouldn't deprive people of blessings! Amen.

March 23—Loving Choices

Scripture reading: Ruth 1:8-18

Love helps the chooser do the hardest thing,
In face of winds of adverse circumstance
In bitter loss, or sickness, or distress
He helps a Ruth, Naomi bless.

Love lets a sister go without a cry
For love respects the choice and will not try
To force the company of one who'd much prefer
   to meet her own deep needs—
Love says "good-bye" nor heeds her own sad
   heart.

Love bleeds—but blesses anyway!
The choice is ours, to go with love to Bethlehem
   or walk away from friendship—fast,
Orpah-like—and stubborn to the last!

Prayer

Lord, Orpah kissed her mother-in-law and went her own way, while Ruth clung to her. Make me like Ruth, able to put others first before my own wants or needs. Amen.

March 24—Real Communion

Scripture reading: 1 John 1:7-10

John explains here what happens when we have real fellowship with God's people. He says we walk in the light, meaning that in our relationships with each other, we relate according to the principles of Scripture. If the Scripture shows me something that is wrong in my relationship with somebody else, then if I'm walking in the light and truly having fellowship with the Father, I will go to them, and vice versa. Then we will sit down together and put right what's wrong with our relationship. If the light shows up something that is wrong in my life, I will confess it and the blood of Jesus Christ will cleanse me from it.

Quite frankly, the church of Jesus Christ tends to be weak at this point of the "communion of saints." We tend to ignore, gloss over, talk around, and talk behind instead of walking in the light and enjoying fellowship with each other, which demonstrates our fellowship with Jesus himself. So it's the easiest thing in the world to say, "I believe in the communion of saints," but it demands a whole new lifestyle to live out that statement.

Prayer

Lord, I know I'm a saint in your book, but I don't always live like one because of my relationships with saints who aren't always saintly either. I'll make a start today by approaching one of the saints and treating him or her exactly as the Word says I should. You will be pleased and they will be surprised—and I will be glad. Amen.

March 25—When Answers Don't Come

Scripture reading: Habakkuk 3:17-19

If there is no heavenly intervention when we pray and pray, we are tempted to think either God isn't there or he just doesn't care. If God isn't there, then at least he cannot be accused of callousness or sheer indifference to our plight. But if he is there and is well aware of what is happening, then doubts are bound to arise concerning his love for us.

A friend told me she was dealing with some terrible memories of childhood abuse. She had been six years of age when her father and some other men began to sexually abuse her. Now, as a young adult, she was struggling with the thought that God had been standing in the corner watching it all happen! "Why didn't God do something?" she asked. "It isn't fair of him to tell us we ought to pray to him and then he ignores our frantic cry for help!"

Unanswered prayer is a big problem indeed. When the human heart cries out, "Is God there? Does he care? It isn't fair!" and there is nothing but silence, the human heart dies a little in despair.

The prophet Habakkuk found a way to praise who God was, despite what God appeared to be doing or not doing. At some point in the midst of our unanswered prayers, we have nothing to do but turn to God and offer our emptiness and desolation. We must depend on the fact that God is God and that he can be trusted.

Prayer

Lord, when I don't see you, I want to affirm my faith in you. You *are* there in my darkest night. Help me believe it. You *are* a God of love and compassion. You do care. Thank you, Lord. Amen.

March 26—Building Bridges

Scripture reading: Philippians 2:1-4

An American went to Africa with a Christian relief organization to find fresh water supplies for poor villages. One day he and his African friends were traveling by jeep when they had to stop because a small bridge on their route had collapsed. The American took one look at the problem and thought to himself, *No big deal. It should only take a couple of minutes to repair, and we can be on our way.*

Two Africans inspected the broken bridge. Patiently they began discussing a possible remedy. This went on for ten minutes, then fifteen, then twenty, then half an hour. The American, glancing at his watch, grew impatient. *For Pete's sake, guys, one of you just take charge and tell the other what to do. We don't have time for all this!*

But the Africans continued their conversation, and only after coming to some sort of agreement did they get the bridge repaired. One of the African hosts explained that neither African had wanted to offend the other by insisting on his method of fixing the bridge. Either method would have worked, but in their culture, maintaining good relationships was more important than maintaining schedules.

Those African men knew that one of the best ways to encourage a brother is to be united in spirit with him. In the same way, Paul wanted the church in Philippi to be united in love, looking to each other's interests. It's a lesson we desperately need to learn.

Prayer

Father, please help me to remember today that relationships are more important than programs in your scheme of things. Amen.

March 27—Sin in Principle and in Practice

Scripture reading: Romans 2:12-16

A little boy and his mother were talking. His mother said, "It's time to get ready for Sunday school."

He said, "Why do I have to go to Sunday school?"

"To learn to be a good little boy."

And here's where the little boy demonstrates tremendous insight into human make-up. He answered, "I already know how to be a better little boy than I want to be."

All right now, have your laugh, and then think about it. How did the boy know the difference? What is it in little boys that enables them to know how to "be better" than they want to be? The same thing that allows big boys and girls to know how to be a whole lot better than they want to be. Why is it that we see the contrast of what we should be and what we really are?

Well, the Bible says we have a moral conscience that reveals right and wrong. But add to that what the early church father Anselm called "the heavy weight of sin." We need to consider that there is a deep root of sin within us that keeps us from living as God wants us to live.

Prayer

Dear Lord, your servant Anselm was absolutely right—we don't consider what a heavy weight sin is. We make excuses for inconsistencies and brush off spiritual deficiencies. I for one need to call sin, sin and in your power turn from it. Through Jesus Christ our Lord. Amen.

March 28—A Peaceful, Grateful Heart

Scripture reading: James 3:17-18

I wish I never heard conversations like the following, but I'm afraid they occur all the time:

"I'm going to do such and such a thing, even though some people tell me it's wrong."

"Doesn't the fact that God tells you not to do it mean anything?"

"I don't care. I've got peace about it."

These confused people nullify an objective truth by their subjective experience of peace. The problem is that subjective peace can be nothing more than the chloroforming of the conscience. Give your conscience a hard time long enough, and in the end your conscience will tell you to go ahead and live as you please. You can call that "peace" if you want to, but that's not what James is writing about here. He is talking about a sense of order in relationships between Christians. We are not called to hassling, fighting, or arguing. We are not called to cliques, schisms, or feuds. We in the church are to be governed by peace.

In Colossians 3:15, Paul adds that this peace is to have a traveling buddy named "thankfulness." One evening our church had a meeting devoted to people declaring one thing in our church for which they were thankful. You walk out on air after a meeting like that. It's amazing what a dash of thankfulness will do. It's amazing what a commitment to peace and order in the fellowship will do.

Prayer

Lord, I want Christ's peace to rule in my relationships with others. Please help me to be thankful, too, regardless of the circumstances. Amen.

March 29—Eternity in Our Hearts

Scripture reading: Hebrews 11:13-16

Think of the greatest vacation you have ever had. What happened when you discovered that you were running out of vacation? You said to yourself or to whoever you were with, "I just wish this would never end." This is a sort of eternity in our hearts.

Of course, kids don't talk like this; they live much more circumscribed lives. But when Mother says, "Come on, kids, bedtime," what is their reaction?

"Just ten more minutes, Mom. Just ten more minutes."

"No, come on, it's bedtime."

"Five minutes, Mom. Just five minutes and I promise I'll do my chores and I promise I'll always be good."

They want to perpetuate what is good. When you eventually get the little rascals into bed, fifteen drinks of water are necessary before they go to sleep. Why? Because they're enjoying what they're enjoying, and they don't want it ever to end. *Eternity in our hearts.*

There is something about our humanity that longs for the good and the beautiful and the glorious to go on and on and on. And it should come as no surprise to us, therefore, that God, having put this desire within us, is open to meeting the desire. There *is* such a thing as life everlasting.

Prayer

Lord, thank you for putting a sense of eternity in our hearts. Here we have no continuing city, and we know it. Help us to hold the things that bind us to earth lightly, not tightly. Amen.

March 30—God's Only Son

Scripture reading: John 5:17-23

J. I. Packer says, "When the Apostles' Creed calls God the 'maker of heaven and earth,' it parts company with Hinduism and Eastern faiths in general. Then by calling Jesus Christ 'God's only Son,' it parts company with Judaism and Islam and stands quite alone."

The little word *only* may seem superfluous there, but I assure you it isn't. On more than one occasion in Scripture, Jesus is described as "the only begotten of the Father." The Greek word translated as "the only begotten" is *monogenes*, which means literally "one of a kind." So Jesus is of the same kind, the same genes, the same nature, the same essence of God. He is God. But there's only one of him; he is unique. He is uniquely God demonstrated in human form.

It's at this point that Christianity must take a stand. There are many people who believe in a vague creator, or who believe that Jesus was a prophet and the Messiah, but who don't believe that he is God himself manifest in the flesh. But if Jesus is less than God, then his death is less than efficacious for the sins of the whole world. He is truly the only Son of God, our Savior.

Prayer

Lord Jesus, the uniqueness of your life and death and resurrection is clear. Help me understand more what it means that you are God's Son, and how I can honor you as your child. Amen.

March 31—The Incredible Journey

Scripture reading: Philippians 2:5-11

Let me trace for you the greatest journey ever made. The first stage of Christ's journey of redemption was his descent. The Scriptures tell us that before the worlds were created, Jesus shared in the glory of God the Father. But when the call came for him to deal with the redemption of the human race, he did not regard this glory as something to cling to. He was prepared to divest himself of it and move on to the second stage of his journey.

In the second stage, the Incarnation, Christ emptied himself of all the trappings and prerogatives of deity. He did not cease to be deity, but he assumed our humanity and accepted all the limitations of life as a human being. The third stage of his journey was his humiliation. Born in the back of nowhere, he was part of a family that nobody particularly knew. He accepted anonymity. The fourth stage in his journey was crucifixion. He submitted himself to death, enduring the torment of the cross.

Our Lord Jesus went from glorification, to incarnation, to humiliation, to crucifixion and death. But through his resurrection, his journey moved upward again. The Resurrection was the sign of his great victory. Then he ascended into heaven and was given the highest place and the greatest title. Christ's journey is not yet complete. For the day is coming when the ascended Lord will receive the glory that is his due—a day when every knee will bow to him and every tongue will confess that Jesus Christ is Lord.

Prayer

What a journey you took for me, Lord! And what a journey you invite me to take for you—a journey to greatness through serving. Thank you, Lord. Amen.

April

April 1—The Father's Love

Scripture reading: Luke 3:21-22

Do you ever think much about the fact that God the Father loved Jesus? From what Scripture says, it appears that Jesus was actually the first object of God's love. Jesus Christ was with God in eternity, living in conscious enjoyment of the love of God (John 1:1-3, 14). But Jesus left heaven and came to earth as a man. There was a glory about the man Jesus, a glory that reminded people of God—legitimately, because he *was* God, the Word who was with God in the beginning. He existed and was loved long before Bethlehem, before he was baptized, and before he walked the dusty lanes and hills of Galilee. God has an eternal affection for Jesus Christ, his Son. And as Jesus approached the awesome cross of crucifixion, he leaned on the Father's love.

Being a part of the holy Trinity, Jesus was loved as a member of the eternal "family." But God had other reasons to love him. Jesus kept the greatest commandment: to love God with all his heart, soul, mind, and strength, and to love his neighbor as himself. Jesus sought his Father's will and his Father's kingdom. Jesus gave God his undivided attention and devotion. God also had reason to love Jesus because he offered himself—became a human being, lived, died, and faced hell itself—so that God could gain back the creation he had lost: us.

Prayer

Heavenly Father, your eternal love for the Son was born in your heart of love. You loved him because you are love, but he made loving easy. You love me too, Father. I'd like to make loving me easier. Amen.

April 2—The Suffering of Rejection

Scripture reading: Luke 22:66-71

When we talk about Jesus' suffering, we are usually talking about the inhumane flogging and beatings that he was subjected to before his crucifixion. When we study it more carefully, however, it's not particularly the physical sufferings that demand our attention.

Following his arrest, Jesus was brought before the Jewish council of the elders, the chief priests and the teachers of the law. They asked him if he was the Christ. He answered, "What's the point of telling you? You wouldn't believe me if I told you." Then they asked him specifically, "Are you the Son of God?" His answer was, "You said it." That may seem a little ambiguous to us, but there was no ambiguity as far as the people examining him were concerned, for their response was, "Why do we need any more testimony? We've heard it from his own mouth."

The charge became blasphemy, and Jesus was subjected to phenomenal hostility by these ecclesiastical leaders. They could not deny what he had done. They chose to deny who he was. There was tremendous hatred and antipathy towards him as they all screamed for his death. I believe that this emotional suffering was far deeper and more devastating to Jesus than the physical torture he endured. The very people who should have understood what God was about totally rejected him.

Prayer

Lord, the chances of my sharing in your sufferings by being crucified are nil. But when I think of the repudiation you suffered and the rejection you encountered, I can relate. Help me seek to respond in love as you did. Amen.

April 3—Christ's Suffering for Us

Scripture reading: Mark 15:25-34

What must it have been like, that dark day on Calvary? To have been one with the Father for all eternity, and suddenly to have your prayers hit a brassy heaven, and to cry from the depths of your soul, "My God, my God, why have you forsaken me?" At that moment, Christ suffered the total emptiness of loneliness and abandonment. It was our sin—societal sin, corporate sin, national sin, international sin, and individual sin—that separated Jesus and his God. Therein is the suffering of the Cross.

What do you believe about Jesus? Do you believe, as the writer of the Hebrews believed, that he tasted death for every person? Do you believe that he empathizes with our suffering because he suffered? Do you believe that he paid the price of your sin before a holy, righteous God? In these days before Easter, contemplate Christ's love for you.

Prayer

Lord, as I think about your death, help me say with the hymnist:

When I survey the wondrous cross
On which the Prince of glory died,
My richest gain I count but loss
And pour contempt on all my pride.
Were the whole realm of nature mine
That were an offering far too small,
Love so amazing, so divine,
Demands my soul, my life, my all. Amen.

(Isaac Watts)

April 4—Finding a Way Through

Scripture reading: Mark 15:42—16:3

On the very first Easter morning, three women hurried to the burial place carrying spices to anoint Jesus' body. They knew there would be a huge stone in front of the tomb and naturally wondered aloud, "Who will roll the stone away from the entrance of the tomb?" Yet they kept on going toward the tomb.

When we are in new, frightening, or surprising situations, we face the same problem. Perhaps you face a seemingly immovable situation that you are powerless to change. Maybe you are thinking that God is unable to help you this time and are stymied with a sense of inadequacy. But love doesn't give up and run away. Love always walks on.

The thing to do in the face of insurmountable problems is to walk right up to them with every intention of walking right on through them. If you can't walk through, walk around—find a way past *to the Lord,* who may or may not move the stone or intervene on your behalf. The women on Easter morning were first and foremost looking for their Lord. Somehow we need to live life with the attitude "I love the Lord, and one way or the other, I will find him on the other side of the problem."

Prayer

Lord, today at the tomb of my troubles, I wonder if my stone will be moved away. It is so big, such a barrier. Please accept my gifts of acceptance and submission to your will. Hear my prayer and answer it as you wish. Amen.

April 5—God Moves Stones

Scripture reading: Mark 16:4-11

I have spent many years anticipating the blockages ahead and practicing rolling them away in my imagination. I have tried to peer apprehensively into the future, convinced there are mountains to move just out of sight. "Don't borrow what hasn't happened," advised a dear friend of mine as she saw me struggling to move an obstacle that I believed would face me six months into the future. "Why don't you wait until you get there?" she continued. "Somebody has discovered that 80 percent of the things we worry about never happen anyway!"

The women hurried on that early morning toward that huge rock that separated them from the body of their beloved Christ. They were frightened, yes, but they kept going. Don't wait until you are not afraid before you walk up to the sepulcher. If you can't walk up to it unafraid, walk up to it afraid. And maybe, just maybe, when you get there, you will find that the stone has been rolled away.

Christ cannot be contained within the tombs of our troubles, inside the sepulchers of our sorrows, or behind the doors of our doubts. No stone can shut him up or keep him away. The stone still stood beside the tomb in that quiet garden, a reminder of the reality of the problems we all must live with. But the angels had moved it to one side so very easily, demonstrating God's resurrection power on our behalf.

Prayer

Roll this obstacle away for me, Lord. It stands in the way of my faith. Bring your life into this doubt and despair I'm experiencing. Surprise me, Jesus, and I thank you in advance for what you are going to do. Amen.

April 6—Resurrection Life

Scripture reading: John 20:1-18

Thank you, Lord Jesus,
   that Your death on the cross made us fit for
      heaven,
   and Your resurrection life makes us fit for earth.

Because You live we can, by Your grace,
   become partakers of Your divine nature.
Your life in us gives us God in the garden of our
   lives,
   meeting us even among the weeds.

Lord, some of us, like Mary, have wept
   until we can weep no more;
   and some, like Peter and John,
   find it hard to believe there is hope at all.

Greet us today with Your great glad cry of
   triumph!
Help us to trust Your power to raise us
   above ourselves and our circumstances and our
      sin.
And send us on our way celebrating Easter
   in our hearts, our lives, and in our families.
Amen.

Prayer

Dear Lord, I offer myself for your service, and my praise
and love, for Jesus' sake, who died and rose again. Amen.

April 7—Alive and Available

Scripture reading: Colossians 2:9-13

It has often been said that Christianity is not so much a religion as a relationship. This is easy to say and is often misunderstood. The point of it is this: The major religions of the world are attempts by people to follow the teachings of dead prophets. Christianity, on the other hand, is the incredible privilege of a redeemed man or woman living in relationship with a risen, living, exalted Lord.

The essence of Christianity is not found in trying to follow the teachings of a dead Jesus. The essence of Christianity is that you and I can be related to God through Jesus, the divine Son of God, who was incarnate, was crucified, is risen, and lives in the power of an endless life. That is why Colossians 2:9-13 is riddled with the expressions "in him" and "with him." It is in Christ (in relationship to him) and with him (in relationship with him) that genuine spiritual experience is to be found.

It's possible to find all kinds of spiritual experiences outside of Christ. People do it all the time. But if you want the real thing that satisfies, fulfills, strengthens, completes, comforts, and delights, you'll never find it until you search for it, grasp it, and rest in it in Christ.

Prayer

Thank you, Father, that the Leader we follow is not dead but very much alive and available to us. Lead us to become increasingly available to him. Amen.

April 8—Practice What You Preach

Scripture reading: Matthew 23:1-4

I remember a time when our eldest child was about one year old, staggering around the kitchen, holding on to things to keep himself upright. I saw him stumble over toward some bright red tomatoes. A smile crept over his face as he picked up one to look closer. Then, *Splat!* It was on the wall.

"David, do not do that!" I commanded. He looked at me, all twelve months of him, and picked up a second one. *Splat!*

"Don't do it, David, don't you do it. I'll spank you if you do." He picked up another one. *Splat!*

We were getting low on tomatoes by this time. So when he picked up the fourth tomato, he held his other little hand out and said, "Spank it, Daddy." Then he was ready. *Splat!*

My wife walked in. "Admit it, you're beaten," she advised. She was right, unfortunately. It's hard to model submission to authority and hard to teach your kids obedience. That's why we simply give up on it so often and why our society is marked by lack of respect for authority.

What's the problem? The problem is back home. Rather than dealing with children in a way that firmly yet gently leads them along, parents often give up, and ironically, they end up embittering and discouraging their kids.

Prayer

Father, please help me to be a good example to the children who watch me—by obeying you and the authorities you've placed over me. Amen.

April 9—The Love over All Others

Scripture reading: 1 John 4:9-16

Agape. One of the three Greek words for love. The word that describes God's absolute and unconditional love for us. He loved us so much, even when we did not return the favor, that he sent his Son for our salvation. Agape is the fruit of the Spirit. Agape is the love that is to be directed toward God, neighbor, and enemy.

In contrast, *eros* (sexual love) and *phileo* (friendship love) are usually related to sensual considerations or physical attractiveness. They depend on a harmonious atmosphere, winsome coaxing, or tender wooing. Agape is the fruit of a decision that commits itself to the well-being of the beloved, regardless of the condition or reaction of the one loved.

When eros comes under the umbrella of agape, sexual abuse and infidelity are out of the question, because both would fail to foster the well-being of the loved one. Agape love protects eros in the bond of marriage and provides deep satisfaction without abusing the other person. When phileo wants to walk out in a rage and slam the door, agape love says, "Hold it a moment, slamming the door might injure this person more. Why not swallow hard, stick around, and do something kind and helpful, or maybe just keep quiet!"

Agape is the love that crowns all our loves. Without it, all other forms of love will fall short.

Prayer

Lord, my loving is too often reserved for those who are lovely, loving, and lovable. Fortunately your love knows no such boundaries. Teach me to love as you love and please be patient as I struggle to learn. Amen.

April 10—Open Doors

Scripture reading: Acts 8:26-38

God has to open doors if anything is to happen. Philip experienced a supernatural open door to share the gospel with the Ethiopian eunuch. After Paul and Barnabas had gone on their missionary journey, they returned to their sending church in Antioch and reported that God had opened the door of faith to the Gentiles (Acts 14:27).

Unless God intervenes, nothing of eternal consequence will be accomplished. Ministry is a battle. And because the opposition is formidable, we need resources greater than our own technology, methodology, enthusiasm, and money. We need God to open doors.

Currently there are more than thirty countries that restrict missionary activity. Those thirty-plus countries account for two-fifths of the world's population. Humanly speaking, two-fifths of the world is nearly out of reach of the good news of Christ. What shall we do? Do we shrug our shoulders, or do we pray that God might open doors?

Andrew Murray put it this way: "There is a world with its needs entirely dependent upon and waiting to be helped by intercession. There is a God in heaven with his all-sufficient supply for all those needs, waiting to be asked." What are some "closed doors" that you can pray regularly for God to open?

Prayer

Heavenly Father, please open the way for your people to share the gospel with those who have never heard. Amen.

April 11—Prayer Works

Scripture reading: Ephesians 6:18-20

I got a letter one day from my friend Thomas Samuel, a missionary working among the unreached tribal villages of India. Christians had been praying that God would intervene in the spiritual ignorance of these tribes. The area was suffering through a terrible drought, and believers began praying that God would send rain. He did.

The villagers who heard these prayers were convinced that God had heard and answered. They had lived through other droughts and knew the horrors they could bring. Now they began to turn to the Lord. God was opening doors for the gospel.

Why does this happen? It happens because people take seriously the instruction of Scripture to pray that God will move. God works in response to the prevailing prayer of his people. He will change lives. He will change circumstances. He will intervene in governments. He will intervene in nature. He will intervene wherever, whenever, however he deems best in response to the prayers of his people.

Prayer

It's true, Lord, that "more things are wrought through prayer" than this world knows of. Touch my heart, sharpen my focus, and deepen my prayers. Amen.

April 12—The Joy of Team Work

Scripture reading: Colossians 4:2-18

Evangelism is a team effort. Notice that Paul said: "And pray for us, too, that God may open a door." Who is the "us" he refers to? The rest of the chapter lists all the people who worked with him, people with wonderful names like Tychicus and Aristarchus and Barnabas, Epaphras, Demas, Nympha, and Archippus. Paul called them fellow soldiers, fellow servants, fellow sufferers. God often works through people who are knit together in a team.

It's obvious from his letters that people are with him, even as he is in prison. He is "in chains" as he writes this letter, but his friends are with him even there. They are part of the team. Paul says it is imperative that you pray for the team. Why? For one simple yet profound reason. If the devil wants to stop evangelism, all he has to do is get Christians fighting with each other. It's so easy for him. If he wants to deflect people from what they're supposed to be doing, all he has to do is to get them squabbling. If he wants to make the work of Christ grind to a halt, he'll get people to major on minors.

When the apostle says, "Pray for us," he means it. He had a job to do, and he couldn't afford to get waylaid because people failed to pray for his team. Who are the people on your team? Who do you pray for and work with for the kingdom?

Prayer

Lord, you place individuals in families, members in bodies, and servants in teams. Sometimes when I go my own way, I wish I hadn't. You know best, so please make me a team player. For Christ's sake. Amen.

April 13—Growing through Prayer

Scripture reading: Colossians 4:12-13

Not all great heroes have famous names. Some do their mighty works quietly, out of the limelight. The Colossians had a man like that in their corner. Epaphras was a man of prayer, and his prayer for the people in Colosse was that those who had started well might stand firm. He prayed that those who had moved into newness of life might become fully assured of it. He thoroughly believed that prayer helps growing believers to mature.

Can you think of a person who began to show signs of spiritual life but who never matured? Can you think of people who began to learn the things of Christ but then had the ground taken out from under them and are no longer assured of the truth of the gospel?

Prayer moves God to help believers to grow. Are you engaging in that kind of prayer? What a tremendous need there is for people who will take this seriously. John Wesley said, "Give me one hundred preachers who fear nothing but sin and desire nothing but God, and I care not a straw whether they be clergy or laity. Such alone will shake the gates of hell and set up the kingdom of heaven on earth. God does nothing but in answer to prayer."

Who can you pray fervently and regularly for, to be assured and grow in their faith?

Prayer

Father, please help me to see people the way you see them and to pray for them in the way they need to be prayed for. Amen.

April 14—Compassion in the Flesh

Scripture reading: Matthew 15:29-32

Human beings need a clear, flesh-and-blood demonstration of compassion. For many, God himself feels too remote. Knowing this, God sent his Son, who laid aside his glory, assumed our humanity, was born in our likeness, and lived among us. And as he lived among us, he modeled compassion.

On one occasion, Jesus saw the people wandering aimlessly like sheep without a shepherd. He knew their society was disintegrating. He knew that they were physically hungry and that many among them were sick. What was his reaction? He was moved with compassion. Our Lord Jesus began to reach out to people. He healed the ill, fed the hungry, brought back the lost. He spoke to their broken society. He gave of himself to them. He became compassion in action.

Prayer

Acts of compassion please you, Lord—they help people and they encourage emulation. So why don't I do more of them? Show me how to avoid being so self-centered that I refrain from that which brings blessing on every hand because I can't be bothered. Amen.

April 15—The Straitjacket of Legalism

Scripture reading: Colossians 2:16-23

Apparently there were some legalistic teachers in the church at Colosse who were insisting that people should observe religious festivals, New Moon celebrations, and the Sabbath day in a particular way. Some of us have been exposed to this kind of legalism. People have tried to lay on us rules of behavior that have nothing to do with Scripture.

People straining under legalism are in bondage. They become nervous and uptight, wondering if it's OK to do this and not that. Legalists not only lay out a system of behavior, but often they go a step further and say, "If you don't do it this way, then you're not spiritual." They judge you on the basis of their own principles of operation. Notice Paul's rebuttal of this approach: "Don't let those kinds of people judge you."

First, these people don't understand that the things they are particularly concerned about are merely a shadow of what was fulfilled in Christ. They are confusing shadow with substance. Second, while these people are frequently deeply into ritual, they're not especially interested in the spiritual reality of which the ritual speaks.

Rules can't make you holy. Legalism can't produce righteousness. We need a fresh appreciation for the grace and freedom that is in Christ Jesus, a grace and freedom that lead to true godliness as the Holy Spirit brings the truth of God's Word to bear on your life.

Prayer

Dear Lord, please help me to stay close to you so I can know what you want me to do—not so I can judge others, but in order to live in a way that pleases you. Amen.

April 16—The Choice of Marriage

Scripture reading: Matthew 19:4-6

I know some men who have it pretty good with their fathers and mothers. They are single and well cared for. Somebody does their laundry. They don't even have to pay room and board. They have life by the tail—and then they throw it all away. They leave mother and father, giving up all that security, and get married. Why on earth would they do that? Because God, from the very beginning of creation, "made them male and female." For that reason the man chooses to leave the old life and move into a whole new situation.

But notice the key: he *chooses* to leave. Although the situation is different today, this matter of choice still applies. Marriages often get into difficulty because people do not live out this basic choice. They choose to get married. Accepting responsibility, they say they will leave the old life. But they don't. They say they are prepared to move fully into this new experience, but they look back. As a result, the new union is never really complete. And it isn't long before problems start to arise.

Prayer

Lord, some people have a tendency to want to enjoy the blessings of marriage while reserving the right to the freedom of singleness. That's not fair, and it's not good enough. I pray for my marriage and the marriages of others I know. Teach us to embrace wholeheartedly these relationships. Amen.

April 17—Remembering the Good

Scripture reading: Philippians 1:1-11

Happy memories were partially responsible for Paul's ability to rejoice in jail. He did not sit in his place of confinement feeling sorry for himself. Rather, Paul's recollections of the days in Philippi brought him joy (see Acts 16). He remembered fondly the girl who had been delivered from demons. He thought of being chained to the slimy wall of the cell as the earth beneath him quaked, and the jailer who believed. Lydia, the skilled businesswoman, and her group of faithful women came to his mind. And as he remembered the experiences, he had a great sense of joy.

As he thought of them all, one thing captivated his mind: God had been at work in those days in Philippi; he had worked during the pleasant times by the river and the ugly times in the cell, the placid days of prayer and teaching and the fearful days of pain and terror. In fact, God had done such a beautiful work in the lives of the Philippian believers that they had joined Paul in his evangelism.

When you find yourself in prison, or in a hospital bed, or tied to a kitchen sink, or anchored to an office desk, instead of moaning about your present status, try to remember what God has been doing in your life. That will remind you of what he is still committed to doing.

Prayer

Lord, I can't forget the negative recollections of my life, but I can certainly try to accentuate the positives, like what you have done and how great people have been. The more I do this, the more blessed life becomes. Thank you. Amen.

April 18—Godly Humility

Scripture reading: John 3:26-30

John was the prophet of the day. Crowds had been flocking to him. One day someone pointed out that he was losing part of his audience to Jesus of Nazareth. He said, "Sure, I realize that. I sent some of them over myself, because I must beome less, but he is the One who must become greater and greater."

There's nothing phony about John's humility. He had come to grips with who he really was in relation to Jesus. A humble man is not afraid to admit who he is, and who he isn't. Various symbols illustrate the relationship between Jesus and John. Jesus was the Light; John was the lamp. Jesus was the Way; John was the signpost. Jesus was the Message; John was the messenger. Jesus was the Word; John was the voice. John didn't like to talk about himself. His main concern was to understand himself in the light of who Jesus Christ is.

When we come to terms with who we are compared to Jesus Christ, we find it's not too difficult to be humble.

Prayer

Lord, I've got a lot to learn from John. He achieved much; he walked tall; he proclaimed the truth; he stood for righteousness. But not one of these was an end in itself. They were all done to glorify God. That's what mattered to him. I want it to matter to me. Amen.

April 19—Being Vulnerable

Scripture reading: Matthew 11:2-6

Now John the Baptist was in prison for confronting King Herod's sin. As he sat there in his cell, he began to wonder about some things. So he asked his disciples, "Would you go back to Jesus and ask him if he is really the Messiah? Is he really the One we are looking for?"

What an interesting insight this gives us into the mind of John the Baptist. In his doubt, he reveals a winsome vulnerability. According to research, the five most difficult statements for the modern person to make are (1) I don't know; (2) I was wrong; (3) I need help; (4) I'm afraid; and (5) I'm sorry. In other words, according to the world's definition, real men and women do not admit any neediness. But John was not afraid to admit his vulnerability.

He had followed God's call—all the way to prison. It was only human to sit there and wonder if something had gone wrong, if he had been mistaken. John needed some reassurance. And Jesus sent some: "Of course I'm the One. See all that is happening here? See how God's kingdom is manifesting itself?" I can imagine John relaxing against his cell wall. He could not have received this reassurance from Jesus had he not asked the question.

Sometimes we need reassurance. We need to hear from the Lord even what we already know to be true. Vulnerability allows us to ask for that reassurance. And God does not chastise us for needing it.

Prayer

Lord, let me be vulnerable enough to ask the troubling questions born of nagging doubt. Otherwise I may never hear the answers. Amen.

April 20—Turning to God

Scripture reading: 1 Thessalonians 1:9-10

"Turning to God" is a lovely expression that describes the essence of spiritual experience. There's something about us that naturally turns away from God. There's something about us that wants our own way rather than God's way. But to become a Christian there has to come a time in our lives when we turn to him.

When that turning takes place, we become open about ourselves, and we demonstrate our desire to have a relationship with him. Then we begin to draw from him what he offers, and we move constantly closer to him.

When we turn to God, we are automatically turning from anything else that rules our lives. We cannot serve God and that which is opposed to God. We must come to God in submission, which means we reject that which is counter to him. We can't have our God and our idols. If we face north, we do not have the privilege of facing south. Often we are like the children of Israel, who turned their backs on God, but not their faces. That's why they were called a "stiff-necked people." They wanted it both ways—God and the local idols. But it doesn't work. Are you turned toward God's direction today?

Prayer

Teach me, Lord, that turning to you involves turning from the things that offend you. I want to go your way. Amen.

April 21—Love's Discipline

Scripture reading: Hebrews 12:5-11

Some years ago I spoke to a large group of high-school students at a summer camp. Some of them behaved badly all week, and when it became apparent no one was going to say anything, I did! I said that the next ten minutes would apply only to those who didn't know how to behave in a worship service, and I knew six of the large crowd who fit into that category. So that there wouldn't be any doubt about who they were, I pointed them out. Then I proceeded.

At the end of my talk a young giant came bustling up to me with a red face and shouted, "Were you talking to me?"

"You know perfectly well that I was talking to you," I replied. There was a pause; then his face crumpled and he said, "Gee, thanks. You're the first person who cared enough about me to tell me where I was wrong."

About four years later, as I was registering new students in an English Bible school, a young lady said to me, "Do you remember me? You pointed me out in a crowd of kids in a youth conference four years ago. I did not appreciate it at the time, but I decided that if ever I wanted Christian training, I would go where they care enough about young people to discipline them."

Love exercises discipline and discernment in its associations and relationships. Genuine love wants what is best for the loved one, and what is best for all of us at some time or other is discipline.

Prayer

Father, I know you sometimes show your love by disciplining me. When I have to lovingly do to others what they need, deliver me from being unlovingly harsh. Amen.

April 22—Let Your Joy Show

Scripture reading: Acts 3:1-10

God approves of joy. He instructs us to come before him with joy. And Zephaniah 3:17 tells us that God is utterly delighted in us, rejoicing over us with singing. The Bible uses several words for various expressions of joy.

When David returned home after defeating Goliath, he got a hero's welcome as the women met him with joyful songs and dancing. The Hebrew word used is *simchah*, which has connections with the idea of something bright and shining. The eyes of a two-year-old at a Christmas tree or a bride walking down the aisle to meet her bride-groom shine with a brightness and sparkle that testify clearly to joy that may be inexpressible in any other way.

Another word for joy is *masos*, which means "leaping" or "jumping." The man who was healed as he sat at the temple gate is a good example of leaping and jumping joy. He insisted on going to worship with Peter and John, and his joy knew no bounds (pardon the pun!). No doubt he caused quite a stir by his unconventional entrance. But this kind of joy is perfectly permissible in biblical thinking.

Rinnah is yet another word that conveys the idea of exuberant expression of joy, with particular reference to "shouting." There are some Christians who like this kind of expressive, even explosive, demonstration of joy, and others who are not so sure. How do you show the joy of the Lord?

Prayer

Lord, some of us are gregarious and some more gloomy, some leap while others lie low, some shout and others remain silent. However I do it, Lord, please make sure my joy shows. Amen.

April 23—The Danger of Lying

Scripture reading: John 8:43-45

Jesus' statement here immediately put the dangerous business of lying into perspective. When we lie, we are speaking the devil's native language. Satan doesn't know the truth, and Jesus says he reproduces people who do not know the truth, and lying becomes their first language too.

Lying may seem harmless at times. But involving ourselves in lying means connecting ourselves with the devil. Jesus came to speak the truth. His words outline a spiritual war between the Father of righteousness and the father of lies. All of us are in this conflict.

As God builds up what is good, Satan intently moves to destroy that good by bringing lies and untruth into areas of truth and reality. That's why God so adamantly opposes lying and so totally supports truth. When we are blinded by the lies of Satan, God longs to shine his truth and love into our spiritual darkness.

Prayer

Father of truth, it's so easy to tell white lies to defend ourselves. But help me fight against Satan's ploys and speak your language of truth. Amen.

April 24—Needs or Wants?

Scripture reading: Psalm 24

Many people come to the Lord out of deep distress. Their lives are in a terrible mess. They've tried everything to sort them out. As a last resort they turn to God because they've been told that he will meet their needs (which is absolutely true). But if they're not careful, they may begin to picture God as nothing more than the "Need meeter" in the sky. Projecting that further, very quickly they begin to have a relationship with God where he serves them, which is exactly the opposite of what it should be. God does not exist to serve us. We exist to serve him.

So who can "ascend the hill of the Lord"? How we can relate the gospel to people in deep need and convey the beauty of God's provision for that need, but at the same time bring them to the point of wanting to serve him? The only solution I know is to concentrate on who God is, rather than on what the person is.

If we can concentrate on God in all his majesty and wonder, and encourage needy people to come to him with a pure heart and a desire to honor him, then we can tell them, "Your hearts are now right for God to meet your needs." But if people simply come on the basis of "God meets my needs and makes no demands," then their spiritual experience is highly questionable.

Prayer

Lord, none of us deserve to stand in your holy place. Help me to see you as the majestic Lord who deserves my undying allegiance and who can meet my needs, but not necessarily my wants. Amen.

April 25—The Work of the Master

Scripture reading: Ephesians 2:10; Philippians 1:4-6

Sometimes I think that we talk a little too glibly about "God's work in our lives." To really believe that the Lord from heaven is at work in a tiny little life is either arrogant nonsense or magnificent truth. A convinced Christian, of course, rules out the nonsense theory and is locked into the truth theory. But to take this lightly is to do a massive truth grave injustice.

Whenever the Lord did anything in terms of work, it was a superb work done by the master workman. And I believe that he has not changed. Therefore, I am dissatisfied with anything that claims to be related to the work of Christ in a person's life that does not bear the stroke of God's genius. God's work in regeneration is not a work that produces a shallow decision, but a deep revolution. His activity in conviction produces broken and contrite hearts, not crocodile tears. And that is only the beginning.

Paul's statement here is that if Christ has started something, he is not about to quit before he has finished it. The beginning of our spiritual experience is not the end. There is sanctifying work to be done, and the motivating force of this work is the One who started the whole thing in the first place.

Prayer

Lord, when I'm discouraged by my lack of growth and maturity, I remember to look back to what I used to be. Then I recognize you have been at work. But I also need to look forward to what I will become. Then I say, "Work on, Lord, there's much to be done." Amen.

April 26—God's Unexplainable Peace

Scripture reading: Isaiah 48:17-18; Philippians 4:6-7

As a pastor I have seen the peace of God work strangely and surely into the ravaged features of the bereaved. On numerous occasions as I have said good-bye to the dying they have expressed only anticipation for glory, compassionate concern for their loved ones, and an insistence that I preach the Word at their funeral! Never a touch of anxiety, except perhaps for the fear of needles or the embarrassment of intimate nursing. Only a sense of psychological order—the peace of God. This is the fruit of the Spirit.

Of course, this kind of peace does not just happen. It comes, as do all the aspects of the fruit of the Spirit, from careful obedience to God's commands as we depend on God's enabling. Those who are habitual worriers, whose lives are shrouded in the gray fogs of anxiety, need to recognize the clear command "Do not be anxious about anything" and act accordingly.

This does not mean that, having spent all their lives worrying, they will suddenly stop, any more than it holds out hope that they will never get depressed and fearful again. It does mean that to the degree that people can respond positively when the anxieties loom large, they will turn the corner and increasingly discover incredible peace permeating mind, emotion, body, and relationships.

Prayer

Lord, there is a peace that cannot be explained except in terms of your working in the heart. All too often I try to organize my life to rid it of all tension and conflict. I need to know your kind of peace, through your Spirit. Amen.

April 27—Jesus and Women

Scripture reading: Luke 8:1-3; 10:38-41

Jesus' treatment of women was revolutionary, to say the least. He acted contrary to the norm wherever he went. That was a new experience for men who regarded women as inferior and irrelevant.

Do you recall his interaction with Martha and Mary? Martha was doing the woman's work—and woman's work is in the kitchen, right? Mary, however, was sitting at Jesus' feet in a Bible study. All upset, Martha said, "Tell her to come and do her job." Jesus replied, "Mary has chosen the better part."

This was a radical statement by Jesus for the times because it was unheard of for a woman to be educated at all, especially in matters of religion. Religious training was of the males, by the males, and for the males. So for Jesus to welcome—even commend—Mary's sitting at his feet to be a learner was a very significant statement on his part.

Prayer

Dear Lord, thank you for making a radical difference in the lives of women by making radical statements about all of us. Thank you for telling me you want me to use my mind to think about you, my spirit to worship you, and my body to serve you. Amen.

April 28—A New Status

Scripture reading: Mark 14:3-9

As we look at this story, we must keep in mind that, in those days, women were regarded as so seductive that if they appeared in public with their hair unbraided or uncovered, they were promptly divorced—no questions asked.

In this situation, Jesus was at dinner, reclining on a couch, a common mealtime posture at the time. And then this woman comes in. Everybody knows who she is, so they're thinking that if Jesus is truly a prophet he'll see through her.

But the woman starts to cry, and then—disgraceful as it was—she uncovered her hair and used it to wipe Jesus' feet. We can only imagine what the onlookers thought of this display. Perhaps they thought she was trying to seduce him. They may have seen her tears and wondered if she'd gone mad. We don't know, but we do know that Jesus allowed her this display. He did not rebuke her.

He ignored the social implications of her loose hair and her blatant appeal for his attention. Because Jesus saw the heart, and he recognized this woman not as a female or a seductress, but as a person whom God loved. As usual, Jesus' response to women was shocking. In allowing this woman to do what she did, he elevated not only her status but also the status of women in general.

Prayer

Thank you, Lord, for treating women and men with dignity even when they were doing something undignified. Thank you for seeing their hearts, hearing their needs, and addressing their sin. Amen.

April 29—Trustworthy Witnesses

Scripture reading: Luke 24:1-12

A fact often overlooked when this familiar Easter story is told is that Jesus considered women reliable witnesses. This was not the case in society at large, and it certainly was not the case in courts of law at that time. Women were not considered reliable witnesses.

Yet, because the men were in hiding, the only witnesses that morning to Jesus' resurrection were women. How ironic! And Jesus met them there and told them to tell others the good news of his resurrection. He entrusted these women with the most important message ever to be relayed from one person to another: There is life after death—because Jesus Christ is alive!

It's not surprising that the women had trouble convincing the men back in town. After all, men weren't used to important information coming from women. But that's the way Jesus managed the situation, and later the men were themselves confronted with his resurrection.

Not only were women the witnesses of Jesus' death, but they were the first to experience the empty tomb. In this way Jesus presented them as reliable witnesses and restored part of the identity as people that society had taken from them. Today, Jesus Christ continues to restore women—and men, and individuals of all situations, races, and social classes—to their full dignity as God's creation.

Prayer

Thank you for the privilege of telling the gospel and for calling women to this task as surely as you call men. Help us all get the job done. Amen.

April 30—A Divine Choice

Scripture reading: Deuteronomy 7:7-9

As we read the Old Testament, we see that people at that time were aware of God's love. He demonstrated his care to them through miracles, such as the Israelites' escape from Egypt and their incredible survival in the wilderness all those years. He demonstrated his love through the laws he gave so that their lives would have order and peace (as long as they followed those laws, of course).

But why did God love them? The Scripture passage tells us plainly: He loved them because he chose to love them. Generations earlier, God had made a promise to Abraham: "I will make you into a great nation and I will bless you" (Gen. 12:2). And God keeps his promises.

So what does God think of people today who deny his existence? Of those who propagate untruths through books and the media and in their teaching? He loves them. Have you ever considered what God thinks of immoral people? He loves them. What might God think of those who oppress others? He loves them. He loves them all, the oppressed and the oppressors. What does God think of thieves and cheats and liars and drunks? He loves them. Of people in business? He loves them. Of parents at home? He loves them. God chooses to love us.

Prayer

What a relief, Lord, to know that your love is a matter of divine decision rather than human deserving. Sometimes I wonder how you can love some people, but in my better moments I stop thinking like that and simply wonder that you choose to love me! Thank you. Amen.

May

May 1—Duty to Whom?

Scripture reading: 1 Corinthians 9:20-22

Ecclesiastes 12:13 says, "Fear God and keep his commandments, for this is the whole duty of man." This defines a sense of responsibility even beyond that to king and country. It declares an allegiance or moral obligation to God himself.

This type of devotion is sadly lacking today. In fact, if people do have a sense of duty in our society, it is likely to be a sense of duty to themselves alone. Their driving concern is their own well-being, their own happiness, their own comfort, their own pleasure. Of course, if we have a society of people primarily interested in their own pleasure, and if the only duty they see is to themselves—not to king and country, not to God, not to neighbor—it's rather obvious we have some major problems.

Tragically, this attitude has infiltrated the Christian community as well. If we're more concerned about individual rights and freedoms than corporate duty, we will have difficulty within the body of Christ.

Prayer

Lord, selfishness comes easily. Egocentricity is natural. You understood that your obligation was to do the Father's will, and you did your duty. Where would I be if you had decided you owed it to yourself to avoid costly sacrifice? Teach me to do my duty—and to enjoy it! Amen.

May 2—The Place for Personal Rights

Scripture reading: 1 Corinthians 9:1-12

Paul doesn't suggest for a moment that rights are unimportant. On the contrary, he says that rights must be recognized. From the very beginning of 1 Corinthians 9, he points out that, because he is an apostle, he has certain rights. He mentions his right to be recognized as one in whom very specific authority resides and upon whom certain responsibilities rest (vv. 1-2). In verses 3-6, he points out his right to be respected as a human being. In verses 7-12, he shows he has every right to be remunerated for his work as a minister. So when the apostle Paul talks about duty to the Lord Jesus, he is not suggesting there are no such things as individual rights.

But notice that Paul talks about his rights in relation to his calling as a Christian and an apostle. In other passages, he talks of relinquishing personal rights for the sake of the kingdom. Individual rights, in and of themselves, will not ensure peace and cooperation among people. Those rights must always be balanced by mutual submission and sensitivity to others.

Prayer

Lord, you know that in our modern culture "rights" are big and responsibilities are few. Help me to understand I have rights, but help me to concentrate on my responsibilities. Amen.

May 3—Moving at God's Speed

Scripture reading: 1 Peter 3:8-9

Delays can teach mighty lessons when they are accepted as being from God and used for his glory.

Jill had planned to use our car one day, but I inadvertently took the car keys. Frustrated, she committed the day to the Lord and asked him to work despite the delay. Two hours later, she found another key and set off. Almost immediately she picked up some German girls who were hitchhiking. Since she was going to a youth center where many German young people were holding a Christian conference, she invited them to go with her. They finally agreed. As a result, one of these girls committed her life to Christ.

She told us her story. Several months before, she had delivered an ultimatum to God, whose existence she doubted. She told him that if he were there, he should show himself to her within three months. If he didn't, she told him, "I'll quit my schooling, quit religion, and I *think* I'll quit living, because there's nothing to live for." After explaining this, she turned to Jill and said, with great emotion, "The three months end today."

Prayer

Dear God, your timing may not always fit my plans, but you're never late. Thank you that you bring blessing even in delays. Amen.

May 4—Patience As a Viewpoint

Scripture reading: James 5:7-11

In today's passage, James tells us to be patient and look to the prophets. He also points to Job as an example. Job's story shows us that those who have a sense of God's overruling in the face of deprivation are those who can afford to approach the unpleasantness of life with much less indignation and much more patience. Pity the person whose horizons are limited to selfish considerations, whose world is no greater than his own well-being, whose vision extends no farther than the tip of his own nose! When suffering comes, he rages at his luck running out and is angry that others far more deserving of fate's blunders get off. He even rails against God, whom he has chosen to rationalize into a state of irrelevance.

The unique concept of the church requires considerable patience if it is to become more than a nice idea. Paul made this clear when he wrote, "Be completely humble and gentle; be patient, bearing with one another in love. Make every effort to keep the unity of the Spirit through the bond of peace" (Eph. 4:2-3).

Prayer

Lord, there are many opportunities in this world to become irate, irrational and ill-tempered—even in the church. But help me to see every frustrating circumstance as a potential patience producer. Let it be, dear Lord, let it be so. Amen.

May 5—The Model of Marriage

*Scripture reading: Isaiah 61:10-11; 62:5;
Ephesians 5:21-27*

The Bible repeatedly uses the idea of marriage to illustrate a theological truth.

In the Old Testament, God promises or "covenants" to be our God eternally, and he invites us to respond by being his family. To help people grasp that truth, God used the model of marriage. In exactly the same way that a wife and husband make a covenant with one another, so God commits himself to his people, and they to him.

The theme continues into the New Testament. There, the marriage relationship between a husband and wife is paralleled to the relationship between Christ and the church. What a challenge to realize the significance of marriage is enhanced by its linkage to two of Scripture's most powerful truths! Paul is saying, "Come on, you Christians, show us that you are holy and distinctive. Make mutual submission the basis of a living, caring relationship. Show this crazy world of ours what it's really like to keep your marriage covenant."

Prayer

Lord, even when we take marriage seriously we often limit its meaning. Help me to broaden my vision so I can see how marriage models your covenant and Christ's relationship to the church. Amen.

May 6—A Living Gratitude

Scripture reading: 1 Corinthians 15:9-11

Paul felt unworthy to be called an apostle. But God's grace overwhelmed and thrilled him. "How can I express my gratitude, Lord?" asks the apostle. The Lord replies, "By doing wholeheartedly what I've told you to do."

"Great! What do you want me to do?"

"I want you to be an apostle."

"Oh, good. To the Jews?"

"No, to the Gentiles."

Now Paul, the true-blue Jew, gags on that one. Try to understand how utterly unacceptable this was to him. But what happens subsequently? He becomes the superlative apostle to the Gentiles. He remains constant and consistent, giving of himself to Gentiles who beat him up, throw him in jail, and eventually take his life. Why? Because the Gentiles are so great? No. Because he had such a tremendous love for Gentiles? No. Why on earth did he do it then? Out of gratefulness for his own salvation. Paul's gratitude attitude kept on and kept on.

If you know people who've got this fire in their bones, you know what I'm talking about. You can see them going on, faint, yet pursuing. They keep going because they're doing it as unto Jesus Christ.

Prayer

Lord, help me wholeheartedly do what you want me to do, even if at first I don't want to. So I won't just *say* thank-you—I'll live a daily thanks. Amen.

May 7—Love Doesn't Discriminate

Scripture reading: Matthew 22:37-40

I (Stuart) was born in England in 1930. World War II started in 1939, so during my adolescence, our family had bombs whistling around our ears. The bombs came from Germany. We did not like Germans.

Then several German prisoners were quartered nearby. The authorities contacted the neighborhood boys and asked us to put together a soccer team to play the prisoners of war. We said, "Sure!" We planned to kick their ankles and shins to get even with them. But something strange happened. Once the games began, we discovered the Germans were pretty good—and so were we. We had fun! They were just like us. As we got to know them, we discovered how wrong we had been. We had been prisoners of our own prejudices.

What were the actions of the Lord Jesus Christ toward those who were being discriminated against? Jesus came as God's Anointed One to *all* people. He's our example. So attitudes and actions that are discriminatory are totally out of order for believers. Love never discriminates.

Prayer

Lord, I do not always give people the benefit of the doubt I expect them to give to me. I ask that I may learn to see people through your eyes rather than through my prejudices. Amen.

May 8—God's Seal on Marriage

Scripture reading: Genesis 2:24-25; Hebrews 13:4

When God unites the bride and groom, he takes all their qualities and fuses them into a new entity. He takes the best and the worst, the strengths and weaknesses of both, and fuses them into each other so they might be mutually complementary and enriching.

In marriage, sex demonstrates this in a unique and beautiful way. Outside the marital relationship, sexual intercourse has no reality behind it. The subjects have not been joined together by God. Their oneness is a lie, a sham. In marriage, sexual fusion serves to enhance union in all its dimensions.

The sexual act is intended to demonstrate that, as two people surrender and fuse their bodies, they have surrendered and fused themselves for richer, for poorer, in sickness, in health, till death do them part. And God has sealed it.

Prayer

Lord, you made us fearfully and wonderfully. And you make married couples uniquely and beautifully too. But so often marriages slide into mediocrity or worse and undoubtedly disappoint you. Teach us to do marriage your way and thus discover your wonders. Amen.

May 9—Pressure Within and Without

Scripture reading: 2 Corinthians 4:7-12

An old pastor once advised me, "There are two wrong approaches you can take to the pastorate, Stuart. You can be as idle as the day is long and get away with it. The other alternative is to send yourself to an early grave by assuming you alone carry the weight of the burden of that church, and you alone are responsible for turning that city around for God. You're not very smart if you take either tack."

Some people put no pressure on themselves at all. Others put such excruciating pressure on themselves that they burn out while trying to live up to their own unrealistic expectations. They expect of themselves only success, always victory. They expect perfection. Inevitably they will forget why God put them here, because their criteria have nothing to do with what Jesus wants. In situations like that, we must keep in mind that we are privileged to be servants of God, and there's only one thing we must do: be faithful.

Prayer

Life is so full of challenges and opportunities, Lord. Challenges to do right or go wrong, opportunities to achieve or atrophy. Deliver me from a wasted life either from underachievement or from overextension. Amen.

May 10—Identified with Christ

Scripture reading: Romans 13:11-14

It's amazing what uniforms do for people. You can take a man and dress him in a sweat shirt and jeans and he's just ordinary. Put him in a uniform, though, and he suddenly becomes a different person, one with a high sense of identification and privilege. He really feels that he belongs. And, consequently, he begins to move in a different manner.

You could say that in Christ we take on a certain uniform, one that motivates us to act differently. Once we are new creatures in Christ, we begin to collect a new wardrobe as well; we put on aspects of Christ's very character. And we become aware that we're dressed differently from how we used to be dressed. This becomes a powerful motivation to live in a different way.

Prayer

Lord, in calling myself a Christian, I have taken your name. I wear your uniform; I identify with your cause; I represent you. Deliver me from disgracing you and make me so live that people know whose I am and whom I serve—and may they like what they see, and glorify you. Amen.

May 11—The Gift of Suffering

Scripture reading: Philippians 1:27-30

Do you know that the gift of grace is not only to believe but also to suffer? Suffering is as much a gracious provision of a gracious God as is the opportunity to believe. Because, while belief produces spiritual life, suffering produces spiritual muscles.

I have seen countless examples of churches full of unchallenged, unmotivated saints doing little but putting in time till the Millennium. I've seen these same people revolutionized because they began to act on what they believed, got out where the action is, took some knocks, and grew beyond all recognition. Suffering is God's precious gift to us. Don't miss it.

I am not suggesting, though, that you should go out and start looking for trouble. That won't be necessary! Just do what God expects a recipient of grace to do, and the trouble will come looking for you. There is no quick trip to maturity, and there is no instant recipe for growth. But there are principles for behavior. When they are followed, growth and maturity have a habit of coming right along.

Prayer

Dear Lord, at times I have questioned the things you allow without considering the fact that no disciple is greater than his or her master and that to suffer for Christ's sake is more privilege than punishment. Forgive me. Amen.

May 12—Part of the Answer

Scripture reading: Luke 10:30-37

Compassion is action motivated by the understanding that God's concern for me is the sole reason I exist and survive. Because he understood that, the Good Samaritan climbed off his donkey, got down in the muck and the nettles (ripping his own clothes in the process), poured oil and wine on the man's wounds, and bound them up. All the while he was in robber-infested country, knowing that at any moment he too could be clubbed on the back of the head. He picked the man up, put him on his donkey, took him to an inn, paid for the room, and promised to return. That's compassion. Not just a warm feeling. Not just a bleeding heart or "liberal" tendencies. Not just giving handouts.

Motivated by God's compassion on my behalf, I long to meet others at their point of need, in Jesus' name. I want to be the means by which God answers their prayers and longings. Powerful things will begin to happen in our lives as we allow our hearts to be touched by the Spirit. We will grow to have the compassion to fulfill our own role as God's Good Samaritans for the world.

Prayer

Lord, I'd like very much to be part of the answer rather than someone who exacerbates the problem. Work in me to bring compassion to the surface so that I will actively involve myself, in your name, to do what you would have me to do. Amen.

May 13—Teach the Children

Scripture reading: Deuteronomy 6:1-9, 20-25

It is all too easy to ignore our responsibility to give moral and spiritual direction to our children. We want to shift the responsibility to other people. But who, besides us, is going to teach our children biblical, spiritual values?

We need to help our children evaluate their learning so that it includes fundamental moral and spiritual principles. In line with this, Deuteronomy tells us to talk about these principles when we sit at home, when we walk along the road, when we lie down, and when we get up. We are to tie them as symbols on our hands, bind them on our foreheads, and write them on the door frames of our houses and on our gates. Instead of keeping our spiritual life in a watertight compartment, we are to make sure each part of our day is saturated with our experience of God.

What is the Lord saying here? "Be natural about it." Be perfectly natural about teaching moral and spiritual principles. Do it in the course of everyday living, in a consistent way. Do it in a practical way. Just make sure you do it!

Prayer

Lord, help us to be so in touch with you that our children see the reality of our love for you all the time—wherever we are, whatever we do. Amen.

May 14—Cautions about "Should"

Scripture reading: Proverbs 22:6; 29:15

The wise writer of Proverbs said, "Train a child in the way he should go, and when he is old he will not turn from it." The problem is figuring out which way our children should go. Parents must walk a fine line between letting their children do whatever pleases them and being so strict they thwart their children's development into the unique persons God wants them to be.

How do we find out what our children should do? We must be sensitive to their God-given potential. "The way he or she should go" must be aligned with God's "should." God has a number of "shoulds" for us, but he actually gives us broad principles and a lot of room in how we understand and teach them.

Jesus spoke harshly with religious leaders for making so many "shoulds" that it was impossible for anyone to follow them all. This is a good lesson for parents. Our job is not to bury our children with rules and regulations but to guide them into the life principles God has provided for their well-being.

Prayer

Lord, may I never impose my will on others but always encourage them to discover and do your will. Amen.

May 15—Powerless to Change

Scripture reading: Romans 5:6; 7:18-19

Powerless is not a very popular word. Everyone talks about having power and being empowered. But the Bible is clear: we don't possess enough power to change our own lives.

There's no question that human beings are remarkable creatures and have achieved great things. But the problem is that although we can send a man to the moon and bring him back again, we are powerless to make him fit to live on earth. Look at humankind's history. People have tried to make life a better experience, but ultimately they have encountered defeat. We have great psychological power, even great creative power and physical power, but—because of sin—we do not have moral, spiritual power. Consequently, we are powerless when it comes to living and expressing true *agape* love.

But Paul makes the point that, even while were sinners, Christ died for us because God loves us. That's the wonderful good news of the gospel. This is why Jesus had to come, to live, die, and rise again: so we could have access to *God's* power. In Jesus Christ we have power—the power to love.

Prayer

Lord, until I discover my own powerlessness, I will have little or no interest in discovering your power. So keep reminding me, Lord. But gently, please! Amen.

May 16—In on the Mystery

Scripture reading: 1 Corinthians 4:1; 1 Peter 1:10-12

The Greek word *mysterion* has nothing to do with our modern concept of the mysterious. When the New Testament uses the word, it is talking about things now revealed to you that you previously didn't know—and that are still secret to many other people.

The mysteries of God have been revealed to the initiated, says Paul. But he adds an admonition: Those of us who have received the mysteries, who have had our eyes opened, must understand that we have received this insight as a sacred trust.

That's what Paul means when he says we are privileged people. God has opened our eyes to things other people don't understand; he has entrusted this information to us in order that we might do with it what he wishes—and, ultimately, that we might disseminate it to others who don't know.

Prayer

Lord, I am overwhelmed by the things I have learned about you because you have opened my eyes. But help me not to overlook the spiritual darkness in which others live. May I be eager to share what I've discovered so others might be blessed. Amen.

May 17—Strife among Christians

Scripture reading: Philippians 2:1-4

We Christians seem to have a hard time learning from the mistakes of the past, for the same old things keep happening. This is particularly obvious in the area of interpersonal relations among Christians. Although we see encouraging signs of improvement, we still have a long way to go.

Besides obscuring our evangelistic message to others, inter-Christian strife dissipates the energies of Christians themselves. It diverts us from the real object of our warfare: Satan and his cohorts. The effectiveness of a body of believers in thwarting Satan is largely related to how much that body is fighting itself. The more energy we expend in fighting each other, the less there will be for the real task to which we have been called. On the other hand, the more we fight the real enemy, the more we'll gladly accept the help and fellowship of all who will identify with us.

Prayer

Lord, you tell us that our struggle is not against flesh and blood. We say amen and then struggle with flesh and blood. Help me to see the real enemy and recognize that those I am fighting are being used by him—and so am I. Then perhaps we can unite in fighting him. Amen.

May 18—God's Goodness

Scripture reading: Mark 10:17-18

Biblical concepts of goodness must have a different point of reference than human concepts of goodness.

The Lord Jesus, when confronted by the young man who called him "good teacher," retorted, "Why do you call me good?" His statement "No one is good—except God alone" showed the necessity of challenging the underlying misconceptions about goodness. God, not man, is the measure of all things, including goodness. This idea is crucial to our understanding of goodness.

We need to seek after a divine revelation of goodness rather than being satisfied with human rationalization. Human goodness certainly helps make life pleasant, but only God's goodness will accomplish God's goals in the world.

Prayer

It hurts my pride, Lord, to be told I am not good by your standards, particularly when I am highly regarded by my friends and relatives. But it's good for me to recognize that without you I am nothing. Help me to earnestly seek your enabling that I may grow in grace—and goodness. Amen.

May 19—In Transition

Scripture reading: Luke 2:41-52

Teen-agers are people in that very difficult transition time between childhood and adulthood. Some aspects of their personality are still childlike (some would even say childish), but in other areas they are surprisingly mature. This uneasy mix of characteristics causes significant difficulty and tension.

Luke 2:52 speaks of Jesus' being in a transitional stage: "And Jesus grew in wisdom and stature, and in favor with God and men." The Greek word for *grew* here means "to progress, to advance, to move." Adolescence is characterized by tremendous progress, movement, and growth.

Parents, teachers, and other adults in a teen's life must take care to remind that young woman or man of just how much potential she or he possesses. The possibilities for reaching goals and developing strengths and gifts are enormous.

Prayer

Lord, I was a teen-ager once, and it was not pretty. Help me to bear that in mind when I deal with the youth I encounter. May I never forget that teens are people making progress under pressure. May I contribute to their well-being rather than criticize their wrongdoing. Amen.

May 20—Growing in Wisdom

Scripture reading: James 3:13-18

What does wisdom mean? It's more than just *learning* information; it's understanding how to properly *apply* information. If we begin to apply information, our attitudes will change. And if our attitudes are changed, our activities and our actions will change. Thus, wisdom means getting information, knowing how to apply it, and changing our attitudes and behavior accordingly.

Jesus grew in wisdom, and so do young adults today. Depending on their source of information and how they apply it, their attitudes and actions will change for the better—or for the worse. James says if you get the wrong information and apply it to your life, it will affect your attitude, and your actions will identify your source of information. Similarly, if you get your information from God, it will affect you as you apply it; your attitudes will be changed and your activities will demonstrate it. This is a tremendous process for teens, because they are beginning to learn concepts and principles and to discover what it means to act on them.

Prayer

May I be a source of encouragement, a mine of godly information, and a reflection of you, Lord, so that the young people whom I influence may be assisted in the adventure of growth and development. Amen.

May 21—Serve while You're Young

Scripture reading: Ecclesiastes 12

We shouldn't wait until we are old to be what we were created to be. We need to encourage young people to take advantage of their incredible potential now, while they are at their best. As we grow older, we do not function as well physically as we did in our youth.

"Remember him—before the silver cord is severed, or the golden bowl is broken; before the pitcher is shattered . . . or the wheel broken." (vs. 6). In the days when this was written, light was provided by golden bowls of oil suspended on a silver cord. When the silver cord wore thin and broke, the golden bowl would spill, and the light would go out. Our lives are like this.

While we are young, we have a strong silver cord and a bright shiny bowl; we are full of vigor and enthusiasm. God can set our bowl alight so that we can do what we were intended to do. We must not wait until the old cord has snapped and all the oil has spilled. The time to serve God is now.

Prayer

Lord, sometimes it is easier to criticize young adults than encourage them or to do something myself rather than let them learn by making mistakes. Teach me to recognize that the next generation needs encouragement and opportunity. Amen.

May 22—Open to New Directions

Scripture reading: Jonah 1:1-3

When Stuart and I first came to Elmbrook Church, I struggled when God began to give me opportunities to teach women. Working with young people was what I loved. So I had an attitude problem. Like Jonah, I gritted my teeth and said, "All right, I'll do it because I've got to. I'll do it to obey God."

One day, a friend said, "Jill, you have God-given abilities, but you don't love these women." She was right, but I was stubborn. Finally, I prayed that God would give me his *agape* love. I prayed that the women might know I loved them. And I do.

God gives each of us the special ability to love beyond ourselves. The only way God can minister to all the needs in the world is for us to say, "I'm willing to love whoever needs it. But without your empowering love, this situation only frustrates, discourages, and disgusts me." Real love for people is a gift directly from the heart of God. It is a gift that is released as we trust him and obey.

Prayer

Lord, teach me that I cannot pick and choose those I want to love, serve, teach. You want me to love everyone unconditionally, like you do. Help me to let you choose for me. Amen.

May 23—A Sense of Privilege

Scripture reading: 1 Corinthians 4:1-7

Why would the people referred to in this passage want to
be faithful? Because they have such a sense of pride in
their privileged position that they say, in effect, "Imagine,
God calling me, choosing me, deciding to do it this way.
It's wonderful." As a result, they don't want to blow it.
Therein lies their sense of privilege, and they are appropriately proud.

What is the driving motivational attitude in *your* Christian life? Are you thinking, *I've lost my sense of privilege,
that sense of pride in being called by Jesus*? If so, it's time
to ask for a new sense of motivation. It's time to meditate
on Scripture so that gratefulness and a sense of privilege
can become part of your thinking again. And faithfulness,
as a result, can be renewed.

Prayer

Lord, you are on record as being as deeply concerned
about motives as you are about actions. Help me therefore
to be as aware of my reasons for doing what I do as I am
about the consequences of my doings. Amen.

May 24—Total Faithfulness

Scripture reading: 1 Corinthians 1:7-9

God is faithful always to mean what he says and say what he means. The significance of this is clear in statements such as, "He will keep you strong to the end, so that you will be blameless on the day of our Lord Jesus Christ" (1 Cor. 1:8). A promise of such dimensions stirs the most exhilarating hope in the human heart.

Yet hope has its doubts, and sooner or later a little voice will ask, "But how can I be sure he will keep me?" The answer: "God, who has called you into fellowship with his Son Jesus Christ our Lord, is faithful" (1 Cor. 1:9). The faith that breeds assurance is rooted in the faithfulness of a God who cannot lie and who must always be true to himself. The ultimate experience of our salvation is laid up in heaven for us, guaranteed by the faithful God.

Prayer

Lord, if you are not totally reliable and utterly trustworthy, there can be no such thing as certainty or stability. But thank you that you reaffirm your faithfulness on a daily basis and, in so doing, encourage my confidence in you to grow. Amen.

May 25—Fragmented by Factions

Scripture reading: 1 Corinthians 1:10-17

Paul talks about two serious causes of conflict among Christians: factions and empty pride. The Corinthian fellowship had degenerated into groups of "Paul people" and "Apollos people" and "Peter people." Instead of being united in Christ, they were fragmented by personalities. No doubt some had been helped more by one than another or were more compatible temperamentally with one than another—but this was no cause for a campaign to boost their man and defeat the other.

We have the same kind of situation in the Christian world today. We have our personalities, and they have their followers. That in itself may be fine, but fighting over it isn't. It is great to be thrilled by someone so long as you are not threatened by someone else. But if we promote the one who thrills and attack the one who threatens, conflict and confusion result. In what ways does the church today exalt its leaders over the supremacy of Christ and the fellowship of believers? How can the church combat such misplaced pride?

Prayer

Lord, I do like some people more than others, and I find it easy to agree with one and almost impossible with another. Help me to handle these preferences and even prejudices so they do not create problems and encourage party strife. Amen.

May 26—Specially Single

Scripture reading: Matthew 19:11-12

Jesus said it is perfectly legitimate to be single, but there are different reasons for singleness. Some are born with the propensity toward singleness, some have been put into that situation by other people, and others have chosen singleness. This reminds me of the quote from Shakespeare's *Twelfth Night:* "Some are born great, some achieve greatness, and some have greatness thrust upon them." I suppose that you could say that some people are born single, some people achieve singleness, and others have singleness thrust upon them.

Jesus outlines a fourth aspect of singleness in Matthew 19:11-12. He states that those who choose singleness for the sake of the kingdom are very special people indeed. This idea is amplified in 1 Corinthians 7:7, where Paul suggests that singleness can be a high calling, given by God to some people as a special gift, so they can serve God without distraction.

Prayer

Lord, help me to see your hand at work in the lives of all of your children—and to live out faithfully the special call you have given me personally. Amen.

May 27—Love Keeps No Record of Wrongs

Scripture reading: Isaiah 43:18-26

I once visited a primitive tribe in South America. Noticing odd objects hanging from the ceilings of their huts, I asked about them. The people explained: "We have many enemies. Each time someone hurts us or does us wrong, we hang up a remembrance of it to make sure we never forget." Some of our minds are like that. We hang all sorts of remembrances of what "he did to me twenty years ago" and "what she did last week" all over our minds in case we forget.

But God tells us to forgive, just as he has forgiven our own malice, hatred, selfishness, pettiness, immorality, etc. We can only forgive with the love God gives to us, the love that must be transplanted and grow inside us. So, don't be surprised when forgiveness is difficult, even excruciating. Take it as a cue to pray more desperately for God to do the forgiving in you, by his love in you reaching out to others—especially those who've been so hurtful.

Prayer

Lord, it's too easy for people to say, "Forgive and forget." I can't always control the memories that crash unbidden into my mind, but I can choose through your grace neither to dwell on the injury nor to make matters worse. Help me forgive again when I cannot seem to forget. Amen.

May 28—Love Doesn't Assume the Worst

Scripture reading: Romans 14:10-13

There is no lower blow than to attribute a bad motive to someone who is acting in good faith with loving intentions. Yet it is a common practice in our dog-eat-dog society. We can be so cynical, harsh, and unloving that our instant reflex is to think the worst of other people. When you go in with accusations about a person's motives, you have left love behind.

Love always gives a person the benefit of the doubt. We don't have the power or wisdom to truly know what is going on inside others' minds and hearts. Love does not attribute evil motives. Love does not keep account of wrongs. Love does not calculate evil. Instead, love considers all the possible causes for a person's hurtful words or actions.

What are some factors in daily life that can cause us to wrong others, even though we're not out to hurt anyone? Stress at work? Fatigue? Anger at something completely unrelated? Ask the Holy Spirit to search your heart, helping you overcome your own tendency to hurt others. Ask also for help in refraining from attributing evil motives to others when they hurt you.

Prayer

Lord, help me to believe the best about others until I have conclusive evidence to the contrary. Amen.

May 29—Love Always Trusts

Scripture reading: 1 Corinthians 13:7; Hebrews 11:1

Love is always prepared to retain faith in a person, because love never believes that anyone is beyond redemption. Love doesn't cut someone off finally and irrevocably. Love always maintains faith for something greater than is in evidence at present. Compare these scenarios: A son tells his father, "Dad, you drive me up the wall, and I see absolutely no way I can survive in the same house with you." But a loving son might come to his dad and say, "Dad, I don't really know what it is about you and about me that we rub each other the wrong way. But I honestly believe it can be resolved. I'm going to work on it." The same thing can happen in a marriage. A spouse might say, "I've had it up to here, and I'm leaving!" instead of saying, "I've had it up to here, but it's not over my head yet! I honestly believe there is hope for us." That's love.

Is there some relationship in which you are having a difficult time with trust? What kinds of statements are you tempted to say about this person? What kinds of statements would love's kind of trust help you to make?

Prayer

Lord, I'm so glad you have not written me off as a hopeless case. But I'm afraid I have taken the liberty to do it to others. Help me to change. Amen.

May 30—Love and Letting Go

Scripture reading: Matthew 16:24-28

> Relinquishment doesn't grab or clutch.
> Clutching crushes love.
> Love can't breathe easily
>   when it's controlled
>   by possessive hands.
>
> Trust grows best
>   when it's planted in respect.
> It flowers in profusion
>   when joys are shared.
>
> Letting go is a learned art—
> Jesus is the best teacher.
> I need to be the best pupil.
> Love will help me
>   let go—
>   if I ask Him to.

Prayer

We seem to clutch, grab, and hold onto our lives and people we love. Take my fingers, one by one, and open them, Lord. Help me to hold those I love lightly not tightly. Amen.

May 31—More Than a Movement

Scripture reading: Acts 1:1-5

History holds many examples of the process that starts with a man, becomes a movement, and ends a monument. While many empty cathedrals, dusty tombstones, and failed ministries might suggest that Christ has become just another outmoded and irrelevant relic, the fact remains that never have there been so many disciples of Christ as there are now.

Jesus' invitation has been accepted by more people in the present generation than in any previous generation. The reason is not hard to find: He has always delivered exactly what he promised. Modern-day disciples on factory floors and in surgical suites are not part of a moribund movement struggling for survival. They are intimately related to the Christ who invites them now to share his risen life through his Spirit, in much the same way he invited the Twelve to share his earthly life on the dusty roads of the Middle East.

The invitation today is essentially the same: "Come to me" and "Follow me."

Prayer

Lord, deliver me from ever accepting a Christianity that is moribund and mediocre. There's nothing outmoded about you; there should be nothing mediocre about me— unless of course I lose contact with you and stop following. Amen.

June

June 1—Down Is Up

Scripture reading: Philippians 2:5-11

When I was a child I heard Dr. Donald Gray Barnhouse speak at the Keswick Convention in England. He began his sermon by saying, "The way to up is down." He paused. There was a nervous rustle among the British crowd. He went on, "The way to down is up." And I looked at him from my hard seat in the back row and said to myself, "That American preacher is a nut." I switched him off, and I'm sorry I did.

What Dr. Barnhouse was saying was this: The way to heavenly success is through humility. But if you insist on pushing yourself up, God will accept full responsibility for pushing you right down. That's the way God works.

We have the loveliest of all illustrations in Christ. The way to the throne was through the tomb. The way to the crown was through the cross. The way to a life lived in the power of God down here on earth is through humility and bowing the knee to Christ as Lord.

Prayer

Lord, I would never have guessed that "the way to up is down." But you showed me it is, and you continue to remind me of that. However contrary it is to my assumptions, it's still true! Thank you. Amen.

June 2—Trouble in This World

Scripture reading: John 15:18-21; Revelation 2:8-11

The Lord pulled no punches when he told the disciples that they would have trouble in the world. They were trained with the knowledge that they were enrolled in a conflict of cosmic proportions. Their enemies were not flesh and blood, but spiritual, powerful, and utterly evil. In practical terms this meant a great amount of physical abuse and appalling danger, sometimes even leading to martyrdom.

The Greek word for *witness* is *martus*, meaning "martyr," a connection that never let the disciples forget that martyrs are witnesses who meet hostility in its most aggressive form. Yet, no matter what the experience, they reminded believers of the privilege of suffering for the One who suffered the ultimate trouble; of the unlimited resources of resolve and courage in the Holy Spirit, the Word, and the believing community; and of the necessity for faithfulness—perseverance while under pressure.

Prayer

Lord, our culture is committed to embracing pleasure and avoiding pain. The results are often ugly. You ask me to find my delight in those things that please you and to embrace those things I would prefer to sidestep, which you have allowed to come my way. Show me how, Lord. Amen.

June 3—Hell Is Emptiness

Scripture reading: Psalm 16:5-11

"You will not abandon me to the grave," the psalmist says. Some translations use the Hebrew word *Sheol* for "the grave," meaning "to be hollow." Sheol is described as a bottomless, silent space where no bird sings, no child laughs, no wind rustles through the trees. No one talks to anyone, for the sense of isolation overwhelms the consciousness and locks a person into the lostness.

It is hard to describe emptiness, but the Bible tries to help us picture Sheol by painting it in shadows and gray tones. In *The Great Divorce*, C. S. Lewis pictures hell as eternal twilight hanging heavy in the damp moldy air. Perhaps we could say hell is like living with everlasting cataracts and unfortunately just enough sight to see that there is nothing to see!

Have you ever dragged yourself out of a nightmare? Somehow you know the horrors are only a dream and it is possible with an incredible effort to wake yourself up. Imagine doing that only to find the nightmare is reality and it is not even possible to escape into sleep again. Think of awaking eternally to bottomless misery. This is hell, the fate God desires for none of us.

Prayer

O God, there is so much emptiness in people's lives. It mirrors the emptiness in eternity reserved for those who don't know you. Save me from this bottomless misery. Give me forgiveness and life for Jesus' sake. Amen.

June 4—Encouraged by Friends

Scripture reading: Proverbs 27:6-9

Two delightful expressions here remind us of the results of genuine friendship: a friend's counsel is helpful and brings joy, and a real friend sometimes will tell us what we do not want to hear. In such circumstances, "wounds from a friend can be trusted."

How do we grow? By developing relationships in which we demonstrate loving concern for each other. As we develop this loving concern, we counsel each other. If a relationship has been established, we hear what we need to hear, not just what we *want* to hear. And because of the relationship, we accept what our friend says and respond accordingly. A real friend will help us grow into the kind of people God wants us to be.

Prayer

Lord, in your friendship and your lordship I find fellowship and discipleship for you to speak to me lovingly, firmly, constructively, critically, and productively. And even when your words hurt, I never doubt their preciousness. Thank you. Amen.

June 5—Second Chances

Scripture reading: Romans 15:1-4

One day the apostle Paul said he needed two people to accompany him on a missionary journey. Barnabas said, "I'm your man. And why don't we take young John Mark?" Paul agreed and the journey began. Then, in the middle of the toughest assignment they had ever had, John Mark got scared and ran home.

When it was time for another missionary journey, Barnabas said, "Let's give John Mark another chance." No, Paul said, and the Bible says the contention was so strong between Paul and Barnabas that they split up.

Barnabas took John Mark's side, and there's no doubt in my mind that he was right. If there had been nothing redeemable in that young man, we wouldn't have the Gospel of Mark today. Who do you know who has "failed" in some way in their Christian walk? How can you love them in a way that covers their failings and aids in healing and restoration?

Prayer

Lord, you are in the business of reconciliation and restoration. I'm afraid I engage in rejection and retaliation. Thank you for the Barnabases of this world who put a human face on divine grace—and please help me do it too! Amen.

June 6—True Charity

Scripture reading: Leviticus 25:8–38

Peter Ustinov, the actor, playwright, director, raconteur, linguist, and humorist, once observed, "Charity is more common than compassion, because charity is tax-deductible while compassion is merely time-consuming." There's something humorous about that. But there's also something cutting and terribly compelling about it, because he's absolutely right.

We're grateful that we live in a nation where it is possible to get tax-deductible receipts for our charity. But there's a danger to such a luxury. It allows us to do something about needs, but to do it at arm's length. It allows us to do something for others, while at the same time feeling satisfaction in gaining something for ourselves. There's a great difference between cold charity and warm-hearted compassion. Charity can be purely external, coldly calculated. True compassion is internal, a motivation of the heart that is pure, rich, and absolutely vital.

Prayer

Lord, I cannot escape the fact that when I'm helpful or gracious I derive a considerable degree of satisfaction from it. But I ask you, please don't let me behave like a disciple for any other reasons than those that please you. Amen.

June 7—Our New Significance

Scripture reading: Philippians 2:12-13

Perhaps you have heard the phrase "We all have a little divine spark in us, and we must try to fan it." This is not what the Scriptures teach. They say that until we receive Christ we are dead to God. Only when we are regenerated through the work of the Holy Spirit does God take up his residence within our bodies. But when he does, he really does!

When Christ's presence graced a stable under an inn in Bethlehem, the inn took on new significance. When he enters any place, he makes it strangely different. When God in Christ entered your life at the moment of your commitment to him, you took on new significance. You were no longer little ol' you against the big, cold world. You became little ol' you, along with the mighty, eternal God who now resides in you. God is willing to energize you to do his will. Are you willing to receive his energy?

Prayer

Deliver me, dear Lord, from the "little ol' me" syndrome, with its defeatist attitudes and small ambitions, and reveal to me the privilege and potential of being your dwelling place. Amen.

June 8—Walking in the Truth

Scripture reading: 3 John 2-4

Twenty centuries after Christ's time on earth we have become accustomed to the broad sweep of Christian theology, modern criticisms, and attempted revisions of it and what we regard as the fundamentals of the faith. But in the formative years of the church, many issues concerning the nature and deity of Christ, the means of grace, and Christian ethics were being fiercely debated.

People from a Jewish background struggled with the concept of a suffering Messiah instead of a popular hero-deliverer. Others from a Greek background, which stressed the evilness of matter, were appalled at the suggestion that God would assume bodily form. Gnosticism attacked on a different, but no less powerful, front. And in the middle stood believers committed to the truth delivered to them through the apostles.

The apostles were not intimidated by their opponents, waging serious war against every threat to their gospel. They expected believers to be able to recognize truth from error and embrace the one and shun the other. To them, this was the essence of faithfulness.

Prayer

Lord, people regularly try to persuade me that there is no such thing as "truth"—only truths. Help your people who find themselves debating such a situation not only to hold to the truth but also to walk in it too. Amen.

June 9—Friends Are Honest

Scripture reading: Proverbs 28:23

There is honesty and then there is *honesty*. As believers concerned about building unity and community, we must beware of the wrong kind of candor. Proverbs 16:28 says, "A perverse man stirs up dissension, and a gossip separates close friends." "He who covers over an offense promotes love, but whoever repeats the matter separates close friends" (Prov. 17:9).

Genuine friendship requires that we be honest with one another. Yet, to maintain a relationship, we need to know when to speak and when to keep silent, what to say and what to avoid. One of the quickest ways to destroy a friendship is through gossip. This is something we need to guard against. Unfortunately, in the church, what passes for candor and "speaking the truth in love" often is sheer, naked gossip, and it is destructive in the extreme.

What kind of friends do you have? How do you protect and develop your friendships? Are you cautious? Are you careful? Are you committed and candid? These are qualities we need to strive for to ensure healthy, productive, and godly relationships.

Prayer

Lord, help us to see friendship as a precious gift to be cherished and cultivated. Help me personally to encourage my friends to grow in grace. Amen.

June 10—Perseverance

Scripture reading: James 1:2-8

During World War II there was a ship called the HMS *Eskimo.* It had been in a horrendous sea battle and taken a torpedo hit that destroyed its bows and effectively cut the ship in half. Everybody thought that was the end of the *Eskimo,* but one day it sailed into Barrow Shipyard. As it slid into port, multitudes were there cheering, crying, and waving. The crew stood at attention on the shattered deck, saluted the flag that, though ripped to shreds, still waved bravely, and sang the national anthem. I will never forget seeing that ship—or what was left of it—arriving battered but safely into port.

Throughout church history, many, many believers in Jesus have endured the unimaginable. Read the stories, however, and you'll find that they persevered unto death, and they were at peace. How? Because they knew where they were going and to whom they belonged; with that knowledge they were able to endure the worst. This life is insignificant when compared to eternity with God and his Son. There are times when that larger view of things is what we must have to get through the present.

Prayer

Lord, I'm so glad you don't just tell me to keep sailing when I've taken a hit. Thank you for keeping me afloat and bringing me into harbor with you. Amen.

June 11—Roadblocks to Caring

Scripture reading: Psalm 14

Understanding God's compassion and realizing we ought to be motivated by it to express compassion to others is only the first step. There are roadblocks. Some Christians reason, "This world is full of con artists. If I start being compassionate, they're going to take me to the cleaners." Others contend, "If people have needs, it's their own fault. To give them a handout is the worst possible thing you can do." All the arguments fail to erase the fact that Jesus said quite simply, "If you have been shown compassion, then you need to show it too." But how—especially if we have deep feelings to the contrary? Psalm 14 offers an answer.

The crux of this psalm is located in the last verse and contains only two letters: *Oh.* Notice that you can say *Oh* in a variety of ways: as an exclamation; as a mere statement; even with a touch of surprise. Or you can read it the way the psalmist intended it to be read— "Ooooohhhhh!"—conveying God's deep, gut-wrenching concern for the needy people of the world.

Prayer

A world full of need can easily be eclipsed by absorption in our own selfish interests. But the enormity of a lost world's rejection of you, Lord, and the resultant chaos and disintegration must lead me to a deep heart concern. May it ever be so for me, Lord. Amen.

June 12—In His Name

Scripture reading: John 14:13-14; 15:7-8

The study and application of Scripture is integrally linked to the practice and enjoyment of prayer. The Master made a wonderfully sweeping promise in John 15:7: "Ask whatever you wish, and it will be given you."

Taken out of context, this could make a superb rationale for all kinds of irresponsible praying. But Jesus had just said, "You may ask for anything in my name and I will do it." To ask *in his name* is to ask as his representative, on his behalf.

When children are young, it is not unusual for a parent to ask them to run next door to the neighbor's to borrow some household item. The neighbor recognizes a perfectly normal request and hands over the item. But if the same kids were to go to the bank and ask the teller to give them ten thousand dollars on their father's behalf, they would immediately be put on inquiry. To ask in their parents' name, children need to make legitimate requests with their parents' backing.

When disciples relish their friendship with the Master, study and apply his Word to their lives, and then ask him for legitimate things they need to fulfill his stated objectives, there are results. Fruit grows all over the place.

Prayer

Deliver me, Lord, from the kind of irresponsible praying that is based on my whims and wants, rather than on my needs and your name. Amen.

June 13—Instructed to Rejoice

Scripture reading: Philippians 3:1; 4:4

"Rejoice in the Lord," Paul tells the Philippians. And notice: It is an instruction, not a suggestion. Rejoicing in the Lord is not of marginal importance, nor is it an optional extra for evangelical extroverts. As the Old Testament tells us, "The joy of the Lord is your strength" (Neh. 8:10).

Strong Christians are strong because they enjoy the Lord. People who don't enjoy him live their lives apart from him and, accordingly, know nothing of his strength. Rejoicing in the Lord may mean thinking through how to rejoice when we don't feel like it. It may mean acting as if everything will turn out all right—when we have no guarantees we can see at the moment.

One thing is certain. There is no way a mere human can live in this world as if he belongs to the next world without the strength of the Lord.

Prayer

Lord, I have to admit that sometimes things come my way that don't delight me, so I struggle against my circumstances. Until, that is, I turn my thoughts to you. Even though my situation does not change, thanks for changing my attitude and helping me to once again find my strength in you. Amen.

June 14—Paying Attention to the Word

Scripture reading: Matthew 7:24-29

The sensible people are those who pay attention to the teachings of Jesus Christ. Many people claim to believe the Bible from cover to cover, but they never spend time in it. They lack an apetite for it, or they have no concern for what it says, or they just fail to study it.

It makes sense to heed Jesus' teachings because his words always project authority. This authority is what aroused his enemies to oppose him so strongly. And this same authority should encourage us to follow him faithfully. Christ's teaching also produces amazement, and then action. The sensible person acts on Jesus' teachings. This is a wisdom for living, a practical rather than theoretical wisdom. A truly wise person can put Jesus' principles into operation.

If the church is to produce wise people, they must be people of the Book. This is the only authoritative source of true wisdom.

Prayer

Dear Father, so often I neglect the gift of your Word. Fill me again with a hunger to read, study, meditate, and then give me grace to act on what I read. Amen.

June 15—Work As Cooperation

Scripture reading: 1 Corinthians 3:5-9

When God told Adam and Eve to till the Garden, what he was really saying was, "Let's cooperate." Paul picks up on the same idea; we are "workers together with God."

A preacher visited a farmer one day. Standing on a hill looking over the farm, they beheld a beautiful field of corn. It was a great sight—lovely, long, straight lines; tall, green shoots; large ears of corn all ready to be picked. "Oh," the preacher said, "just look how the Lord has sent the rain and has given you the soil, the seed, and the increase! Isn't the Lord wonderful? You must praise the Lord every day." The old farmer nodded. "Yes, I do. But you should have seen what this place was like when he had it on his own."

If you are going to grow corn to feed people, you need a farmer. But the farmer can't invent the soil, create rain, or perform the miracle of reproduction. God does that. Today's Scripture points out that one of the high and noble privileges of being a human being is that we are called to cooperate with God in the work going on in the universe.

Prayer

Teach me what is my work and what is yours, Lord. If you don't, I know I may neglect what you gave me to do and get in the way of what you wish to do. I really do want to cooperate. Amen.

June 16—Love Always Counts

Scripture reading: 1 Corinthians 13:8-10

The final description of love in this "love chapter" is that love is eternally relevant. Saying that "love never fails" doesn't mean that loving is a simplistic answer to anything, that love always works. If a girl determines to love a man, there is no guarantee he will love her in return. If he doesn't respond, nothing can be done. "Love never fails" doesn't mean that love will always achieve whatever you want. It doesn't mean that love never fails to get a response, but rather that love never fails to love! It never gives up. It always abides. Love is of eternal significance.

"Love never fails" says to us that love will ultimately win over lack of love, just as God's love through Jesus' death and resurrection triumphed over death and hatred. In other words, whatever we do out of love will count. We may not see it counting at this moment, but because love is the essence of God, any loving we do has an eternal place and purpose. Love may be ignored, but it is never wasted and—in God's book—never discounted.

Prayer

I rejoice in your love, Lord—the love that doesn't change and never quits. I regret that my love does both. With the model of your love before me and the power of your Spirit within me, things can change. I pray they will. Amen.

June 17—Marriage Mathematics

Scripture reading: Mark 10:7-9

Many people in our society do not recognize marriage as a divine institution and are not committed to it. But when the wedding vows include a deep commitment, a couple can build on that commitment a superstructure of thoroughly mature living.

It is a beautiful thing to observe couples who have truly committed themselves to their marriage. Believe it or not, love can grow! I know couples who have been married forty, fifty, and even sixty years. Over the years they have faced pain and pleasure, gain and loss, but in and through it all, their love is growing more Christlike as they serve one another.

Jesus said, "The two will become one flesh. . . . They are no longer two, but one. Therefore, what God has joined together, let man not separate" (vv. 8-9). Thus, when two people marry, they become a unique entity. God has a special kind of mathematics. He can make one plus one equal one. It's in the commitment to the new, divinely crafted one-ness that strength to persevere is discovered and the ability to mature is found.

Prayer

Lord, if one plus one equals one, it must be because they were halves to begin with! That shows me how much I need to contribute myself to the new one-ness and to embrace my spouse as my other, indispensable half. My better half! Help me to mean it, Lord. Amen.

June 18—Prejudice in Church

Scripture reading: James 2:1-9

Imagine the situation that may have prompted James's words. You've got a small group of believers, and James is the leader of this little church. It's made up mostly of poor people—some of them slaves—and very few wealthy or influential people at all. One day, to their delight, someone very wealthy, very influential, and very powerful comes in. Of course, the people say, "Wow! That's great! Double the offering overnight." They fawn over him, ushering him to the best seat. But they discover a shabby little man in the seat, so they try to get him out of there.

It's a perfect example of prejudice. The believers are prejudging both men on purely external and material criteria. They are not showing any interest in the spiritual realities of the people. They don't seem to act as if Jesus is Lord and Savior of both. They have committed prejudice in the church of Jesus Christ.

What type of person might feel uncomfortable in your church, and why? How can you help eliminate such prejudice in love?

Prayer

Lord, I need to be willing to see everyone as created by you and therefore significant, fallen and therefore needy, redeemable and therefore deserving of my loving care. Aid me in my shortcomings, Father. Amen.

June 19—Beauty in Diversity

Scripture reading: 1 Corinthians 12:12-30

In verse 13, Paul identifies those within the body at Corinth: some are Jews, some are Greeks, some are slaves, and some are free. We would put it differently in our own historical framework, but Paul is simply saying it would be ridiculous to suggest we're all identical. We're not. We have come from widely differing circumstances. Not only that, he points out that we have different callings. According to verse 18, God has taken individual Christians from differing circumstances and placed them in the body in different ways to do different things. If we ever become locked into complete uniformity, we will destroy the beauty and the uniqueness of the body of believers.

To the church, God has said, "I'm going to bring together the most diverse people imaginable. They will possess a fundamental unity, and I'm going to allow that unity to become something for which they will live and for which they would die if necessary. It will never, however, be a unity that possesses a dull uniformity. It will be a unity that allows for untold diversity." And so it is.

Prayer

There's a great challenge for me, Lord, in your commitment to bring unity out of diversity. It's the challenge to be open, understanding, patient, flexible, unafraid, and much more. I can't do it alone. Thankfully, I have you! Amen.

June 20—Basking in His Love

Scripture reading: Ephesians 3:14-19

I have often talked to men and women who are having problems with their spouses and asked them, "Do you love your spouse? Does your spouse love you?" "Yes," they often reply, but there is no spark there. No delight. They believe, but they don't enjoy it. I tell a person in this situation to wake up in the morning and tell his or her spouse, "I love you," and to stop work for a minute in the middle of the day and think, *Wow, there's someone who loves me.* I tell them to bask in it, talk about it, enjoy it.

It is just the same with our enjoyment of the Lord. Think of him and his love in the morning when you wake up; remember him in the daytime when nerves are fraying; rejoice in him at night as you go to rest. For example, if your spouse forgets your anniversary (remember, it's not just *your* anniversary) and you retire to your mirror to pout, convinced that nobody loves you, remember Jesus does. Spend your pouting time praying and praising him instead. You'll be so strong in the Lord, you'll be teasing your spouse about the omission instead of freezing him or her for the mistake.

Prayer

Help me, Lord, to bask in, luxuriate in, relax in, and rejoice in your love. Today, Lord, I'm going to do just that—whatever happens. Thank you, Lord. Amen.

June 21—Growing the New Nature

Scripture reading: 2 Peter 1:3-11

There is no such thing as automatic spiritual growth or painless escape from corruption. They come about through attention to a succession of understandings and attitudes that lead to self-control.

If I want to enjoy the power of God in my life, I must control the attitudes and reactions springing from my own sinful heart. I cannot have the new godly nature and the old sinful nature living in tandem. It's one or the other. In the same way, if I am serious about escaping the corruption in the world, I must practice self-control. God is not going to wave a magic wand that will banish the demons I have been happily entertaining. Neither will he send his celestial cavalry to rescue me at the last minute from the marauding bands of enemies I have been secretly cultivating. I have to say "Be gone!" to the demons and "Get lost!" to the marauders if I am serious about growth in grace.

Prayer

It doesn't make sense for me to ask you to deliver me from the things I secretly delight in. I need to draw on the vast resources of grace you make available in order to be free of the things I covertly cherish and thereby prove again the reality of your work in my life. Help me, Lord. Amen.

June 22—Management Problems

*Scripture reading: Ecclesiastes 5:18-20;
Ephesians 6:5-8*

A lot of people need to look closely at their employment situations. We should ask ourselves some basic questions:

- Why am I doing what I am doing?

- What is my attitude toward what I am doing?

- Do I continually find myself challenged in my place of employment?

- Am I doing what I feel God really wants me to do?

If you are where God wants you, enjoy it. If you need to change employment, ask yourself why you are contemplating a change. What are the factors leading to it, and how do they match what Scripture says about the Christian's approach to work? Commit your goals and desires to the Lord, and seek his kingdom first.

Prayer

Lord, I know we sometimes hum to ourselves, "I owe, I owe, it's off to work I go," but deep down I know there's much more to employment than economics. Today, let my workday be *your* day, Lord. Amen.

June 23—Love Makes Unlikely Friends

Scripture reading: 1 Samuel 16:6-13

The prophet Samuel thought that surely God would choose one of Jesse's strong, elder sons for anointing. But God reminded him that outward appearances can be misleading. I learned this lesson too.

My first night in the Royal Marines, I waited until all the men in my barracks were all busy in the other end of the room, before slipping down beside my bed to pray. I knew they'd seen me when a loud silence descended upon the room. "Have you lost something?" one of them asked. "He was praying," pitched in another. "Who to?" said another. "God!" "Is he under the bed?" They were amused, and I felt awfully stupid.

And then a man with the ugliest, meanest-looking face I ever saw said, "Consider the lilies. They toil not. Neither do they spin. But I say unto you that Solomon, in all his glory, is not arrayed like unto one of these." Everybody stared at him.

This man who looked like such a cutthroat could recite Scripture by the yard! He was one of the most courageous people I have ever known, and we became inextricably bound up in each other's lives. I did eventually find out the reason for his incredible face; he was the middleweight boxing champion of England.

Prayer

Forgive me for looking at people you love with eyes that judge unfairly. Help me to be discerning enough to see in each individual a person for whom you died. Amen.

June 24—When Depression Comes

Scripture reading: Psalm 42

Depression is all too common in today's world. Offices of doctors, psychiatrists, pastors, and counselors overflow with despairing people. But it's nothing new. Winston Churchill, one of the great leaders of the twentieth century, suffered terribly from depression. He said it followed him like "a black dog." Charles Spurgeon, one of the greatest preachers of all time, had a lifetime battle with depression caused by the disease of gout.

Great men of the Bible were not immune to depression. David's experience recorded in Psalm 42 is particularly helpful because he so candidly tells how he felt and what he did about it. The details of David's circumstances may differ from ours, but the experience of his depression is not at all removed from the symptoms suffered by so many. Self-pity, brooding, withdrawal, introspection have been the painful lot of many.

David admitted his feelings openly, turned his broken heart to the Lord, and even praised him (vs. 5). Perhaps there's no better cure for depression than praise. Not the empty noise that some people mistake for praise. Nor do I mean the evasion of truth or escape into unreality that some call victory. But the intelligent concentration of the mind on the Lord, to such a degree that the heart becomes warm from the truth the mind is pondering.

Prayer

Loving Father, when I'm feeling helpless and hopeless, give me strength to turn my mind toward you. Thank you that you can handle my feelings—good and bad. Amen.

June 25—Destroyers in the Body

Scripture reading: Philippians 3:2-3

The Philippians were in danger from "dogs, those men who do evil, those mutilators of the flesh," and Paul gives a strong dose of "Watch outs."

The "dogs" were those who were always looking for a fight. They destroy your joy by arguing with you about the choir or the sermon or a favorite preacher before you know what's happening. Watch out!

The "men who do evil" never miss a chance to stir things up. They rock the boat and wreck the work wherever they go. Watch out!

The "mutilators of the flesh" are those who discount reality and put ritual at a premium. They pick at people's experiences of Christ and devote their considerable abilities and energies to negative causes. Watch out!

While it might be thought Paul at this point was as negative as those he criticized, he went on to explain his warnings: "For it is we who are the circumcision, we who worship by the Spirit of God, who glory in Christ Jesus, and who put no confidence in the flesh."

Prayer

Lord, the enemy of the church sometimes attacks from outside and other times from within. We've all met the dogs, the people who do evil, and the mutilators. Help me to keep my eyes open for them, and please help me to ensure that I don't become one of them. Amen.

June 26—Self-Control

Scripture reading: 1 Thessalonians 5:4-10

Paul's doctrine of self-control stemmed from the truth of the Spirit's presence in the life of the believer to give courage and determination where previously they did not exist. Paul called for a monumental dependence upon and obedience to the indwelling Spirit, which would glorify God through self-control rather than feeding human pride through successful self-effort and self-improvement.

When Paul spoke of self-control, he had in mind not so much the personal improvement of the believer as the well-being of those among whom he lived, the success of the ministry in which the believer was involved, and, above all else, the glory of God. Self-control, rather than being an effort to make things better for the Christian, was an expression of appreciation for the miracle of redeeming grace and God's unlimited forgiveness for sin. It was a warm-hearted demonstration of gratitude for salvation offered at no cost to the recipient, but at awful cost to the donor.

Prayer

Lord, I'm appalled at my own weakness, horrified by my fallen frailty. I've tried to reform and renew, to turn over a new leaf and make New Year's resolutions—and I see again my weakness. Thank you for showing me the great truth that "when I am weak, then I am strong"—in you. And let me live in the good of it. Amen.

June 27—Where Is the Enemy?

Scripture reading: 1 Corinthians 5:9-13

Some years ago, when Jill and I visited Edinburgh, Scotland, we toured the magnificent castle that towers over the city. It had been built on a steep precipice overlooking a lake.

When the castle was built, its location had made it practically impregnable. In fact, the Edinburgh castle was captured only once in its long history, and not because of outside attack. A traitor on the inside opened the doors and let the enemy in.

Similarly, some people think that the major problem confronting our church and society is not external but internal. For them, the enemy lies within in the sense that we have failed to apply the moral implications of our faith. What do you think? Have Christians failed to link belief and behavior to form a distinctive lifestyle? Has that failure compromised our integrity as people of God?

Prayer

Lord, there is a fine line between being judicious and being judgmental, between being discerning and being discriminatory. It's difficult to know which to embrace and which to eschew—for the good of the church. Teach me, Lord. Amen.

June 28—Loving God

Scripture reading: Mark 12:28-31

The Bible speaks of us loving God. But what does it mean to love God? The Bible tells us from the beginning what is involved: We are to love God with all our heart, all our soul, and all our strength (Deut. 6:5).

The heart is that part of us that discerns. To love God is first of all to discern the truth about him. It's an intelligent thing, a grasping of truth about God. We love God not because of feelings but because of truth. But the truth is not a dry, desiccated truth. It's a truth that involves our soul, the part of us that desires. So having *discerned* the truth of God, we *desire* to know more of him and respond to what he is. But it's not merely desire, because we love him with our *strength*—the part of us that decides and acts on a decision.

What does it mean to love God? It means to have an all-around relationship where, discerning him and desiring him, we put him first with all our strength.

Prayer

My desiring, discerning, and deciding are frequently suspect, Father. This has led me into inappropriate perceptions, motivations, and actions. But—worse—these inner dynamics have shown my lack of love for you, Lord. Help me not to forget this lesson. Amen.

June 29—The Power of Kindness

Scripture reading: Romans 2:1-4

Late one evening Jill was surprised to receive a call from one of our children, who was baby-sitting for a friend. "Is everything all right?" Jill asked. "What's wrong?" The child said, "Mom, I wanted to call and say I am sorry for being such a little snot lately. I've just been sitting here thinking about you, Mom, and your kindness got to me. The worse I became, the more kind you became." There was a great homecoming that night after the baby-sitting duties were complete!

Kindness is worth the effort. In the fellowship of believers it is a necessary part of Spirit life. But kindness of Spirit life must extend to the unbeliever, too. There are many motivations for ministry and numerous incentives to evangelism. None is more winsome nor effective than the loving-kindness that reaches out in genuine sympathy to the spiritually forlorn and, regardless of personal cost, generously and unstintingly communicates the reality of Christ.

There are no substitutes for kindness in the lives of those who know the loving-kindness of God. This is Spirit life.

Prayer

Lord, Scripture teaches that your kindness leads to repentance, and a little reflection and experience have shown me it is true. Your kindness has also radically challenged my attitudes and changed my approach to people. Thank you for being so kind to me. Amen.

June 30—Staying on Course

Scripture reading: Colossians 2:6-8

The passengers were flying along at thirty-five thousand feet when the captain came on the intercom. "I have some good news for you, and I have some bad news. First the bad news: I regret to inform you that we are lost. And now for the good news: We are making excellent time."

Similarly, Paul says that once we have begun our spiritual odyssey, we need to beware of being taken off course. The words translated "see to it" (vs. 8) actually mean "beware," or "keep your wits about you." There are people who can "take you captive." *Kidnap* would be the word today, or *hijack*. In either case, you start off the way you want to go and finish up where you don't want to be. When people try to hijack your faith, they will divert your attention from what is right and good and true. They will pervert the gospel by putting other things in its place. Rather than base all spiritual reality and life itself on Christ, they will build all kinds of highly intriguing, wonderfully attractive structures that are, at their core, empty and destructive. Before you know it, Christ is no longer the real authority in your life.

Has somebody hijacked your faith? Are you continuing in the faith as you began? Are you aware of the spiritual dangers that come your way? Are you getting off track? It needn't happen. When faith hijackers turn up, recognize them, resist them, and stand fast in the truth you have learned in Christ.

Prayer

Dear heavenly Father, please help me to be on the alert for deceptive and hollow teachings and always look to you to keep me on a straight course. Amen.

July

July 1—Loving My Neighbor

Scripture reading: Leviticus 19:13-18

The corollary to loving God is to love my neighbor as myself. But who is my neighbor? Somebody once asked that question of Jesus. So Jesus sat the man down and told him the story of the good Samaritan. At the end of it, the man knew the answer to his question: My neighbor is the person within my sphere of influence who needs me.

Have you noticed how many people keep shut up tight in their own houses and yards? They want their privacy— they don't want neighbors to see them too closely. The flip side of that is that they don't want to see their neighbors too closely, either. After all, if we look too closely, we'll see the needs: the man who batters his wife inside their $300,000 suburban home; the children alienated from parents; the person suffering in silence from depression, despair, and loneliness. It's much easier not to see any of that; then we won't be aware of how we should be loving our neighbors. But love doesn't hide its eyes and hurry by.

Prayer

I have discovered that loving my neighbor can be costly, time-consuming, and sometimes downright challenging. But it is part of being human according to you, Lord. So help me to evaluate my own involvement and outreach and make the necessary changes. Amen.

July 2—Listening Love

Scripture reading: 1 Peter 4:8-11

Sometimes we need to learn to love through the more intuitive, poetic parts of ourselves. Listening and hearing with the heart can often be the most loving thing we can do. Meditate on the following statements.

Love listens—using silence to talk louder than a thousand words—bending near the sick one, focusing attention on the need, looking as though there's no one else in the wide, wide world except the one who needs to talk.

Love is watertight, never leaking the confidences shared at midnight—or at dawn—or in the middle of the day. Time is irrelevant to love.

Love borrows wisdom from on high, passing on eternity's information at the right time and in the right way.

Love's ears are open to a shriek or groan, complaints or angry shouts. It matters not: No one listens like Love!

Prayer

I am such a talker, Lord; teach me to listen to you and others first, and talk next. You're a great listener, Lord; help me to be like you. Amen.

July 3—Knowing Christ Better

Scripture reading: Philippians 3:8-11

When a little boy fell out of bed and his mother asked how it happened, he replied, "I stayed too near where I got in!" That's exactly how it is with many people in their spiritual experience. Satisfied that their sins are forgiven and that their reservations for heaven have been confirmed, they stay "where they got in." This is a sure way to spiritual boredom and ineffectiveness.

Paul could never be accused of settling for where he got in! For him, knowing Christ was totally radical and revolutionary. It changed everything. But note that the most important aspiration he had was to know Christ better: "I want to know Christ and the power of his resurrection and the fellowship of sharing in his sufferings" (Phil. 3:10). In short, Paul believes the greatest thing that ever happened to him was knowing Christ—and the greatest thing that is going to happen to him during his lifetime is getting to know Christ better.

Prayer

Lord, I rejoice in the ways in which you have revealed yourself to me and chosen to introduce me to the Father. I love knowing you, and I genuinely long to know you better. Show me how, Lord. Amen.

July 4—Distinctive People

Scripture reading: Ephesians 5:1-10

Scripture tells us that a distinct, holy lifestyle is the result of living in God's love. We live as holy people when we live in the light: "For you were once darkness, but now you are light in the Lord. Live as children of light" (Eph. 5:8). Living out of touch with God is like living in darkness, where evil and confusion reign. But when we come to know Christ, we are introduced to the light and get a new perspective on life. Because we can see with new eyes and new hearts, we are able to live in new ways.

Living in the light requires three separate actions. First, we must reject the darkness. Next, we need to reflect the fruit of light, which Paul describes in verse 9: "The light consists in all goodness, righteousness and truth." When we live in the light of the knowledge of God through our Lord Jesus Christ, we become interested in what is good, right, and true. Third, we must respect the Lord's wishes, as indicated in verse 10: "Find out what pleases the Lord." Many people are only interested in pleasing themselves. But the distinctive person seeks to please the Lord.

Prayer

Lord, may I at the end of this day dare to lift its events and actions to you, asking if you're pleased. This is my desire and my prayer. Amen.

July 5—Beyond Circumstances

Scripture reading: Philippians 4:10-13

We were having dinner with a friend in Belfast, Ireland, when the police called and told our host, Bill, that his office building was on fire.

There was hardly anything left. I will never forget Bill's face as he stood among the ruins of his business. He was composed and relaxed. A firefighter came up to Bill in tears, saying, "Mr. Fitch, we know what you've tried to do for our city. We're going to work all night here to try to salvage some of these things for you." Bill just looked up and said, "No, you're not. I want you boys to go home. It's too dangerous here, and you're tired." And then he said, "Tomorrow is the Lord's day. We must be up bright and early to worship him."

Bill Fitch is a man who knows joy and contentment because he is confident in God's love for him, and it shows. His dependency is not on the abundance of the things that he possesses but on a loving Lord.

Prayer

Sometimes it takes a disaster to show us what's important. Teach me that people matter more than things. And help me always to keep my focus firmly on you, Lord. Amen.

July 6—Responding to Love

Scripture reading: Psalm 25

I was brought up in a home behind my parents' candy store. I had been taught from my earliest days, though, that the candy was not mine.

One day, when I thought nobody was around, I took a piece of candy without asking. Suddenly I heard a voice say, "Stuart, come here."

I remember the awful starched whiteness of my father's apron as I stood before him. The depth of his voice seemed to come from the height of heaven, and the effect was awe-inspiring. Then he gave me a talk about whose candies they were, what I was to do if I wanted one, and the fact that I had taken one without permission. He reminded me that my action was stealing. The impact was phenomenal, and I never took another candy again.

I was able to handle that kind of fatherly reprimand because of the love in his eyes. His sternness and judgment were not divorced from his love. I knew he was right, and I responded to it. Each of us must come to see God like that. And then we must respond to him appropriately.

Prayer

Thank you, Lord, that you rebuke us in love. And thank you that your awesome holiness is married to your generous grace. Thus your rebukes are designed not to destroy but rather to discipline and develop us. Thank you, Lord. Amen.

July 7—Counting the Cost

Scripture reading: 1 Peter 4:12-19

There is no shortage of people in the world today who are longing for intimacy and commitment. And there is no shortage of earthly answers to these expressed needs. But often they are absent of any idea of cost or suffering involved.

When we look at Scripture, we find no room for a painless commitment. There is no resurrection without a crucifixion. "Know me," says Christ. "Know my suffering." Peter put it this way: "Dear friends, do not be surprised at the painful trial you are suffering. . . . But rejoice that you participate in the sufferings of Christ" (vv. 12-13).

Christ suffered the attacks of Satan; fellowship with Christ's suffering will open the Christian to possible attacks in this area. In hell's game plan, sleeping saints are allowed to lie; but once they wake up, they are targets for attack. There is no shortcut to knowing Christ's person, Christ's power, and his passion. It's a long road that ends in heaven, and then, and then only, we will know as we are known.

Prayer

Lord, you don't expect me to go looking for trouble, but neither do you expect me to be surprised or upset when it comes my way. But just as your sufferings were redemptive, so mine, under your gracious hand, become arenas of blessing. Thank you, Lord. Amen.

July 8—The Nature of God's Forgiveness

Scripture reading: Psalm 103

The question is often asked, "Why do bad things happen to good people?" The unspoken assumption being that God should give us more good stuff and exempt us from the bad. But God indicates that if we get what we deserve, we'll be in a fine mess. And if he gives us what we've really earned, we'll be in an even bigger mess. Instead, he deals with us on the basis of love and grace. His love forgives us and gives us the gift of pardon.

Our difficulty in understanding the concepts of pardon and forgiveness, grace and mercy shows how limited our understanding of God's love truly is—and how exaggerated is our view of our own goodness. We seem to think we merit divine favor. However, the Scriptures teach that God gave us what he gave us for no other reason than that he is a loving God. We must come to terms with that in order to be the humble, repentant people God requires us to be.

Prayer

Lord, my prayer is that I will see myself as you see me, rather than through my self-congratulatory perspectives, in order that I might be overwhelmed all over again by your grace. Amen.

July 9—Love Leads to Forgiveness

Scripture reading: Ephesians 4:32—5:2

The perfection of love is seen completely in the forgiveness of God the Father. The Greek word for forgiveness is *charizomai,* related to *charis,* which means "grace." Forgiveness is a gift of grace, totally undeserved and unmerited. Yet when we set out to forgive others, we often require that they earn or deserve it. They must feel sorry enough, and say it in just the right way. Even after we've said we've forgiven them, inside there is a reserve toward them, in case they offend us again.

This is not the forgiveness into which love leads us. Love learns to expect the best from people, to give them the benefit of the doubt. God certainly gives us the benefit of the doubt; this is the least we can do for one another. Ask the Holy Spirit to search your heart and show you where your forgiveness is not in character with God's forgiveness.

Prayer

Lord, I know that only the repentant experience forgiveness but you extend it in advance. Help me, therefore, to do the same and thus demonstrate your grace in my life. Amen.

July 10—Submitting Out of Reverence

Scripture reading: Ephesians 5:21

Why are we to submit to one another out of reverence for the Lord? Because every person we deal with is someone God made. We are dealing with beings of infinite and eternal consequence, created by God, and we'll answer to him for the way we handle them.

We could cut the divorce rate dramatically if people would simply fear the Lord in their marriages, if they honestly believed in their hearts that they're going to answer to him for what they're doing. I'm also firmly convinced that we could dramatically improve our marriages if we brought a sense of reverence for the Lord into our relationships with each other.

Think of the dramatic changes we could see in the church as a result of reverence for one another. How often do we see the people around us as eternal beings, created by an eternal, wise, and loving God? In creating these people around us, God has purposes in mind—divine purposes—and we must live in reverence of this fact.

Prayer

Part of my problem in relationships, Lord, is that I am so earthbound in my perceptions of people that I forget the heavenly view of those same individuals. Because I don't respect them, I fail to reverence you. Forgive me, Lord. Amen.

July 11—Fear of People or Fear of the Lord?

Scripture reading: Acts 9:26-31

Saul of Tarsus created havoc in the Christian church. His persecution of believers was dreadful. Then God solved the problem—Saul was converted. Suddenly the church had peace. Not that they put their feet up and said, "Oh, what a break!" No, the church used their newfound freedom to move ahead. They replaced their fear of Saul of Tarsus with fear of the Lord. This was a very sensible thing to do, because Jesus once said, in effect: "Listen, folks. Don't fear people, who can kill the body. Rather, fear God, who, after the body has been killed, can cast the soul into hell." That's the perspective Jesus wanted to make clear to his followers.

What a lovely thing it is for the church to live in the fear of the Lord. When people respond to each other, not on the basis of like or dislike or agreement or disagreement, but on the basis of accountability to the Lord, then we see real concern. What a delightful thing it is to rightly understand the Lord and appropriately respond to him.

Prayer

Lord, help me not to be a people pleaser but a God pleaser. Deliver me from having to have everyone be like me. Give me a reverential trust and a hatred of all that wounds and displeases you. Amen.

July 12—Praying about Problems

Scripture reading: Philippians 4:4-7

Sooner or later everybody has problems. Problems have to be met, and God's Word says how it is to be done: "Do not be anxious about anything, but in everything, by prayer and petition, with thanksgiving, present your requests to God" (Phil. 4:6).

To be anxious for people's well-being is natural, but anxiety in a Christian must accomplish more; it is intended to stimulate prayer. In addition, our prayer requests should be presented with a great degree of intensity. God wants you to be serious about your problems if you want him to deal with them seriously.

The person who has a problem will be grateful for the fact that he can share the burden and know the concern of God's loving heart. On top of that, the Holy Spirit may assure him that God is acting positively on his request, and gratitude will fill his soul.

Whatever we do with our problems, we must not hesitate to speak to the Lord about them, making requests with a sense of reverence, intensity, and gratitude.

Prayer

If we never had a problem, Lord, we'd never know that you would solve it. Teach me to trust you and be obedient to your command not to be consumed with anxiety. Thank you there is such a thing as prayer. Help me to meet you here today. Amen.

July 13—Taking Love to the Pub

Scripture reading: Luke 14:15-24

When we lived in England and Stuart was traveling the world preaching, I decided something had to be done about our neighborhood. So a bunch of us set out for the local pubs to sing some hymns around the bar piano and to speak to the customers. Bibles in hand, we'd come into a bar full of drinking people and announce, "Hello, everybody. We've just come in to talk with you and visit. We thought we might have a hymn sing tonight." After a sort of shocked silence, someone would say, "Come on, then, love."

And they loved it. They would settle us at the piano and start requesting their favorite hymns. Sometimes tears ran down their faces. We had a tremendous time.

As soon as they saw the Bibles and heard our announcement of who we were and where we'd come from, everyone reached for his or her wallet. This was their picture of the church: a few hymns and then a passing of the plate. How sad, especially when love involves so much more. We can't expect many of these people to look for love in the church. No, love must seek out those people who need to know it.

Prayer

Lord, love is all about giving, not getting. Teach me to reach out in love wherever I find people who need to know you. Live out your love in me, Lord. Amen.

July 14—Victory Means Battle

Scripture reading: 1 Corinthians 15:57-58

It is unfortunate that sometimes preachers, in their enthusiasm, have encouraged people to become Christians by assuring them that if they do, everything will suddenly be fine. If we give people the impression that Christianity will exempt them from all the problems and difficulties of life, we are grossly misleading them.

Some time ago, the expression "the victorious Christian life" was in vogue. Unfortunately, this phrase implied that a true Christian lived in a state of constant victory. Everything was always marvelous—a smile on your face and a song in your heart. However, thinking people soon realized that the only way to truly experience a *victory* is by first having a *battle*. God never called us to a blissful existence or suggested to us that the Christian life would be anything less than a struggle. In fact, repeatedly in Scripture we are told that it is going to be a rough, tough situation. But, in the roughness and toughness of it all, in the challenge of the fight, we are to keep on keeping on.

Prayer

Lord, it's so easy to give up, especially when I'm in the heat of battle. Steel my will and inspire me in the fight. And remind me that I am on the winning side. Amen.

July 15—A Fortress of Peace

Scripture reading: John 14:27; Philippians 4:7

"The peace of God will guard your hearts." *To guard* means "to act as a garrison of soldiers"—to protect and defend and make an impregnable defense. That is what the peace of God can do.

A few years ago I stood with the widow of one of my best friends, who had just been killed in his airplane. She was smitten with grief, but we spoke of "the peace that passes all understanding." She said, "I never realized what that verse meant. But now I know how it feels." It was a garrison to her mind, to maintain her mental equilibrium, and to her heart, to give her emotional stability.

Handled according to divine principles, the unpredictable things of life can become the means of the unexplainable peace of God acting as a garrison in our hearts and minds. This must be our experience as we meet the situations and the people and the problems that make up our daily lives.

What does "the peace that passes all understanding" mean to you? Are you claiming that peace as you deal with the blessings and burdens of each day?

Prayer

Defend me and befriend me, O Lord. Guard my heart and mind, and help me claim your promise of peace and live in the good of it. Amen.

July 16—Seeing Others through Divine Eyes

Scripture reading: Matthew 9:35-38

In this Scripture from Matthew, Jesus looks out over a crowd of selfish, miserable, sinful, demanding people—and what does he see? Needs. He had a special perspective, looking through love's eyes. When we begin to see with love's eyes, we don't see people who must be tolerated or people we like or dislike. Neither do we see people to be used, to be hired or fired, to fight, or to take advantage of. We've turned our back on the "worldly point of view." What we see now is people who in their deep need are loved, redeemable, and significant in God's sight.

This point of view is life-changing. As children of God we develop a vision for broken lives being mended, for fragmented and sinful people becoming whole. That's what happens when you understand the love of God. The love of God flowing from you changes your attitude toward your own life, your attitude toward people, and the emphasis of your being. Whatever your vocation, occupation, calling, residence, your overriding concern will be not to exacerbate the pain and disruption people already have to contend with, but to throw your energies into being a part of their restoration, not condemnation.

Prayer

Lord, when I see a multitude of need, help me respond and not react. Make me like you. You were able to put your own personal pain aside and minister to others. I'd like to do the same. Amen.

July 17—In the Palm of God's Hand

Scripture reading: John 10:27-30

When I was a young boy, I remember a preacher who stayed in our home. One day he took a penny out of his pocket and put it on his palm. "You're the penny, Stuart, and this hand is your Savior, the Lord Jesus. You may fall in the hand of the Lord, but you won't fall out of the hand of the Lord. I'll tell you why." Then he put his other hand over the one holding the coin, wrapping the first hand in the second. "Now," he said, "can you see the penny?"

"No. I know where it is, though. It's inside the first hand and inside the second hand."

The preacher nodded and explained, "The first hand is Jesus, and the second hand is the Father. When you are held there, you are secure in the Father and the Son—and they are one." And then he added something I've never forgotten. "Of course, that doesn't mean you can't fall. But it does mean that every time you fall, you fall in the pierced hand of the Lord Jesus, and it hurts both him and you. And this in itself should be an encouragement to you to be secure in the Lord and desire to go on with him."

Prayer

Lord, what happiness to know I may fall down but never fall out of your hand! Yet, Lord, what grief to realize my sin hurts you. May these thoughts guide my actions today. Amen.

July 18—Serious, Not Frivolous

Scripture reading: Exodus 32:1-20

Christianity is serious business. Perhaps it is the very seriousness of our faith that frightens us into frivolous excess, simply because we feel that we can't cope with the solemnity of it all. Beware at this point, for only the serious-minded will do the will of God. The frivolous will do nothing more than pass the hours until they have no more to pass.

I'm not speaking against humor and laughter—they are divine inventions created for the well-being of human society. But their abuse, along with the fixation on trivia, has led many a Christian into the paths of impotence. Moses and Aaron illustrate the point. Moses on the mountain, alone with God, was being made the recipient of God's law for his people. Meanwhile, down in the valley, Aaron and his people were having a party. Aaron fiddled while the mountain burned, and the people fiddled along with him and finished up badly burned themselves.

To fill your mind with the frivolous at the expense of the serious is a mistake for any Christian.

Prayer

What do you see in my life, Lord—frivolity or faith? Show me the difference between the joy of doing your will and light laughter about nothing. Make me rightly serious about Jesus. Amen.

July 19—The Restored Image

Scripture reading: Titus 3:3-7

My mother acquired a lot of antiques for her beautiful manor house in England. To me, they were rather ugly lumps of wood. I remember her bringing one piece in, and I said, "Oh, Mother, what on earth is that?" She replied, "It's the most beautiful piece!" and told me all about it. I said that it just looked like an old piece of wood. Her answer: "It's lost its image."

Well, my mother worked and worked on that piece. Eventually the image that had been lost came through. And it was indeed a beautiful piece of furniture. It's one of the precious things we brought with us from England. It stands in our home now, reminding me of a spiritual principle: that it cost my mom almost more to restore it than to buy it.

I cannot help thinking of my own life as an "ugly lump of wood"—loveless, carnal, selfish, irritable, impatient. And yet I know that somewhere in me is the image of God that needs to be restored. As you read your Bible during the next few days, look for clues about the divine image that God is restoring in you. What will you look and act like eventually, as that image becomes more defined?

Prayer

Lord, I need to remember what I used to be—it keeps me humble! But I must bear in mind what I will be—that keeps me going. Thank you, Lord. Amen.

July 20—For Jesus' Sake

Scripture reading: 2 Corinthians 4:5-11

Paul is telling the Corinthians, "I am your servant. Not for what I get out of it, and not for what you get out of it—but for Jesus' sake." The lovely thing about being the servant of the Corinthians for Jesus' sake is this: When Paul has "had it up to here" with Corinth, that's irrelevant. And when the Corinthians aren't very nice to him, that's irrelevant. Paul isn't there for his own sake; he's not even there for their sake. He's there for Jesus' sake. Paul's sole reason to work among the Corinthians is so that the Corinthians might likewise fall in love with Jesus and give him honor and praise.

Paul goes on to say he's not only committed to endure for Jesus' sake, but he's prepared to suffer for it too. Why? Because as he suffers, people will notice. And when their curiosity gets the better of them, Paul will have the opportunity to explain the gospel. The apostle looks at his circumstances and reacts by saying, "I do not lose heart." He listens to the complaints and criticisms and replies, "I endure all things." His detractors wonder why and he responds, "Because I understand God's mercy and I'm concerned for Christ's honor. I'm doing it for him."

Prayer

Lord, help me to live in such a way that people will want to know why I do what I do. Then I can tell them you are my Lord, that I live for you. Please take that message to their hearts. Amen.

July 21—Passing It On

Scripture reading: Philippians 4:8-9

It's obvious that we need to feed our stomachs. But we often forget the absolute importance of feeding our minds. And the basis of all wholesome mind food is the truth of God.

To grow in spiritual and mental dimensions, it is necessary to use the mind to learn, the ears to hear, and the eyes to see. Paul had given ample food for the minds of the Philippians through his intelligent presentation of the gospel in his teaching ministry. They had taken time to hear the Word of God preached. And—don't miss this—they had kept their eyes open to what he was doing, as well as what he was teaching and preaching. Those three methods are beyond reproach.

We do well to remember that to be correctly fed, a mind needs plenty of nourishment served through teaching, preaching, and example. Make sure that you attend to the in-depth teaching of the Word. Don't be conspicuous by your absence when the Word is being preached. Learn all you can from the example of the leaders whom God has given you.

Prayer

There are so many ways for me to learn, Lord. Help me to stay alert and use them all. And there are so many ways I can communicate, too. Help me to remember that people are watching as well as listening. May they see no inconsistencies. Amen.

July 22—No Greater Love

Scripture reading: John 15:12-13

There was a young couple in Cromwell's time. The young man was a soldier who evidently did something wrong, and Cromwell condemned him to death. Cromwell said that when the curfew bell rang, the young soldier would be put to death. And so the people gathered in the village square to watch him hang. The young wife of this soldier knew that when the huge bell in the tower rang, her beloved would die. So she climbed up the tower and hung onto the clapper of the bell. When it was time, the old sexton began to pull the rope. The young girl was smashed against the side of the bell again and again and again. And everybody stood in the square, waiting for the execution of the soldier. Finally, the puzzled sexton finished trying to ring the bell. Cromwell asked him why the bell had not been rung. And the young girl climbed down, bleeding and bruised, and told Cromwell what she had done. "Girl," he replied, "your love will live this evening. Curfew will not ring tonight."

If we love, then we're willing even to die for those we love. Today, many are suffering for their faith, condemned to death by those antagonistic to Christianity. Who can you pray for today?

Prayer

Lord, there's something sadly wrong with the attitude that takes for granted your sacrifice of love and assumes our loving requires no pain or loss. Deliver me from such gross impertinence, Lord. Amen.

July 23—Temporary or Eternal?

Scripture reading: 2 Corinthians 4:16-18

When my children come home for a visit, they love to get out the old pictures of me and say, "You're not the man you used to be, Dad." Of course, they're right! I remember teaching my kids to run. I also remember the day my eldest son took me out for a run and ran me into the ground. I once had hair on top of my head as well as on my chin! I can remember when I could see my congregation without my glasses—and now I have bifocals! Yes, the outward man is perishing.

Let's look again at Paul. When he was shipwrecked in the past, he used to be able to swim out to the life raft. Now he has to be dragged to it. But when they finally get him there, what do they discover? The old codger is full of life! The outward man is perishing, yet the inward man is being renewed daily. And if you were to ask Paul why this is so, he'd reply as he does in verses 17-18, "Our light and momentary troubles are achieving for us an eternal glory that far outweighs them all."

Prayer

Lord, there's not a lot I can do about physical deterioration. But there is no excuse for spiritual atrophy. Deliver me from the narrowness of cramped vision, the pettiness of shriveled desire, and the crabbiness of frustrated ambition. Make me mellow with age, Lord. Amen.

July 24—Welcome the Lonely Times

Scripture reading: Lamentations 3:25-28

Make no mistake about it: sometimes God wants you to be alone. For it is in those alone times that our hearts and minds can turn completely to him and his purposes.

Consider the apostle Paul. If the Philippians had looked after his every whim and caprice, Paul might grow blasé and flabby. So God allowed a little neglect once in a while to remind him that God is the source of his adequacy (Phil. 4:11-13).

In our busy, pragmatic society, quietness and aloneness are almost nonexistent. One of the scarcest commodities in the world today is quiet stillness. "Be still, and know that I am God" the psalmist challenges us. But it is so contrary to our lifestyle that often we don't even understand it or see the necessity for it. So sometimes God has to intervene and lay some aloneness or neglect or uncertainty on us so we can get things into proper perspective again.

What has been your response to periods of loneliness? What do you find most helpful in overcoming loneliness?

Prayer

Lord, I often miss your whispers simply because I'm too busy and my mind is full of noise. Help me to embrace the quiet and welcome the lonely times so that I may not miss a word. Amen.

July 25—Spiritual Realities

Scripture reading: 2 Corinthians 4:1-4

Spiritual realities that involve the forces of evil undoubtedly are at work in our world. These forces blind people's minds to the truth, and it is necessary for God to shine into their hearts. Because of this desperate situation, Paul says, "I cannot quit when there are people in the grip of evil. I can't give up when there are people around me whose eyes are blinded. God wants to shine into their hearts."

This concern for human souls is an important motivational factor, compelling the apostle to persevere. We can easily forget that people live as they do because they are often blind to another way of living. Their choices may be less a result of willful disregard for God and more a simple ignorance of their options. Their plight should motivate us to bring the truth to them through our Christlike words and actions, so they may "see the light of the gospel of the glory of Christ."

Prayer

Father, I don't always sense the plight of the spiritually blind. Enable me to be sensitized to their need to "see the light." Amen.

July 26—Filled Full

Scripture reading: Philippians 4:14-20

When I was a bank inspector, I traveled first class, stayed in good hotels, ate well, and ran up some fairly large bills. But I did it with great peace of heart because the bank was behind me picking up the tab. In the same way, I like sharing because I know God is coming right behind me picking up the tab. He's committed to meeting my needs.

The word *supply* means "fulfill," and that is how God operates with sharing saints. For him, to fulfill is to "fill full." And he does it in a way that brings glory to himself. The prospects are therefore extremely bright for the person who shares. God is committed to looking after him, and doing it in a way that measures up to his standing and status. He does it through Christ Jesus. Paul gets so excited thinking about these truths that he bursts out, "To our God and Father be glory for ever and ever. Amen." May I recommend a similar response from you?

Prayer

Lord, how wonderful it is to know that you stand behind me at all times with unlimited resources to meet my every need. I can afford to be generous, knowing you are there to replenish me constantly. Thank you, Lord! Amen.

July 27—Living Consistently

Scripture reading: Matthew 7:21-27

How do we confirm our belief? By our behavior. Belief unrelated to behavior is not the norm for spiritual experience. When we get our theology straight, our morality will demonstrate that belief eventually.

On the other hand, proper morality doesn't automatically point to correct theology. I cannot say, "I am a very moral person; therefore, I don't need the Lord Jesus Christ and the Spirit of God. I am a very good person; therefore, I don't need to be washed, justified, and sanctified." It's important to remember that people can behave well outwardly but remain unchanged in their basic attitudes toward God.

Belief and behavior must travel in tandem. True belief and true experience result in a newness of lifestyle. Newness of life comes because we understand the dynamics needed to live in the power of the Holy Spirit, in obedience to his Word.

Prayer

Lord, professing is one thing, performing is another. So this I pray: that you will encourage me to confess you as Lord and lead a consistent life that will confuse no one. Amen.

July 28—God, Our Husband

Scripture reading: Isaiah 54:4-8

I was never more aware of this aspect of my relationship with God than when my earthly husband was away from home for long periods of time. I do not sleep very well when Stuart is away. The house seems to be full of creaks and groans.

I remember in the early years of our marriage, asking my "heavenly Husband" to care for me while Stuart was out of town. If God is my Husband, then he would give me that sense of security that makes it easy to fall asleep.

I remember standing beside my bed, struggling against my fears. Would I look under the bed, or wouldn't I? I wouldn't if Stuart were home. I managed to get myself under the sheets without succumbing, but I found myself lying as stiff as a board, waiting to be murdered!

I switched on the light—which I hadn't wanted to turn off in the first place—and reached for my Bible. After a few minutes I discovered this verse: "Indeed, he who watches over Israel will neither slumber nor sleep" (Psalm 121:4). I seemed to hear God say, "Go to sleep, now. There is no use both of us staying awake!" And I went to sleep.

Prayer

What a joy it is to know that knowing you makes such a difference in life's little things such as sleeping and waking, eating and drinking. Thank you, Lord. Amen.

July 29—Soul Healing

Scripture reading: Exodus 16:1-3

A young girl complained to me that her life was fine until she accepted the Lord. Then the sky fell in. Her fiancé dumped her, her father died, and her best friend moved across the country. "It was better in Egypt," she said bitterly.

When the Israelites made this complaint originally (just past the Red Sea), God revealed himself to them as Jehovah-rophe, "the God that heals." This is striking because it was not physical healing they needed! Wouldn't you have thought that the first time God leaned out of heaven to tell humanity he was the Great Physician, it would be in connection with our bodies? But it wasn't. It was at the point of Israel's dashed dreams, hampered hopes, and desperate desires that he came and healed their bitter, disappointed, critical spirits.

This passage seems to indicate that the most important sickness God has to deal with is a spiritual malady. It is our sin nature that causes us to turn against God at the slightest cause. Sin is at the root of all our maladies—physical, social, spiritual, and psychological.

Prayer

Sickness of the spirit is not always diagnosed quickly. Lord, help me to know that my ailment is spiritual and the doctor I need is you—Jehovah-rophe. Amen.

July 30—Lift Up Your Trumpet!

Scripture reading: Judges 7:19-25

Gideon started off with thousands to help him fight the hordes of Midianites. He ended up with a handful of dedicated soldiers. Together they routed Israel's enemies and won the day. They brought peace to their land, and Gideon became their leader and hero.

Amazingly, they did it all with trumpets and jars containing lighted lamps. When Gideon gave the order, they blew the trumpets and broke the jars, and the light shone out into the darkness, bringing panic to the sleeping Midianites. So shall it be with us. When we lift up our voices like trumpets and allow God to break us in order for his light to be released, we'll see and enjoy a great and glorious victory.

First, we must know the peace of God for ourselves, and then we must be obedient to his law and live broken and contrite lives before him. Then and only then will "Jehovah-shalom" rightly get the glory and become the God of those we love.

Prayer

Lord, it was Gideon's core belief that you are Jehovah-shalom in the midst of conflict that gave him the strength to dare to obey your unbelievable instructions and experience your incredible victory. Please keep my focus in the same place, dear Jehovah-shalom. Amen.

July 31—Learning from the Good Shepherd

Scripture reading: John 10:11-18; Psalm 23

The Lord tells us he owns the sheep because he has bought them; they are his, and he is able to instill in us— his under-shepherds—the very same service of caring concern. He also says that he has "other sheep that are not of this sheep pen." Jesus never lost his love for the outcast, the sinner, and the lepers of his day. He intends for us to follow in his steps.

To follow him is one thing, but to follow after those who are lost and not following Jesus is altogether different. Yet, the two must go together if we would truly understand what it means to follow God's example.

All of us are leading someone. Whether it be mothers leading children, friends leading friends, or colleagues leading colleagues. Are we modeling Jesus, owning our ministry? Carefully counting the ninety-nine to make sure they are safe and sound? And are we further seeking the one lost sheep, ever conscious of his or her plight, putting ourselves at risk in order to bring him or her home rejoicing?

Prayer

Only you, Lord, can make shepherds out of sheep. And you're doing it all the time! Please continue this unique work in me, for I often fear my sheepishness is intruding on my shepherding. Amen.

August

August 1—Winds of Evidence

Scripture reading: John 3:5-8; Acts 2:1-4

We may not know where the wind originated or where it is going, but we surely can tell where it has been. We can see the branches moving, the grass waving, the waves in the water and ripples in the sand. The wind works, sometimes quietly and gradually, sometimes with greater force and bluster. But it always leaves evidence of itself.

One dramatic picture of the wind of God is given in Acts 2. This time it is not a gentle breath or a moderate breeze, but a mighty blast. The church is born! The Spirit flooded the upper room—and the people in it—and the sound seemed to fill Jerusalem. The mighty wind spoke of the very presence of God.

When the Spirit of God is working in our lives, the evidence will be there—sometimes in small ways and other times more obviously. Although we might not understand how the Spirit is working in a situation, there will be the telltale signs: hearts turning toward God, if even by small degrees; peace where there could be argument; hope where one would expect cynicism. And, in some cases, profound miracles of both body and soul.

Prayer

Lord, as the wind of your Spirit breezes through my life, may the cobwebs of spiritual careless neglect be blown away. And as I move around, may the zephyrs of your grace leave gently windswept people in my path. Amen.

August 2—Learning to Ask

Scripture reading: John 4:7-26

The Lord knew this Samaritan woman was a thirsty, unsatisfied person. He knew something else about her: she didn't have to be thirsty. It's interesting that, knowing all this, Jesus didn't tell the woman what she needed. He supplied some information and left it to her to ask. Jesus wanted her to ask him for the living water that would quench her life thirst.

What a real experience of deep, soul happiness we find when we receive from Christ the gift of the Holy Spirit and find in him an inexhaustible reservoir of life. Our duty is to come with our bucket of faith, lower it into the well with the rope of prayer, and draw up spiritual blessings. Then, like the woman Jesus met at the well, we can leave our buckets at Jesus' feet and run back to our thirsty, needy world with the good news.

Prayer

Lord, teach me to draw deeply from your well of spiritual blessings and find the living water I thirst for. Amen.

August 3—Tools for the Job

Scripture reading: Ephesians 4:11-16

"Give us the tools, and we'll finish the job," said Winston Churchill, referring to the weapons England would need to win the war against Germany. "Give them the gifts and they'll finish the job!" says the Father to the Holy Spirit, referring to the tools the church will need to win the war against evil.

Spiritual gifts are very important. For the church concerned with the evangelization of the world, it is an exercise in futility to try to serve God's cause without exercising spiritual gifts. The local assembly should understand that gifts are for the common good; in order to keep unity in the church, they should be exercised in love without a competitive spirit. Since the Holy Spirit is the one who gives out the gifts, we do not have the right to insist that others seek certain gifts. Each of us has a job to do, suited to us specifically. And the Spirit gives us the tools with which to do our part.

Prayer

Lord, I need to be clear about my God-given task on earth and convinced that I am rightly equipped for it by you. Clear my head on these matters, Lord. Amen.

August 4—When God's Glory Departs

Scripture reading: Ezekiel 10:18-19

Ezekiel saw God's glory depart from the temple. Why? Apparently, idols of Asherah, the Canaanite goddess of fertility, and animals were being worshiped in Jehovah's house. Tamnuz, a Babylonian fertility god, was also being honored. Sun worshipers too abounded in God's house, as did those who "put the branch to the nose," a ceremonial gesture used in nature worship.

All these practices were detestable to the Lord. No wonder the glory of the Lord departed! How sad that the hardened Israelites didn't even realize it was happening. They continued as if all was well.

Has the glory of the fullness of the Lord departed from your life and the life of the body of believers to which you belong? If so, why? Which idols have found their way into his place? Yes, spiritual gifts may still perhaps be exercised, but the sweet manifestation of God's presence will be strangely lacking. And without a doubt his work will be hindered.

Prayer

Tune my heart, God, to your presence in my life. Reveal the subtle and not-so-subtle things that become idols and squeeze your glory out. Amen.

August 5—Love's Lessons

Scripture reading: 1 Thessalonians 2:1-9

Love works hard to make truth
   clear as crystal, easy to understand.

Love believes in Sunday school
   in little minds needing little lessons—
   about a big God.

Love gently instructs those it loves
   to accept truth's tenets,
   ancient values, moral codes.

Love hopes for a ready response
   but makes allowances for
   human frailty.

Love trusts twice, forgives freely
   while expecting the best.

Love is ever patient
   using time
   to grow a good child;
   replete with the likeness of
   its Maker!

Prayer

Help us grow good children up in their faith. Help them stand tall even when others would try to knock them down. Birth a great love for you in their hearts, please, Lord. Amen.

August 6—Reasoning Together

Scripture reading: Isaiah 1:18-20

How is it that people without the Lord often are open and willing to listen and respond to him, while people who have known him for years refuse to listen and respond anymore? It's a mystery. The greater mystery perhaps is the love of God that persists in not only seeking the lost sinner but in also seeking the hardhearted saint. He offers life to both.

"Come now, let us reason together," God says. This doesn't mean "let's have an argument." It means to agree with his verdict about the heart condition of rebellion and repent of the cold hostility against him that is a result of deliberate sin. It means to acknowledge that one's actions have not been in accordance with divine reason. After all, God's demands are reasonable. It is sin that is unreasonable. If we humans are God's creatures living in God's world, sustained and provided for by God, then to turn our backs on him and go our own willful way doesn't make a bit of sense.

Prayer

Lord, knowing myself as I do, I suspect that if I had a fraction of your authority and power, I would not be very open to inviting those who frustrate my plans to sit down and "reason together." Incredibly, you do, showing me yet again your wondrous grace and love. Thank you. Amen.

August 7—Turning Against Our Heavenly Parent

Scripture reading: Isaiah 1:2-9

One day years ago I was helping our daughter-in-law corral her four-year-old, two-year-old, and twins who were eight months old—no easy task! At last, after a long, hard day, all were bathed, put to bed, read to, and prayed with. A heavenly stillness enveloped us. "If these kids ever rebel, Debbie, after all you do for them," I told their mother, "I'll knock their blocks off!" We laughed.

It was inconceivable that, after the one-hundred percent commitment of each twenty-four hours of loving mothering, these children would ever be anything other than thankful and grateful. Yet we both knew each little one had a will as big as our own; even if everything possible was done the right way, that in itself would not guarantee their positive response.

God understands. "I reared children and brought them up," he noted, "but they have rebelled against me." Despite all God had done for them, the nation of Israel had grown into a bunch of disrespectful adults intent on rebelling against their heavenly Parent's wishes.

Prayer

Lord, I am deeply disappointed when I see ungrateful, demanding kids. But what blinders I wear—for they model for me in their unacceptable behavior the unacceptable responses of my own ungrateful heart toward you. Yet you go on loving me, patiently. How can I thank you? Amen.

August 8—When Sorrow Flees

Scripture reading: Isaiah 35:5-10

"I tried to run away from God," a teenager told me, "but I discovered he had longer legs than I had."

"So what happened?" I asked him.

"I stood still and the sorrow in my life ran away instead," he answered.

I turned to this passage of Isaiah and we read it together: "Gladness and joy will overtake them, and sorrow and sighing will flee away." I explained that Jesus, who is our joy, delights to overtake us, stop us in our tracks, and give us something to sing—rather than sigh—about.

God has given his people a spiritual inheritance, part of which is a deep experience of abiding joy. Joy strengthens us to serve God even in the middle of trouble. "The joy of the Lord is your strength," the Bible says in Nehemiah 8:10. Isaiah speaks for Jehovah when he says he will give us the oil of gladness instead of mourning, a garment of praise instead of a spirit of despair (Is. 61:3).

Prayer

We mere mortals know both agony and ecstasy. But my greatest joy is seeing you replace my sorrows with your joy and gladness. Only you can do that, Lord. Thank you. Amen.

August 9—Don't Neglect the Important Things

Scripture reading: Hebrews 13:5-8, 20-21

Years ago I was talking with David, my elder son, who had been called to pastor a small church in Michigan's Upper Peninsula. Our conversation was interrupted by a telephone call from the church asking if he could arrive a day earlier than originally agreed because some of the men in the church were planning to fix an elderly church member's roof; they thought it would be good if the new pastor could be seen doing that kind of work.

There was no doubt that this was a worthwhile endeavor and that the public-relations benefits for a new pastor would be invaluable. But I said to my son, "This is how it will be. There are so many good things to do—and so many things you will be expected to do—that you will struggle to preserve your own spiritual vitality, without which your ministry will dry up."

He went a day early to work on the roof, but he took with him my parting advice: "By all means work on her roof. But when you stand before the people on Sunday morning, don't *sound* as if you've been on a roof all week."

Prayer

Lord, life is so full of opportunities and demands that I sometimes feel overwhelmed. Teach me not only to discriminate between the good and the evil but also to differentiate between the better and the best, so I can live productively, wisely, and well. Amen.

August 10—Enough Hours in the Day

Scripture reading: Psalm 90:1-12

One day, I said to myself, "There aren't enough hours in the day." Then I stopped to think about it. God knows what he wants me to accomplish. If he knows what needs to be done—and, presumably, knows how long each task will take—it is reasonable for me to assume he will allot the right amount of time to accomplish his purposes.

I came to the astonishing conclusion that there are exactly the right number of hours in the day to accomplish what God wants me to achieve. Instead of making an intense, frustrated, never-ending attempt to meet every need on the horizon, I could strive to fill the hours with the sort of responsible living that allowed me to be a person devoted to ministry rather than a machine driven by guilt, ambition, or even a diluted messianic complex.

Responsible living led to an increased devotion to well-doing. But the well-doing certainly did not require the abandonment of such divinely ordained delights as being a husband and a father—and even, on occasion, an abysmal golfer.

Prayer

Lord, when you returned to heaven, you left a world still full of need. But you said you had finished the work the Father had given you to do. Would you teach those of us who are "driven" people that we will never solve every problem, yet we can fulfill your purpose. Help us to be satisfied with that. Amen.

August 11—Similar Gifts, Different Styles

Scripture reading: 1 Corinthians 12:4-11

Jill and I are quite different in our approaches to speaking. Jill prepares meticulously, making copious notes with various colored pens and all manner of lines and stars and symbols that mean something only to her. She expounds on Scripture well and loves "to peek around the corner of the verse." She uses humor and speaks openly about her own failures and frailties.

My approach is quite different. I speak from my skeleton outline and have more than enough material in my head. As I preach, I adjust. Although I preach the same sermon in all four of our weekend services, they all come out quite differently. I don't often talk about my own failures—not because I don't have any, but because I'm not particularly comfortable talking about myself that way and I can't imagine why anybody would be interested.

Jill and I have some of the same gifts and callings. But the Lord has prepared us to develop and use them in quite different ways. This is just one example of the rich variety found in God's people.

Prayer

Lord of bewildering diversity, creator of a trillion snowflakes, and designer of billions of fingerprints, I believe you made me special, unique, and irreplaceable. Help me to embrace that truth so I might live out that for which you made me ideal. Amen.

August 12—Caught Up in Labels

Scripture reading: Matthew 28:16-20

I became entangled in a conversation with a person once, about the quality of my Christianity. After enduring numerous questions, I responded, "In effect, you want to know if I am a born-again, Spirit-filled, charismatic or Reformed, premillennial, pretribulational Christian." And we haven't even mentioned denominations, sacraments, church government, political involvement, social issues, or the role of women!

"Let me simplify everything by asking you just one question," I went on. "Are you a disciple of Jesus Christ?" The response to that question has usually been most significant. Some people look blankly back at me, suggesting that they have never considered the possibility. Even more disconcertingly, some say, "Well, I wouldn't exactly claim to be a disciple. I'm just an ordinary, born-again Christian." This suggests to me some degree of confusion about what it means to be a disciple. Those "ordinary Christians" who wouldn't claim to be disciples have failed to recognize there is really no justification for differentiating between the two.

Prayer

Lord, sometimes we get so caught up in labels and explanations and categories that we lose sight of our fundamental duty to simply be your disciples. Help me to focus on my disciple relationship with you and let everything else fall into its proper place as far as you're concerned. Amen.

August 13—Nominal Christians

Scripture reading: 2 Corinthians 11:7-15

In the first-century church, being called a Christian meant you were identified as one who had believed and turned to the Lord and who had determined to remain true to the Lord with all your heart. But between the first and twentieth centuries, some strange things happened to the word *Christian*. Depending on who was speaking, it could mean anything from a religious preference ("Of course I'm a Christian. I'm not a Buddhist, am I?") to a designation held by anyone with the slightest church affiliation, without it affecting his or her life in any way.

Vance Havner, the famed Southern preacher, used to say, "I understand about homiletics. I just don't never let them interfere with my preaching." In much the same way, it is possible to be a "Christian" in today's terms but never let it interfere with your living. This is barren nominalism of the worst kind.

Prayer

Lord, I know that calling myself "Christian" means that I bear your name wherever I go. Please remind me that your reputation is on display whenever I call myself Christian, and may this reminder govern my behavior. Amen.

August 14—Disciples of Christ

Scripture reading: Acts 11:19-26

Long before the term *Christian* was invented, those who followed Christ were known as *disciples*. A good case therefore can be made for using *disciple* rather than *Christian*, because Christians were called disciples first. Why bother? Well, I think the word *Christian* is used so much it means so little. Perhaps we should give *disciple* another look.

The people who followed Jesus during his earthly ministry were disciples first. That word defined their relationship to Jesus of Nazareth. Ultimately, it was the disciple qualities in believers that led to their being called Christians. They were so closely identified with the one called the Christ that they were given a name meaning, roughly, "little christs."

I suspect that, if we were very closely identified today with the actual lifestyle and philosophy of Jesus Christ, we would not be labeled Christians because that word has come to mean so many things besides a disciple of Christ. What do you suppose people would call you if they looked at you and saw, clearly and consistently, the integrity, the compassion, the holiness, the servanthood, even the abrasiveness that Jesus' way of life introduces into a culture?

Prayer

Lord, I want to stand out as your disciple. Help me reflect your love and compassion by serving those around me as you did. Amen.

August 15—Discipleship Is Relationship

Scripture reading: Mark 3:13-19

As soon as Jesus embarked on his public ministry, he began calling the disciples who would form the nucleus of his church. The basis of their discipleship was a relationship to Christ.

Being with a person over time usually results in that person's influencing every area of your life. You pick up little habits you didn't have before. You begin seeing life from a new viewpoint. That person's concerns become your concerns.

Anyone who has had a favorite (or least favorite) teacher understands that the actual teaching was but part of the relationship. Spiritual and emotional dynamics were at work as well. The teacher may have been tough as nails when the grades came out, but students were moved to work because of the teacher's encouragement of and confidence in the students' abilities.

These and many other dynamics were involved in the disciples being with Jesus. On how many levels does the Lord Jesus Christ affect your life?

Prayer

Lord, I've often taken comfort in your promise to be "with me," but I've overlooked the obvious corollary—that I am invited to be with you. Make me conscious of this, and ensure that I am aware of being with you to bring you joy and to make me different. Amen.

August 16—Following, Learning, and Imitating

Scripture reading: 1 Thessalonians 1:4-10

Schoolchildren in ancient Greece did not have to sit at desks in classrooms. Instead, they were deposited by their proud parents or long-suffering slaves at a grove where lemons and oranges and olives grew. In the shade of these lovely, aromatic trees stood the teacher, clad in a long white robe and matching beard.

Once the pupils (disciples) were assembled, the teacher would start walking among the trees, sharing with them the lesson for the hour. The pupils would follow their teacher as he walked; no doubt, being kids, they would begin to imitate his every gesture and idiosyncrasy. In time they would learn something despite themselves.

To the Greek mind, discipleship meant following, learning, and imitating. All three concepts are strikingly evident in the impact that Christ had on his disciples and are equally powerful in shaping the modern-day disciple.

Prayer

Father, what a privilege is mine—to be called into fellowship with your Son—to learn of him, to follow him, to imitate him, empowered by the indwelling Holy Spirit. And what a responsibility is mine—to reflect in my life the transforming power of my relationship with him. I give you thanks. Amen.

August 17—The Power of Simple Demonstration

Scripture reading: Mark 1:14-20

Malcolm Muggeridge, the British author, journalist, and critic, was for many years a brilliant and articulate skeptic. One day, on assignment for the BBC, he was sitting in the crypt under the Church of the Nativity in Bethlehem, waiting for the streams of tourists and pilgrims to pass through so that he could film his commentary.

The crypt itself is gloomy and unattractive, with many smoky lamps and threadbare wall hangings. I can think of no place on earth more ideally suited for a skeptic to have a heyday. But when a group of pilgrims entered the crypt, Muggeridge was strangely moved. Some of them fell on their knees in prayer. Others began to sing quietly, while still others appeared to be in a state of ecstasy. The impact on Muggeridge was dramatic, eventually leading him to become a disciple of Jesus Christ himself.

It is easy to see how Simon became so attracted to Jesus; he could observe him "up close and personal." But it takes people like Malcolm Muggeridge to remind us that those who love Jesus can still effectively demonstrate the beauty of his person to a watching world.

Prayer

Lord, I instinctively sense that the answer to skepticism is argument. I forget that the best argument is a winsome life. Forgive me my argumentativeness and help me work on holy attractiveness. Amen.

August 18—In Awe Enough to Follow

Scripture reading: Luke 5:1-11

Luke's account of the call of the disciples is more detailed than those of the other Gospel writers. From him we learn about Christ's teaching from the boat and Simon's willingness to go fishing again simply because Jesus told him to. The results were nothing short of spectacular; the catch was so great that the nets couldn't handle the weight of the fish. When the haul was finally dragged in, Simon "fell at Jesus' knees and said, 'Go away from me, Lord; I am a sinful man!'"

Since there is no record of Jesus preaching on sin and repentance at that particular moment, we must assume that it was his majestic, awesome power so dramatically demonstrated that showed Simon what a weak, ineffectual, unreliable sinner he was.

Jesus, of course, had no intention of "going away." In fact, his work was just beginning. But surely he was delighted to hear Simon's words. They showed that this headstrong fisherman was at last ready to follow.

Prayer

Lord, all too often I forget my inadequacies and waywardness. Thank you for patiently working with Simon Peter; do it again with me. Amen.

August 19—Leaving Sin

Scripture reading: Hebrews 12:1-3

Some time ago a young woman came to me to talk about the fact that she seemed to have lost her joy in the Lord. She requested prayer that joy might be restored to her.

When I endeavored to identify the cause of this sense of loss, she refused to get specific. Couldn't we just ask God to give her back her joy? she wondered. When I persisted, the woman tearfully admitted that she was living with her boyfriend and didn't want the church to know because she thought we might tell her it was wrong.

We didn't need to tell her it was wrong. She knew that instinctively. What she apparently did not know was that when one's affections are alienated from the Master, one does not live in the conscious enjoyment of his presence. The decision to follow Christ presupposes the decision to forsake all that would alienate our affections from him.

Prayer

Lord, I don't know how I can expect to enjoy you when at the same time I'm doing what you don't enjoy. But so often I do. Help me to follow through on the decisions that need to be made if I am to live righteously in your sight. Amen.

August 20—Willing to Follow

Scripture reading: Mark 10:28-31

As the first disciples discovered, following Christ forced them to decide whether they were prepared to acknowledge his general lordship of their lives, and follow wherever he might lead.

For the modern disciple, the issues are much the same. For some people, the call of Christ requires a lifestyle where the comforts of home and the delights of family life are laid aside. Jill and I realized early in our marriage that Christ's call required me to be away on preaching missions for extended periods of time. Frequently I was asked by people who invited me to minister in their country, "How can you justify being away from your family?"

"I can justify it because you apparently thought it was all right to ask me to come!" I replied.

"Yes, but how can you fulfill your biblical role of father and husband and be away from home so much?"

"I'll answer that if you can tell me how I can fulfill my calling as an international evangelist and stay at home!"

Prayer

Lord, it's a matter of willingness, I know. But sometimes I say "I can't" when what I mean is "I won't." Forgive me, and help me to release what I'm holding onto, knowing that you will take it and keep it—and that it couldn't be in safer hands. Amen.

August 21—Being Good Stewards

Scripture reading: Luke 19:11-27

When Jill started her teaching career, she was thrilled to receive her first paycheck. She opened a bank account, but was horrified to learn there was no little box into which her money was placed until she went to collect it. I explained that the bank didn't actually keep her money at the bank. "It has been loaned to other people to pay for their houses and cars."

"You mean they've let my money go and they don't know where it is?"

"Well, they don't know exactly where your money is, but if you go in and ask for it, they are required to return it to you immediately. In the meantime, they put it to work."

As a banker I thought I understood banking until I tried to explain it to my young wife, whose artistic and literary gifts are outstanding but whose economic and accounting skills are of a lesser caliber. But Jill did understand when I explained that stewardship works the same way. When we become Christ's disciples we gladly hand over all we have to him. At that point, he returns those resources to us and we function as his stewards. We put those resources to work, until he calls upon us to relinquish them for his purposes.

Prayer

Lord, your call to us is so all-encompassing that it's a good thing you draw us into it gradually. Help me to ensure that as you invite me to go deeper I will dare to follow. Amen.

August 22—Doing What Comes Naturally

Scripture reading: Romans 8:5-8

I remember as a child arguing with my sister Shirley a lot. When we were very small, my father gave Shirley two sixpences, one for each of us. Later, Shirley told me she had lost mine! How did she know it was *my* sixpence she lost? I wondered. But that's how it is with children. Selfishness comes quite naturally.

A gravestone in England reads: "Here lies a miser who lived for himself, lived for nothing but gathering wealth. Now where he is and how he fares, nobody knows and nobody cares." What a terrible thing! If that man was truly so self-centered, there's a dreadful possibility he's living now in total isolation, for I believe that's what hell is: living with yourself for all eternity. Nobody else will be there, just your thoroughly selfish self, separated from God, apart from any good company at all.

Jesus said we'll be separated from him forever if we do not let him do something about our natural state. The world may say "natural" is good, but Christians cannot believe that if they have any knowledge at all of sin—and its selfish consequences.

Prayer

Jesus, thank you for unselfishly dying for me so I can receive your Spirit and be empowered to be selfless. Amen.

August 23—Change Is Unavoidable

Scripture reading: Genesis 12:1-4

When I joined Britain's Royal Marines as an idealistic, adventuresome eighteen-year-old, I was aware they would make some changes in me. I had no idea how many changes. Would I have volunteered had I known in advance about the gruesome details that go into turning a banker into a Marine? Probably not. But it's a purely hypothetical question; one never knows in advance exactly what he is going to go through. It was no different for Abram when he left his home for who-knew-where.

Disciples of Jesus Christ need to be aware that change is necessary, painful, and inevitable, but there is no way they can or should know what they will be called to go through. They must simply be willing to take it a step at a time.

Perhaps the inevitability of change has escaped some of us. By definition, disciples follow. That means they go where they have never been before—or at least where they aren't at that particular moment! In other words, they progress.

Prayer

Lord, it ought to be obvious that following you leads to progress, that progress involves change, and that change is often painful and threatening. So lead us gently in the discoveries of discipleship, because many of us didn't know what we were getting into! Amen.

August 24—Right Answer, Wrong Expectations

Scripture reading: Mark 8:27-33

When Jesus asked what people were saying about his identity, the disciples quickly gave him the information they had gleaned from their discussions with others and no doubt felt very pleased with themselves. They were not given much time to enjoy their success. "But what about you?" Jesus asked. "Who do you say I am?"

Peter said, "You are the Christ." By this he meant that he recognized that Jesus was specially anointed by God to restore Israel's fortunes, according to prophets. So Peter must have been devastated when Jesus then instructed the disciples not to tell anyone! Why would this be so? The answer to this seeming inconsistency is not hard to find.

Jesus taught the disciples that he would be rejected by the Jewish leaders, die, and rise again. Peter was right about Jesus being the Christ, but he was wrong about the kind of Messiah Jesus was. If Peter had been allowed to propagate his misunderstanding of who Jesus was, the damage would have been considerable. Indeed, Peter reacted so violently to Jesus' statement about his coming death that he actually took the Master aside "and began to rebuke him."

Prayer

Lord, I have a tendency to make you fit conveniently into my plans and assume you have come to fulfill my agenda. Help me see you as you truly are. Amen.

August 25—Disciples Need Rest

Scripture reading: Mark 6:30–32

When adrenalin is flowing, who needs rest? With a world full of needy people, who needs to get alone for quiet? With momentum on your side, who wants to take a break? But these men were disciples, and disciples have to learn!

No doubt you have watched long-distance races where a couple of runners immediately go to the front of the pack and set a fast pace. These front runners are called "rabbits." They are in the race to set a quick pace for the benefit of the other runners, but they themselves have no intention of finishing. They go off in a blaze of glory and fizzle like fireworks on the Fourth of July.

This is exactly what can, and sometimes does, happen to Christians who start at a terrific pace, quickly run out of spiritual gas, and finally drop out of the race. But it doesn't have to happen. Disciples need rest if they are going to gain the stamina they need to minister effectively.

Prayer

Lord, continue reminding those of us who are "task oriented" that it is necessary to care for our own spiritual well-being if we are to make an impression on our world's spiritual wilderness. Amen.

August 26—Disciples Need Depth

Scripture reading: Matthew 16:5-12

I suspect that the Twelve had learned enough about the Lord to become equipped to do the kinds of things they liked doing. Exorcising, preaching, and healing were exciting and rewarding. They had garnered a degree of fame and recognition. No doubt, they were in great demand. So why bother thinking and learning and wrestling with the hard things? What they didn't know was that they weren't doing as well as they imagined. If they didn't get things straight about the Lord, they would end up flat on their evangelical noses.

I am reminded of the kid who got a new bike and quickly learned to ride. He disappeared around the block and returned at great speed shouting, "Look, Mom, no hands!" The next time around: "Look, Mom, no feet!" The third time around: "Look, Mom, no teeth!"

Disciples who think they know enough are the ones who end up confused because they have failed to deepen their knowledge of Christ. And if they have attained positions of prominence and leadership beyond their abilities, they are in danger of losing their spiritual teeth. We need to remember that being a disciple means being a learner.

Prayer

Lord, you know I've sometimes been guilty of speaking with authority from the depth of my ignorance and operating with flair out of spiritual impotence. Help me to do it the right way! Amen.

August 27—Integrity in Business

Scripture reading: Psalm 101

The modern-day Christian is frequently faced with a choice between doing what is right by God's standards or succumbing to the generally accepted standards of business morality, which often leave much to be desired.

I have a friend who had spent his working life in the used-car business. He became a disciple of the Lord Jesus and promptly began to follow him earnestly. One day he called me and said that he could no longer function as a disciple in that particular business, and he was quitting. He had never done anything else, and I knew it might be hard for him to start a new career at that stage of his life. So I urged caution, while commending him for recognizing that disciples must decide whether or not they will do things God's way or man's.

I knew some used-car dealers who were also genuine disciples, so I encouraged him to meet with them and see how it was possible to be honest and successful. Today he is still an effective disciple of Jesus Christ skillfully disguised as a used-car salesman.

Prayer

Lord, it's hard to function Christianly in a non-Christian or a pseudo-Christian environment. But it can be done if we "trust and obey." So please don't let me slide into easy conformity or become an irrelevant, isolated oddity. Make me a gutsy disciple. Amen.

August 28—The Challenge of Self-Denial

Scripture reading: Luke 9:21-27

Apparently, Christ told people right from the beginning that the life he was inviting them to share with him would challenge them to the core of their being. At the same time, he required his disciples to listen again to what they had presumably already heard; they needed a refresher course in what discipleship involved.

We must let people know what discipleship involves right from the beginning of our communication about Christ. And we must go on reminding each other of the challenge of being a follower of the Lord Jesus, because there are many aspects of discipleship that would be easy and convenient to forget.

Look carefully at what Jesus actually said in Luke 9:23. There are four responses he clearly expects from his disciples: (1) Come after me; (2) Deny yourself; (3) Take up your cross; and (4) Follow me.

Prayer

Lord, I must admit that following you is full of surprises. Not because you hide anything from me, but because sometimes I wasn't listening and other times I assumed the hard parts of discipleship were for those other folks and not me! Help me "be real." Amen.

August 29—The Effect of Living Rightly

Scripture reading: Matthew 5:13-16

Percy Robinson was a small man whose diminutive stature was accentuated by a severe curvature of the spine. His wife had died, leaving him alone in a tiny home where he lived quietly and frugally. By day he earned his living as a printer.

When I was a young banker, during my lunch hours I would often eat a sandwich with Percy among the ink and the presses, which looked as if they had been bought cheaply from a print shop in Charles Dickens's time.

He talked always about serving the Lord, and he delivered his printing at such low rates that he barely eked out a living. When I asked Percy about this, he said he didn't want to abuse people. He was unobtrusive, even to the point of being regarded as something of a village eccentric. But when Percy died, a brash businessman who was not known for handing out accolades said, "If ever there was a Christian, it was Percy the printer."

Prayer

Lord, it's the quiet, consistent, unobtrusive Percy Robinsons of this world who make the greatest impact on me. May I be equally quiet, consistent, and unobtrusively yours. Amen.

August 30—The Meaning of the Cross

Scripture reading: Acts 5:17-20, 41-42

We are so familiar with the expression "take up our cross" that we might not be able to realize the shock with which Christ's words must have been received. After all, in that day crucifixion was a Roman means of capital punishment.

For centuries, the cross has been a stark symbol of the Christian faith—and rightly so. It points to the central and unique event—namely, Jesus' death and resurrection—without which our faith would be invalid. It appears on steeples and Communion tables, letterheads and necklaces, even baseball hats and T-shirts.

But as important as symbols are to our faith, we cannot afford to relegate the idea of the disciple's cross bearing either to cross wearing or to church decorating. The Master was talking about an attitude of heart that would so identify his disciples with him and his cause that if it led them to pain, suffering, loss, and even death, they would be found faithful to the end, even "rejoicing because they had been counted worthy of suffering disgrace for the Name."

Prayer

Lord, I'd just as soon avoid pain and stress and major on peace and prosperity. But I know enough about you to be confident that you will permit for me what is necessary in order that I might become what you want me to be. So be it, Lord. Amen.

August 31—Lambs among Wolves

Scripture reading: Luke 10:1-17

The disciples had observed firsthand the conflict that resulted when Jesus challenged the realms of spiritual darkness. Even so, it is doubtful they fully understood the extent of the fight between the kingdom of Satan and the kingdom of God.

The same can be said for the modern disciple who has watched from the sidelines the struggle between the people of God and the strategies of the evil one. Only those who have endeavored to move into enemy territory know the stress and strain involved. Accordingly, they are the only ones who begin to discover the resources of authority and power with which disciples have been invested.

If the Twelve had any doubt about the reality of spiritual warfare, those doubts vanished when the Master said (in a slightly different context), "Go! I am sending you out like lambs among wolves." If disciples have any degree of success, they may forget they are lambs up against wolves and try to roar like lions. It is fatal to rely on our own strengths while underestimating those of the enemy.

Prayer

Lord, a healthy dose of spiritual realism is what I need if I am not going to overestimate my own significance and underestimate the enemy's power. If I make either miscalculation, the results will be ugly. Protect me therefore, please. Amen.

September

September 1—It's Okay to Make Mistakes

Scripture reading: John 21:1-19

The teaching method of allowing mistakes was certainly used by the Master, our Lord Jesus. But such a philosophy has never been overly popular with his followers. One reason for this is undoubtedly the common fear of failure. We are so success-oriented we see anything less than "winning" as unacceptable and to be avoided at all costs.

One of the easiest ways of avoiding defeat is to refuse to enter the contest, and this is exactly what some disciples do. Rather than risk looking foolish or feeling inadequate, they prefer to stick with what is tested and tried, thus never launching out into new areas of endeavor and discovery.

Then others hold the idea that only excellence will do for the Master, an idea which may be commendable in its intent, but which is decidedly debilitating in its outworking. Why chance trying anything new if only excellence is acceptable? And how is excellence to be achieved if people are not encouraged to learn, if necessary, by making mistakes?

Prayer

Lord, you don't expect me to be casual or careless, but you also don't expect perfection this side of glory. I know I'll make mistakes. I trust they will be little ones, that the damage to your name will be minimal, and that I will learn through them. Amen.

September 2—Weapons for a Spiritual War

Scripture reading: Mark 9:14-29

The disciples encountered a desperate man seeking healing for his demon-possessed son. They had responded to the father's request with great enthusiasm only to discover that they were up against a demon that showed no respect whatsoever for them or their attempts at exorcism.

Imagine the scene as crowds gathered around the boy who lay writhing on the ground, while the disciples tried to deal with the situation. We have to give the Twelve credit for trying. Unfortunately, though, they had forgotten that their warfare was spiritual, and so they were failing to use the proper spiritual weapons of prayer and faith. Despite all their efforts and their warmhearted response to the pitiful boy, they came up short by a mile.

At this point, the Master stepped in. He was obviously frustrated with their mistaken approach to the problem. Just as a little knowledge can be a dangerous thing, so can a little success. Given the success of their previous mission, perhaps the disciples concluded that with their ability proven, all that was now required was hard work, enthusiasm, and know-how. They had forgotten the element of spiritual power, without which we are unable to do any of the Lord's work.

Prayer

Lord, your disciples were called, commissioned, and gifted, but still couldn't deliver because they were deficient in prayer and faith. Show me the deficiencies in my spiritual life as well. Amen

September 3—The Fruit of Failure

Scripture reading: Acts 15:36-41; 2 Timothy 4:11

Recently I was talking to the wife of a professional athlete. The player's previous coach had left the ball club, and with a new coach the athlete's play had improved so dramatically that he was the talk of the league. When I asked what had made the difference, she said, "The main reason is that if he made a mistake under the previous coach, he was promptly benched. But under the new coach, he is allowed to make a mistake or two, and this gives him time to settle down and play his game."

John Mark had obviously fallen short of Paul's expectations. But this did not negate his usefulness to Paul later. One of the most endearing things about Jesus' handling of his disciples was his willingness to teach them through their mistakes. He could quite easily have benched them all. But fortunately, this has never been his method—not then, not now.

This is an encouragement to all disciples who have failed and been devastated by their failure, or even for disciples who have never failed only because they have never tried. The good news is that Jesus Christ has many faithful disciples who have done their share of failing.

Prayer

There are so many bad things associated with my failures, Lord. I hinder your work. I disappoint you and discourage my sisters and brothers. But the up-side is that I learn humility. Could I perhaps learn it some other way? Amen.

September 4—Genuine Greatness

Scripture reading: Acts 9:26-28

On my very first preaching tour of the U.S. as a young Britisher, I was quite nervous. When I discovered that the first week I would be sharing the ministry with Dr. Paul Rees, whom I had greatly admired for many years, my nervousness disappeared immediately and was superseded by total fright!

But I need not have worried. Dr. Rees treated me as if I were the most capable preacher he had ever listened to. He sat on the front row taking notes as I preached; he came and asked me questions after I was through; and when he talked to me, he acted as if I were the only person on the planet. To my embarrassment, he also introduced me to everybody as "my dear friend, Stuart."

The amazing thing to me was that it was all genuine.

Greatness is not necessarily being well known. Greatness in this case was a well-known man who, in the name of Christ, received an unknown youngster starting out in ministry, made him feel welcome, affirmed him, and did all that he could to encourage him.

Prayer

Lord, I'll never forget the grace of those who have gone before me. May there be one or two who come after me who find me helpful. Amen.

September 5—Honoring God at Work

Scripture reading: Ephesians 6:5-9

I have no illusions about the difficulties that genuine disciples of Jesus Christ experience as they seek to live by his principles in the workplace. Often in the working environment, advantage will be taken of anything or anyone in order to turn a profit or assure a move ahead. From my own experience in business and that of many godly business people, however, I have observed the following:

1. I should set goals pleasing to the Master in the course of my daily business life. This will mean that my work becomes worship and, accordingly, will be work of the highest caliber.
2. Instead of seeking to beat the competition, I should compete against those attitudes and actions in my life that are displeasing to the Master.
3. I should strive to do only what the Master says and leave the results to him, resting in the assurance that he will work in my circumstances and on my behalf.

It was my mother who taught me as I was about to embark on my business career, "Remember, Stuart, that God says, 'Those who honor me, I will honor.'"

Prayer

Lord, as I move out into the world where you decided I should live my life, I know I am your representative. That's scary. But I also know I am your responsibility. That's a relief. Thank you. Amen.

September 6—Understanding Prayer

Scripture reading: 1 John 5:13-15

Prayer is universally practiced, but it is not universally understood. I remember having a long, interesting discussion with a professed atheist. As we were parting, I said to him, "I'm going to pray for you."

"Don't do that," he remonstrated hastily.

"Why not? As far as you're concerned, God's not there; so it can't do any harm."

"I know that. But I still don't want you praying for me."

"But tell me, why not?" I insisted.

"Because I have a funny feeling it might work!"

Perhaps we are surprised to discover that atheists sometimes have "funny feelings" about prayer, but none of us are surprised to hear that people in tight corners believe in prayer. A man in a foxhole under fire once prayed, "God get me out of this and I'll never bother you again." God did, and he didn't!

But is prayer a matter of ritual or superstition? Is it a pious platitude or a last resort? Do we engage in it as a matter of course, or is it an optional extra like whitewall tires, which make the automobile look good but do not materially affect its performance? Disciples of the Lord Jesus need to examine these kinds of questions.

Prayer

Lord, my prayer is brief and to the point: Teach me to pray. Amen.

September 7—Practicing Prayer

Scripture reading: Matthew 6:5-8

Jesus prayed often, and his disciples knew it. He sent them ahead in the boat while he prayed, and on more than one occasion he took some of them with him to pray, though they did not do very well. He also made it quite clear to them that they were not to pray in the extravagant, unseemly manner of the hypocrites whose prayers were performances designed to impress people rather than petitions intended to implore God. He would have nothing to do with this kind of behavior.

Jesus seemed to approach prayer as yet another area of life to be learned and developed. He talked about it in parables and gave some guidelines for it, but mainly his concern was that his disciples *do* it. For all the books and seminars we can absorb about prayer today, perhaps we too should try simply to do it, day by day, in the spirit of learning—and of discovering this miraculous dimension of discipleship.

Prayer

Lord, I know desire and discipline are ingredients of effective prayer. Sadly I'm often deficient in both, but I do want to be more prayerful, and I promise to follow as you lead and learn as you teach. Amen.

September 8—Come Confidently, as a Child

Scripture reading: Matthew 7:7-11

Much about God as revealed in creation is awesome and perhaps intimidating, but he has shown, primarily in Christ, that he is eminently approachable and abounding in compassion toward those who genuinely seek him. As the Master reminded his disciples, even fallible earthly fathers know how to look after their children. If the kids ask for something appropriate, such as bread, Dad does not give them a useless stone. Likewise, the heavenly Father can be counted on to give his children whatever is necessary for their greatest good.

When our children were young, we lived in a very small house with inadequate facilities for quiet study. I had to find whatever quiet-ish corner was available and do as much study as possible before the inevitable interruptions came. If the children had a problem, they brought it! If they were excited about something, they shouted it! There was an openness about them that was delightful and a desire to share that was winsome and spontaneous. That is how children come to a father, and it is in that spirit that the disciples were encouraged to pray to their Abba Father.

Prayer

Lord, I don't want to be brash in my approach to you, but neither do I wish to be reticent in coming to you. Knowing you love me and welcome me helps. Thank you for revealing yourself in this manner. Amen.

September 9—Prayer Is Conversation

Scripture reading: Luke 11:2-4

There are two ways to have a conversation. One is to dive right in, tell the person all that you want him or her to know, and then leave. The other is to give the person the opportunity to tell you what he or she wants you to know while you listen carefully and then respond appropriately.

The former is a conversation in name only and does very little to deepen a relationship, because one of the parties has shown little or no interest in the other. The latter is truly a conversation and enriches the relationship between the participants, for each has been able to reveal what was in his or her heart and have someone else be interested enough to listen.

Prayer is the talking part of our relationship with God. When we come to the Lord expressing interest in his name, kingdom, and will, we open ourselves up to the very real possibility of getting to know him better, because we are identifying with the things that are on his heart.

Prayer

Lord, I would like my prayers to concentrate more on what is on your heart than what is on my mind. This reminds me that prayer means listening for you as well as talking to you. Amen.

September 10—Legitimate Needs

Scripture reading: Matthew 6:11; John 6:32-35

"Daily bread" relates to our physical needs. We human beings have always had difficulty differentiating between needs and wants—and this causes prayer problems. God is committed to meeting needs, but not necessarily to meeting wants. Daily bread is about as basic as one can get. How much butter and jam we may feel free to expect from God is left to the individual's conscience, but bread on an ongoing basis is a legitimate need, and therefore a legitimate prayer item.

This raises the matter of those who do not even have enough basic necessities for survival, and strongly suggests that such need should be not only a matter of prayer but also a cause for action. Supplying food to the hungry can lead to sharing the true Bread of Life.

Prayer

Lord, forgive my absorption with secondary issues and my neglect of primary matters. Deepen me and let it show in the maturing of my praying. Amen.

September 11—Forgiven to Forgive

Scripture reading: Matthew 6:12-15

In the Lord's prayer we see that forgiveness is something we experience as coming from God and as going from us to others. We also see connections between the two types of forgiveness. When we experience God's forgiveness, we can express our own forgiveness to others. When we do not forgive others, we are unable to fully experience God's forgiveness. This is a mystery, yet it is a spiritual principle very basic to our existence as spiritual people.

We cannot forgive unless we have God's view of people firmly in our minds. God is looking for ways to bring people to himself in reconciliation; he would gladly see us reconciled to himself and to one another. God does not go looking for opportunities to wreak vengeance on people's wrongdoings—and neither should we. God sees people as what they are capable of becoming through the regeneration of the Holy Spirit. He does not see them as hopeless cases or worthless causes—and neither should we.

God has lavished forgiveness and peace upon us, and, rather than feeling superior or vindicated in our own rightness, we must lavish these gifts on others. The immense, transforming forgiveness of God is meant to come full circle—to us, then through us.

Prayer

Lord, as I cannot receive a gift with clenched fists, I cannot enjoy forgiveness with an unforgiving heart. So, for the good of all concerned, teach me about forgiveness and forgiving. Amen.

September 12—Lead Us Not into Temptation

Scripture reading: Matthew 6:13; 4:1-11

The disciples of Jesus became increasingly aware that they were in a spiritual battle with evil forces. So they understood that they would find themselves in situations that would give them every opportunity to go wrong. That is what temptation is. But temptation is also an opportunity to do right, and that is why God allows us to be tempted or tested.

The Lord's Prayer appears to request that the tempting and testing be circumvented, if at all possible. The legitimacy of this kind of prayer is clear because the Master himself prayed in a similar vein in the Garden of Gethsemane. He recognized, of course, that if the testing was unavoidable, grace would be available (and it was).

It is equally legitimate for disciples today to pray that they will not have to go through temptation; but if God knows that this is not in their best interests, then they should pray that they will not be overcome by it. The Holy Spirit led Jesus into the wilderness of temptation. It was a necessary part of his calling. There has never been a disciple in any era who has not needed to pray constantly about this kind of thing.

Prayer

Lord, knowing my own frailty, I would prefer not to be exposed to temptation. But that would not only protect me from going wrong, it would also deny me the chance to do right. So I'll trust you, Lord, to permit what is necessary and provide what is appropriate. Amen.

September 13—The Spread of Hypocrisy

Scripture reading: Luke 12:1-3

While driving home from church with my two younger children, I asked, "What did you think about the sermon this morning?"

"It was fantastic, Dad," said Peter, going on to point out specific details which had impressed him.

"You hypocrite!" shouted my daughter.

"Judy, that's enough of that kind of talk. You will not call your brother a hypocrite," I reproved.

"He went into church with me, picked up a copy of the outline, sat on the back row, and memorized your three main points. Then he slept through the whole service."

"Pete, is this true?" I asked, turning to look at my mildly embarrassed son.

"Yes, Dad. I was tired, and your sermons are boring."

"There you are, Dad," said Judy. "Now what do we call him?"

"*Hypocrite*, unfortunately, is appropriate, but it's still a very unpleasant word to apply to anyone," I admitted reluctantly.

The Lord Jesus called hypocrisy *yeast*, pointing out its insidious nature. As yeast works quietly and unobtrusively until it permeates everything, so hypocrisy's penchant for covering up reality and acting out a lie can become a way of life.

Prayer

Lord, I'm more skilled at seeing the hypocrisy in others than the hypocrisy in myself. Make me more honest and more consistent. Help me slow down the yeast effect. Amen.

September 14—What Will People Think?

Scripture reading: Luke 12:4-5

The tragedy of all hypocrisy is that it illustrates that the hypocrite is more concerned about what people think than about what God knows; is more worried about what people might do than about what God could do; and is more interested in the immediate circumstances, where people reside, than the ultimate glory, in which God reigns.

There was (and still is) a danger of spiritual hypocrisy working out in two entirely different ways. On the one hand, some people might believe in their hearts, but be afraid to confess they are following the Lord. To such men and women, Jesus said, "He who disowns me before men will be disowned before the angels of God" (Luke 12:9).

On the other hand, there may be those who, for whatever reason, might wish to be accepted as genuine believers, but whose hearts are actually far from the Lord. To them, he will one day say, "I don't know you or where you come from. Away from me, all you evildoers!" (Luke 13:27).

Prayer

It's what they used to call the "credibility gap," Father— that great divide between what's true and what I want people to think is true. There's only one remedy, and that is for you to keep me honest. Do it, Lord! Amen.

September 15—Safeguards against Hypocrisy

Scripture reading: Luke 12:6-12

Given our natural tendency to play roles that do not always equate with reality, we need safeguards against such behavior. The first is to be aware of the propensity—forewarned is forearmed!

The second safeguard is to be constantly aware that the Lord knows our hearts and is far more significant than any person we may wish to impress.

The third is to recognize the great care our heavenly Father extends toward us. Reminding the disciples that sparrows are practically worthless, yet never beyond the Father's care, Jesus points out his far greater concern and compassion for human beings. This knowledge should warm our hearts and protect us from hypocritical activities.

The fourth safeguard is to recognize the nature of those people who tempt us to cover up the Spirit's work. They fall into the category of people who blaspheme against the Holy Spirit, a sin Jesus called unforgivable. By this he meant that those who go beyond resisting the truth and attribute the Spirit's gracious work to Satan instead, will find no basis for forgiveness. Disciples today should not be intimidated into playacting by such people.

Prayer

My desire to be accepted is so strong, Lord, that sometimes in my weakness I "do" what I don't "believe." This can improve my standing with the wrong people and grieve the One who matters most—you! Forgive me, Lord. Amen.

September 16—What about Possessions?

In the 1830s, Alexis de Tocqueville observed, "No stigma attaches to the love of money in America." The apostle Paul warned, "The love of money is a root of all kinds of evil" (1 Tim. 6:10).

In the 1980s, convicted stockbroker Ivan Boesky said, "Greed is healthy." Jesus taught, "Be on your guard against all kinds of greed."

There is a clear tension between the commonly accepted view of our society and the teaching of Scripture on the subject of materialism.

Between the poles where possessions are regarded as either evil or everything, a balance must exist. To demonstrate that balance, Jesus told a parable about a successful farmer so engrossed with material things that he had overlooked the major issues of life. God called him a fool, told him that he would die rather than enjoy the fruits of his labor, and asked, "Then who will get what you have prepared for yourself?"

Turning to the crowd, Jesus added the punch line, "This is how it will be with anyone who stores up things for himself but is not rich toward God." The Master criticized the farmer not for being successful or for having considerable resources, but for storing everything up for himself and not being rich toward God. We can own, use, and enjoy material things, but we must understand their appropriate place in our lives.

Prayer

Lord, the allure of possessing more is so compelling. I know that I'm intrinsically selfish, so help me combat my natural tendencies by learning to share and to give. Amen.

September 17—Giving Is Serving God

Scripture reading: Luke 12:32-34

Jesus used dramatic instructions such as, "Sell your possessions and give to the poor," adding that the result would be purses "that will not wear out, a treasure in heaven that will not be exhausted." The extent to which this is done must be determined by each of us, but the principle is clear.

We know that the Master said, "It is more blessed to give than to receive" (Acts 20:35), but it takes a certain degree of spiritual maturity to believe it. That is why it has often been said that the last thing to be converted is the pocketbook.

Our spiritual wealth could be measured, not by the possessions we have stored up, but by the ones we have given away. In other words, possessions are the means to an end—they are to be used to glorify God, whether that be to provide food and clothing for our children or to make it possible for ministries to do their work.

Prayer

Lord, I believe it because you said it—"It is more blessed to give than to receive." And every time I've done it, I've experienced the blessing! So why do I still struggle with it? There's clearly room for growth here, Lord. Amen.

September 18—Live by Your Convictions

Scripture reading: Matthew 10:32-33

How many disciples of Christ have carefully avoided stating their convictions at a job interview for fear of losing a possible promotion? And how many young men and women have allowed their affections to so control them that they have never openly admitted their Christianity to the one to whom they are attracted?

Eric Liddell was a man who knew what was in his heart and allowed it to flow from his lips. He was a member of the 1924 British Olympic team, and when he discovered that his race was to be run on a Sunday, he declined to compete. Intense pressure was brought to bear upon him. He was the talk of the Paris games. Even the Prince of Wales and the British Olympic Committee tried to dissuade him, but to no avail. He stood firm, despite the fact that, as world record holder, he was favored to win the gold medal. Liddell did run another race later in the games, which he won, but he did not run against his convictions.

When Liddell died at the age of forty-three in a Japanese prison camp during World War II, a leading Scottish newspaper wrote, "Scotland has lost a son who did her proud every hour of his life." Here, truly, was a disciple of Jesus Christ skillfully disguised as an Olympic gold medalist, missionary, and patriot.

Prayer

When I pass on, the newspapers may not notice. But you will, Lord, and, while the media may be silent about my departure, may heaven reverberate with your "well done." Amen.

September 19—Money Isn't Everything

Scripture reading: Matthew 6:19-24

Our society is committed to the idea that economies should grow so that more and more people can enjoy a better standard of living. This seems appropriate, but there is a hidden hook to the idea that needs to be recognized. Economies grow as production increases. Production increases as demand expands. Demand expands as it is stimulated. Stimulation is achieved by addressing inbred psychological factors to the point of manipulation and exploitation.

So advertising, which can be an immensely helpful tool, has instead become a powerful weapon playing on such human factors as fear, pride, desire, and greed. And if people cannot afford the "necessities of life," credit is always available; they can have the goods now and pay later.

Thus we find the natural human desires to acquire goods, to be accepted, and to have positive feelings about oneself perverted and turned against us. The material is close to being reckoned as everything, money is king, and Mammon calls the shots.

Prayer

Lord, you gave us bodies and put us on earth, so we know there's nothing intrinsically wrong with material things. It's the commitment to them, the amassing of them, the dependence upon them that is the problem. Help me, Lord, to enjoy what you give me but not so much that I enjoy it more than you—the giver. Amen.

September 20—The Mark of a Disciple

Scripture reading: John 13:34-35

The Lord Jesus Christ issued no uniforms to his disciples. He gave them no ID badges. But this was not because he wanted them to be incognito. On the contrary, he wanted them to be readily recognizable. In fact, he stipulated a specific way of ensuring this very thing. It is revealed in today's verses: love for one another.

This highly significant expression requires considerable thought because, while it is easy to articulate, it is not at all easy to understand or to implement. Fortunately, Jesus amplified what he meant in striking fashion. Talking about love as the hallmark of a disciple, he gave the Twelve a fitting analogy: "As I have loved you, so you must love one another." That statement alone immediately got the idea of loving out of the amorphous abstract into the down-to-earth practical, because every one of those disciples could point to specific ways that Christ's love for them had taken on form and content.

Prayer

Lord, I've been pondering all the ways you loved people. And each example is a model to me of acceptable behavior. So, with your earthly life as my example and your indwelling life as my enabling, I'd like to make progress in my loving. Amen.

September 21—Power to Shine

Scripture reading: Matthew 5:14-16

My dad used to tell the story of a man who, at his wife's urging, bought an electric doorbell and installed it on his front door. When the installation was completed, he connected the wires to a battery, called his wife to his side, pressed the button, and the bell rang out loud and clear.

His wife, sensing the time was ripe, then said, "All we need now is a light over the front door so people can see the doorbell." With a typical masculine sigh, the man returned to the store, bought the light, fixed the wiring, attached it to the battery, and with a flourish flicked the switch. But nothing happened.

Crestfallen, he checked everything and tried again, with the same negative results. Having depleted the resources of his electrical knowledge, he called a friend and explained what had happened. His friend was amazed that he had linked both the bell and the light to a battery, pointing out that the battery might be powerful enough to ring a bell, but not to shine a light. Said he, "You see, it takes a lot more power to shine than to shout!"

Prayer

That's it, Lord. I can shout on my own, but I can only shine in your power. What I really want to do is shine *and* shout to your glory. Let it be, Lord. Amen.

September 22—Potential in a Son of Thunder

Scripture reading: Luke 9:49-56

Remember that the Lord once gave John and his brother James the nickname "Sons of Thunder." This presumably referred to the tempestuous way they reacted to situations and the stormy relationships they experienced. Here, they were quick to demand that fire and brimstone be rained on the Samaritan villages that did not welcome the disciples, and John was quite ready to rebuke a healer who was not among the Master's immediate followers. The picture that emerges of John is not one of a loving, humble servant, but of an arrogant, intolerant, tunnel-visioned upstart!

It takes the eye and imagination of a sculptor to look at a block of masonry and see in it a work of art. But it also takes much patient chipping away over long tedious hours before the work is completed. In the same way, the Master apparently saw things in the youthful John that were hidden to everyone else (with the possible exception of his mother!). But it took years of patient working with him before the transformed disciple began to appear.

This work was begun in John as the two of them walked the roads together, but it was continued by the Spirit who worked a patient miracle from within. Loving as Christ loved his disciples includes having vision enough to see potential in people and patience enough to see the potential realized.

Prayer

I know you've been chipping away at me, Lord. Thank you for your vision of what I can become and your willingness to make it happen. I'd like to develop the same approach to people around me. Amen.

September 23—The Commandment to Rest

Scripture reading: Exodus 20:8-11

God thought work was so important that he used up one of his Ten Commandments to deal with it. The Ten Commandments, as someone has said, are not Ten Suggestions. They are God's mandate for all people. Sin didn't change God's mind about work—it just made it necessary for him to command us to get it done, how to go about it, and when to stop.

God didn't give many specific instructions to the Hebrew people about how to spend their Sabbath day of rest. He mainly wanted them to refrain from working on that day. It was to be a day different from the other six days of the week.

In our workaholic culture, we need to follow this commandment more than ever. What are some kinds of work that are most likely to creep into our Sabbath days? How can we make our Sabbath different from the rest of the week?

Prayer

Lord, I'm sometimes surprised when I fray around the edges. But it's because I've failed to balance work and worship. Help me to do my work as unto you and to worship you with all of my heart. Amen.

September 24—Known by Their Fruit

Scripture reading: Matthew 7:15-20

A friend of mine and his brothers were occasionally reprimanded by their parents and sent to their rooms as punishment. They did not mind this because they had devised a method to escape detention: climbing down an old fruit tree outside their bedroom window and sneaking away to play.

One day they heard their father propose chopping down the tree because it was no longer bearing any fruit. The young boys decided immediate action should be taken. Pooling their pocket money, they dashed to the village, bought apples and black thread, and busily tied apples all over the tree.

Next morning they heard their father call to their mother, "Mary, the most remarkable thing has happened! The fruit tree is covered with apples this morning. It's a miracle!" The boys beamed with pleasure, knowing that their escape route was saved. But their smiles faded when their dad added, "I don't believe it, because it's a pear tree!"

My friend's parents showed their wisdom and rare good humor by allowing the tree to survive. The point of the story, however, is as simple as it is obvious. Apples do not grow on pear trees, and vice versa.

Prayer

Lord, on the basis of iron discipline and monumental self-control I may be able to see some growth in my life. But I know that it takes the work of your Spirit within to produce the fruit that truly glorifies you. Work on, Lord—I'll cooperate. Amen.

September 25—Submit to His Pruning

Scripture reading: John 15:1-4

If the Master is the vine, the disciples are the branches, and Christlike character the fruit, then the Father is the Gardener who tends the branches so they will produce more and better fruit. And how does he do this? By the uncomfortable but necessary process of pruning.

The Master told the disciples, "He cuts off every branch in me that bears no fruit, while every branch that does bear fruit he prunes clean so that it will be even more fruitful" (John 15:2). In the same way that a vine left to itself will produce all kinds of shoots that only drain the energy of the stock, so disciples, left unattended and unaccountable, will degenerate into an energy-sapped, nonproductive people. In the same way that Israel slipped back into being "a wild vine," the disciple's life has "wild" tendencies that must constantly be held in check.

The Father is committed to seeing that this task is done; and he does it by encouraging us to maintain certain disciplines, such as prayer and the study of his Word. He also places disciples in relationships where they are accountable to those who care for their spiritual well-being. This is one of the functions of the local church as well as a responsibility of concerned friends.

Prayer

I don't particularly like being pruned, but I do have a desire to be productive. If my dislike of the former takes over, then my fruitfulness is diminished. But if my desire for the latter governs my thinking, then my attitude toward your pruning is transformed. That's how it should be, Lord. Amen.

September 26—Growth or Sour Grapes?

Scripture reading: John 15:5-8

Shortly after I resigned my position in the bank at the age of twenty-nine to embark on a career of full-time ministry, I was stricken with a throat ailment so painful that public speaking was impossible and normal conversation difficult. I was devastated because there was doubt that I would be able to resume preaching. I had never been ill in my life, so I had no experience of suffering—and it showed in my attitude! I had given up a secular career in order to devote myself to preaching, and it now looked as if I might be unable to do either.

I had to address this fundamental question: Did I love preaching about the Lord more than I loved the Lord about whom I preached? It did not take long to discover that the idea of being a famous preacher and traveling around the world had been most attractive to me, and may have been a major factor in my decision to leave the bank. But the pruning process was at work, and in the end I reluctantly admitted what was going on in my own heart, reaffirmed my genuine desire to serve the Master however he wished, and agreed that if he did not want me to preach ever again, I would be happy to go on loving him.

Discipline from the Lord produces in some people sweetness and maturity, but in others, bitterness and regression. The reason is simply that those who accept the pruning, produce; and those who reject it grow sour grapes that set everyone's teeth on edge.

Prayer

Teach me, Lord, to embrace what you permit in order that I may produce what you desire. Amen.

September 27—Obedience to Our Friend

Scripture reading: John 15:9-14

If you want to maintain a friendship, you aim to please. You look for practical ways to express how you feel. The way to show Christ our appreciation is to obey. He explained, "You are my friends if you do what I command." Nothing is more pleasing to him than when his disciples do what he wants them to do. And we have to know his commandments in order to obey them.

I have found that many people know more about soap operas than about Christ's words. They relate to what they are watching and instinctively react in the way the actors react. The fact that the secular solution is far removed from the biblical solution is of little concern, because either they do not know what Scripture says on the subject, or they have so much toxicity in their spiritual bloodstream that God's Word has little effect on their thinking and decision making.

Even those who find themselves in positions of mature Christian leadership have fallen morally, not because they were suddenly overwhelmed by an impossible temptation, but because they allowed biblical truth to be swamped by worldly error. Such people often respond to their misdemeanors by talking more about psychology than sin and more about personal fulfillment than individual responsibility and obedience.

Prayer

Lord, there's great joy in knowing you call your disciples *friends*. This makes obedience much more attractive than if it were imposed upon me by dictatorial fiat. It's my Friend telling me to do what's best for me. Thank you for that. Amen.

September 28—A True Team Spirit

Scripture reading: 1 Corinthians 12:4-11

When I joined the Royal Marines, we had to memorize the phrase *esprit de corps*. *Esprit de corps* means literally "spirit of a body." For the Marines, it means individual Marines can achieve certain things, but a regiment can accomplish the unimaginable.

This idea of team spirit, or *esprit de corps,* may sound strange when we think of the church of Jesus Christ, but actually it fits very easily into theological thinking. The Bible teaches that the church of Jesus Christ, the local fellowship of believers, is the body of Christ. Furthermore, people who are part of that body have a spirit, a motivating factor, that they would otherwise not have. In other words, it is possible for Christians to operate Christianly on an individual basis, but they cannot operate fully on that basis. For if they do not understand the *esprit de corps* that comes from being part of the body of Christ, they will lack certain kinds of motivation.

When I experience God working in my life, I must not assume it is purely for my own benefit. God's activity in my life is also for the good of the body of believers to which I belong and with which I identify.

Prayer

Lord, teach me your *esprit de corps*, so I may fully support other members of the body and help contribute to the growth of all believers. Amen.

September 29—Deadwood

Scripture reading: Luke 13:6-9

Living wood needs to be pruned, but deadwood needs to be removed altogether. It is serious when living branches grow wild and become considerably less productive than they are intended to be. But it is much more serious when deadwood clutters the vine. Unpruned wood fails to produce its potential; deadwood has its own vast potential for destruction, decay, and disease—and usually produces it!

Modern disciples need to be aware that the community of believers is always vulnerable to deadwood taking over. Far from producing the character and activity of the living Master, this produces things that militate against him and his cause. Unfortunately, many of us have heard of churches "dying on the vine," but we may not always have known why. Either the living branches became unfruitful through unwillingness to respond to the Gardener's pruning, or the church became a collection of people who failed to recognize that their vitality depended upon their union with Christ.

Prayer

Lord, I'm not discerning enough to distinguish between deadwood and dormant branches, but you are. So I'll trust you to work on your vine, including me, and I'll keep abiding. Amen.

September 30—Cosmic Conflict

Scripture reading: Luke 22:31-38

As Jesus approached his crucifixion, little did the disciples realize that they had become the focal point of a cosmic struggle. The Master announced, "Simon, Simon, Satan has asked to sift you as wheat. But I have prayed for you, Simon, that your faith may not fail."

Down in the trenches, these men were going to be fighting against a hostile crowd and their human tendencies to save their own skins. But in the High Command the struggle was much greater. It was the prince of darkness versus the Prince of Peace. Satan was committed to undoing all that the Father had planned; the Father, on the other hand, was committed to seeing his Son accomplish against all odds his purpose for coming to earth.

While only the Master could do the work of redemption, the disciples' involvement would become absolutely crucial after the Resurrection. It was profoundly important to Satan that they be stopped, but even more important to the Master that they survive. Jesus, knowing all this, allowed his disciples to be put to the test. If they were going to be his people, they had to go through their baptism of fire. But not alone! He was praying for them.

How many times have we felt betrayed, as though we had been set up to fail, and guilty because we did not do as well as we should have? But Jesus knows and he is praying!

Prayer

What a comfort to know that when I'm so overwhelmed I cannot pray, that you, Lord, are praying. And how satisfying it is to realize that even Satan's attacks when rightly handled, serve only to further your purposes. Thank you. Amen.

October

October 1—Jesus Offers Restoration

Scripture reading: Luke 24:9-12, 36-39

People react differently to their circumstances. For some it's difficult to admit they have been terribly wrong. Perhaps this was Peter's problem. Or maybe he was thinking, *If Jesus really is risen, then I will have to face him. And what can I possibly say to him about my denial and desertion?*

Peter was not left wondering long, for that evening the Master appeared to the disciples together. To say that they were dumbstruck and shamed is to put it mildly. Yet Jesus spent no time upbraiding them for their failure; instead, he addressed what was more significant—their lack of faith.

He had told the disciples repeatedly that he would rise again. He found it hard to believe that they found it hard to believe!

There was no easy road back for these wounded men, but the Master had time. That is the good news for all injured disciples who have gone through Satan's attacks with less-than-flying colors. The Lord understands the tremendous odds we face, and while the hurt and disappointment that we feel remains, his love and care prevail, leading to his gracious restoration of our lives.

Prayer

What great good news it is, Lord, that failure is not final! This is not an invitation to irresponsibility, but it is an introduction to hope, and for this I give you thanks. Amen.

October 2—Three Questions of Healing

Scripture reading: John 21:15-17

"Simon son of John, do you truly love me more than these?" The address was formal, but the voice was warm. And there was no doubting the identity of the speaker. That voice was too familiar to doubt. It was the Lord, and he was asking the most important question of all.

Peter promptly answered in the affirmative, as if to say, "You are asking me? You of all people know what's going on inside me."

Twice again Christ asked the same question; twice Peter repeated the answer.

Wait a minute! Three times before the crucifixion Peter had been asked if he knew Jesus, and three times he had denied any knowledge of him. Three questions, three denials. Now three questions and three affirmations from Jesus. The fire in the courtyard, the fire on the shore. This surely could not be coincidence!

See how careful and deliberate Jesus is in this tremendous healing process. And if he could be this careful handling Peter's wounds—Peter, who failed so miserably—how much more do you think he longs to care for all the failures we face in each day?

Prayer

Lord, you are the original wounded healer. How thankful I am for your tender mercies. Teach me, when healed, to use my self-inflicted wounds as credentials to be a wounded healer, too. Amen.

October 3—How Deep Is Your Love?

Scripture reading: John 21:15-17

In his first two questions to Peter, Jesus used the stronger Greek word for love, *agape*, while Peter replied with the weaker word *phileo*. It would be unwise to make too much of this difference, but we cannot ignore it. We can reasonably conclude that Peter was affirming his love for the Master, but not at the depth the Master was asking. Yet he gave Peter a chance to dig out what was at the bottom of his own heart—a love that had survived, battered and bruised, but intact.

The situation is not unlike one we encounter at times in counseling. A happily married man is attracted to another woman and becomes unfaithful to his wife and unfair to the other woman. When the affair is discovered, the man turns from his sin and seeks his wife's forgiveness. Although profoundly hurt, she freely extends it to him. He could have learned this lesson and saved everyone considerable pain by resisting the temptation to start with. The one bright spot, however, is that he, like Peter, learned through tragic and sad experience how deeply his love truly ran.

Prayer

Lord, may I never fall to the bottom of the pit to learn the depths of love. But, should I do so, give me insight into loving such as I never dreamed possible. Amen.

October 4—Keep on Following

Scripture reading: John 21:18-19

Recently I talked to a man who was understandably distraught about the breakdown of his marriage. He told me that he had prayed that the Lord would intervene, but he hadn't. At first, this caused him to question the Lord's love for him; but as time went on, he had begun to question whether the Lord even existed. His case is not atypical. But it is serious. When spiritual discouragement sets in, disciples are particularly vulnerable.

Immediately after Jesus had given Peter the benefit of his total attention and had outlined for him the ministry of shepherding to which Peter was now called, the Master added, "When you were younger you dressed yourself and went where you wanted; but when you are old you will stretch out your hands, and someone else will dress you and lead you where you do not want to go." Then Christ dropped the clincher: "Follow me!" Tradition confirms that Peter was subsequently crucified for his faith, and that at his request, he was executed upside-down. Evidently Jesus was gently forewarning Peter that when the going got particularly tough, he would need to be particularly conscious of following one step at a time.

Prayer

Some steps on the rocky road to glory are so hard they appear impossible. I'm tempted to turn back in dismay or disgust. Remind me then, Lord, that you have gone before and through the Spirit are with me on the way. Keep me moving ahead one step at a time. Amen.

October 5—Minding Our Own Business

Scripture reading: John 21:20-23

Gladys Aylward was a tiny, fiery missionary whose work with children in China during the Japanese occupation was memorialized in the film, *The Inn of the Sixth Happiness*. One day as she read in her Bible that the Lord would supply her needs, she told him, "I need a husband. You promised to supply my needs, so I expect you to send me a husband."

I remember hearing her tell the story with such effect that, as she came to this part, she paused, looked around the room, and said, "Somewhere in this world is a man to whom God said, 'Go to China and marry Gladys Aylward.' And he never came! So I said to God, 'God, why don't you do something about this man, whoever he is and wherever he is?' And God leaned out of heaven and said, 'Gladys Aylward, mind your own business!'"

It really is not our business how God chooses to work with another person. Sometimes he seems to be gentle on people who, to us, seem hardheaded enough to get rougher discipline. Other times it seems that God lets gentle people suffer so much for no apparent reason. And often, we are entirely too interested in why someone else is getting the answer to the very prayer we have been praying for ourselves!

Prayer

Lord, your business, I know, is to lead. Mine is to follow. Unfortunately, I tend to interfere in your business and neglect mine. Sorry, Lord. I'll try to remember who does what! Amen.

October 6—The Work of Love

Scripture reading: 1 Corinthians 13:4-7

Love always overcomes bitterness,
  regardless of how love feels,
  despite manifold reasons
  to harbor a grudge—

Love works at forgiving,
  rising early,
  looking for the hurt one,
  chasing down the wounded,
  binding up the hurts with
  words of reconciliation.

Love retires late, tired with trying
  to make amends,
  sleeping swiftly,
  eager to rise and begin again.

Love never gives up.
Love that gives up—
  isn't love.

Prayer

It's hard to think of love as work, Lord God, but it is.
Perseverance is love at work. Work that work in me, for
Jesus' sake. Amen.

October 7—Security in Any Language

Scripture reading: Matthew 28:18-20

More than thirty years ago, I was surprised to receive an invitation to speak at the "Polish Millennium," the thousandth anniversary of Christianity in Poland. So one cold winter's day, I flew into Warsaw. No one was at the airport to meet me, and I had no contact names. Other passengers collected their bags and left, but I waited . . . and waited.

After what seemed an eternity, I was startled by a voice behind me. "Briscoe?" Whirling around, I saw a man wearing a long coat and a hat pulled down over his eyes. I did not realize how insecure I could feel until that moment. But a great grin spread across his face, and, to my astonishment, he hugged me and kissed me three times! Then, grabbing my bag, he hurried me out onto a bus, where he talked to me in a loud voice about the Lord Jesus. I noticed people were listening, and he said, "Oh, many of them speak English, so speak up loudly. Your ministry in Poland has begun." I suddenly felt very much at home with this man, for he was with me and he knew what he was doing!

"Surely I am with you" spells security in any language. Armed with this sense of adequacy and security, the eleven disciples were to embark on the mission for which Jesus had been preparing them.

Prayer

There's safety in numbers, we say. And there's security in friendship. But there's no safety and security like that of the believer who moves out into the world with you, Lord. Amen.

October 8—Reverence for the Consuming Fire

Scripture reading: Ezekiel 1:1-9, 25-28

We find here an essential reminder of God's towering majesty. When Ezekiel's forefathers were in the wilderness, they had been reminded daily of the imposing Presence in the cloud by day and the pillar of fire by night. But Ezekiel's contemporaries had no such revelation. They were exiled and for years they had been convinced that if their God was still around, he certainly was not imposing enough to get a grip on their situation. They had come to the conclusion that their problems were considerably bigger than their God, and hopelessness was their daily diet.

Moses had made it quite clear that the Lord was not about to be pushed around, but that he was, among other things, "a consuming fire" (Deut. 4:24). The writer of Hebrews later picked up the idea and encouraged readers to "worship God acceptably with reverence and awe; for our God is a consuming fire" (Heb. 12:28-29).

There is little doubt that the Israelites had not only lost sight of the greatness and grandeur of their God because of the disastrous experience they were going through, but they had also forgotten that God is to be treated with great reverence and respect. The Lord refused to accept such a situation and was determined to speak to Ezekiel and through him to the people. But first Ezekiel himself had to become acutely aware of the reality of God in his own life.

Prayer

May the fear of God take away my fear of other people and imposing circumstances as I do your work, dear Lord. Amen.

October 9—The Loud Silence of God

Scripture reading: Ezekiel 20:1-5; Luke 23:8-9

Herod was excited about meeting Jesus, not because he believed that the Lord was who he claimed to be, but because Herod was always glad to meet a celebrity. So he plied Jesus with one question after another, but he never got a single answer. The Lord was not about to waste his breath entertaining someone who needed something much more than entertainment.

There is a solemn truth to be learned from the leaders of Tel-Abib whom Ezekiel describes and the men who met the Lord Jesus in the final days of his earthly ministry. It is that God reserves the right to talk as long as he wishes and to be silent when he has said enough. Perhaps to modern ears, the silence of God is a strange sound, startling in its impact, because they have not learned that to ply God with questions and subjects for discussion is an exercise in futility when he decides he has had enough.

In Ezekiel's day, so that there would be no misunderstanding, the Lord instructed his prophet to explain why he had no interest in further debate and discussion with the elders. In effect, God said, "Give them a brief review of the history of Israel, Ezekiel, and show them that I have been talking to them for centuries, but they have not obeyed me" (Ezek. 20:5).

Prayer

We are so used to getting our own way, God, that it is inconceivable to us that you would not be available when we demand it. Teach me that I am are not God—you are! Amen.

October 10—Get a New Heart

Scripture reading: Ezekiel 18:21-32

The Lord made clear through his servant Ezekiel that contrary to what some people seemed to think, he took no pleasure in anyone's death. He urged the Israelites, therefore, to come to the point of making individual commitments and responses to the Lord. "Get a new heart and a new spirit. Why will you die?" he said.

Before we get overly excited about the command for listeners themselves to get a new heart, let us remember that Ezekiel had already said that *the Lord* had promised to give them "an undivided heart and put a new spirit in them" (Ezek. 11:19). There is no contradiction in these statements, just two sides to the same transaction.

It is not unlike the two-sided statement in Philippians 2:12-13: "Work out your salvation with fear and trembling, for it is God who works in you to will and to act according to his good purpose." There is the human and the divine aspect in all human-divine experiences. We are totally locked into the necessity of God's working in us and giving us a new heart and spirit, yet this cannot happen unless we cooperate by working out our salvation. In other words, when God sees that we are earnest, he moves in power.

Prayer

How I praise you for a new heart and a new spirit. Yet my spirit needs to be renewed moment by moment and day by day. Do your work in my heart, O Lord. Amen.

October 11—Aiming for God's Approval

Scripture reading: John 6:60-65

It is time we took a hard look at the church's methodology for drawing crowds. Our fascination with the "personality cult" and our readiness to accept what is superficial in the place of that which should be life-changing and God-honoring needs prayerful scrutiny. Maybe some of us need to be reminded by the Word of the Lord that instead of using those who are well spoken of and who hear appreciative sounds most of their lives, God's choice is many times a prophet who will speak the truth in love and who may never be vindicated as a prophet in his lifetime.

The size and popularity of a ministry is unimportant. The crying need is for men and women who are so much more concerned with hearts being moved and God's being vindicated that they will be almost oblivious to the size of the crowd or the sounds from the pew. We need men and women who are in tune with heaven and wait only for the eternal "Well done, good and faithful servant."

Prayer

We all like to be liked, Lord Jesus. But sometimes it's not going to be possible—not if we are true to your Word. Help me to get my affirmation from you and not from human beings. Amen.

October 12—Beyond Tears from the Past

Scripture reading: Esther 2:5-8

We need to let God wipe the tears from the eyes of our memories. As a child of the Jewish dispersion, Esther must have done a lot of crying. Though she was probably born in Persia, her parents had apparently died while she was young. To be an orphan, a refugee, and a female was not a very good thing in the year 408 B.C. But I believe Esther allowed God to wipe away the pain of her memories.

I do not believe the good attitudes of this beautiful girl, that we glean from Esther 2, could have flourished in bitter soil. In retrospect, Esther must have been able to see God clearly in the shadows of her life. Surely it was he that provided her with a loving uncle to parent and protect her.

Are you obsessed by memories from a bitter childhood? Have you lost family and home, been displaced, or been mistreated? Have you ever asked God to wipe the tears from the eyes of your memories? You may ask how healing happens. One of the answers lies in prayer. The Bible tells us just who to turn to with our hurts. It is prayer that takes us to the right place.

Prayer

Lord, despite myself I play the hurtful "tape" over and over again. Help me break the cycle of my despondency. Dry my tears and let me smile again. Amen.

October 13—Divided Loyalties

Scripture reading: Esther 2:9-18

You cannot shine in a blue sky! God allowed the shadows to lengthen and the day to flee away in order to have the perfect backdrop to set off his jewel, Esther "But, how can I be expected to shine?" you might object. "It's too hard in my situation. I'm linked so closely with an unbeliever that divided loyalties are tearing me apart!"

Esther must have wrestled with this issue also. She surely struggled with divided loyalties as some of us do. Finding herself (through no fault of her own) married to the king, she knew she must try to please him, and she apparently succeeded. On the other hand, there was another allegiance that claimed her heart. Every good Jew knew that Jehovah, the King of the universe, called his children to love him first and obey his rules and laws. King Xerxes certainly considered himself reason enough to be worshiped heart and soul. But Esther never forgot her true identity and ultimate loyalty.

Prayer

Divided hearts find it hard to love you. Divided lives find it impossible to please you. Divided loyalties bring misery and doubt. Unite my heart to sing your praise, dear Lord. Thank you. Amen.

October 14—The Risk of Sharing the Cure

Scripture reading: Esther 2:19-23

In Esther's day, approaching the King without being bidden could result in death. Should she take the risk and report the plot? She chose to share the news that saved the King's life.

Those of us who are believers in Jesus have a very simple question to answer. Having found the cure for the "cancer" of sin, that is, the knowledge of Christ who can save us, will we share our all-important information with others who could eternally benefit? Having applied the "medicine" of salvation to our own sin-sick souls, will we dispense it to others? Our choice mirrors that of the beautiful Queen Esther. The problem is that there are certain personal risks involved in sharing.

In some parts of the world today, there is risk of the most ultimate kind, and sharing our faith in hostile territory may literally mean giving our life's blood. But for most of us the risk is far less life-threatening, though cost there may be. We might suffer the loss of a relationship or lose face with friends. We may even find our jobs are in jeopardy. The challenge is this: Do we care enough, dare enough, to share enough?

Prayer

Help me not to be afraid of living on risk's edge, Lord. After all, such a position will only force me to depend on you. Amen.

October 15—Faith and Courage

Scripture reading: Esther 4

Faith is doing something without the courage. Faith trusts God as we do something courageous without wanting to! Faith says, "It shall be done—look out, devil, here we come, God and I!" Faith is a very practical thing. It enlists our minds and helps us to believe that we were born for a purpose.

Like Esther, there should be a sense of destiny borne in upon us that says, "I was created for such a time as this." We must come to believe that we are the only ones who can serve the Lord in quite this way. In the words of a well-known hymn, "There's a work for Jesus only you can do." The mind will need to be enlisted to believe this before faith can instruct the body to action.

The mind also needs to stop playing so many horror movies for our entertainment. The awful scenarios our fertile minds conjure up have to be experienced to be believed. The mind always seems to present us with the worst possibilities about a certain course of action in graphic scenes and glorious technicolor. These mind movies need to be monitored by Jesus.

Prayer

Faith is doing the right thing without the courage—isn't that true, Lord? Doing the right thing scared. Give me peace of mind to know you'll never leave me nor forsake me, whether I have the courage or not. Amen.

October 16—Doing the Right Thing

Scripture reading: Esther 5:1-8

The first time I opened my mouth to witness for Christ I lost a friend. It took an enormous amount of courage. It was a risk, but a risk I felt I had to take. Daring to dare, I told my best friend in a faltering voice that I had become a believer during my brief stay in the hospital. She did not hold out the golden scepter, like Xerxes did to Esther. She responded by ending our relationship!

Even after that bad experience, it did not take nearly so much effort to risk witnessing a second time to another close friend. I found faith grows faith, because faith trusts God to enable us to do the right thing in a wrong world.

The person God uses is the one who has stopped giving God conditions for his or her obedience. The only golden scepter any of us should be interested in is the one held out to us in heaven when we finally approach the eternal throne. All of us can be assured of that one!

Prayer

Lord, friends are important to me. I don't want to lose my friends. However, if you ask me to—for you—I will. Amen.

October 17—Filled with Christ

Scripture reading: Colossians 2:9-12

I remember years ago attending a performance of Tchaikovsky's *Pathétique Symphony*. At first I was completely unmoved and untouched by the music, even though the auditorium in which I was sitting was filled with glorious harmony. Later in the program, however, a remarkable change came over me, for I found my heart soaring with the music, my feet tapping to the rhythm, and, at the conclusion, my hands clapping in appreciation. Heart, hands, and feet were affected because the music invaded my soul. The difference in attitude and reaction came about when the music ceased to be all around me and managed to get right into me.

The teaching of the Scriptures is that we are in Christ—the realm of the spiritual experience. Scripture also teaches that Christ is in us—the reality of spiritual experience. The realm of Christian experience is only made reality through the activity of the Lord Jesus Christ himself living and reigning within the heart of the redeemed sinner. It is when the Lord Jesus gets right into you that the heart, hands, and feet move in response to the music of heaven's realm, in which you are seated with Christ.

Prayer

The music of Scripture needs to reverberate through my soul. Then my feet will dance with joy, my God, as I do your will. Amen.

October 18—Scaling Impossible Walls

Scripture reading: Romans 3:19-23; 6:23

Years ago I was watching a party of climbers attempting to scale the North Wall of the Eiger—13,000 feet of sheer rock face high in the Swiss Alps. The climb is extremely dangerous and totally impossible to all but the most expert climbers. As I watched the toiling climbers, a high-altitude balloon from a nearby exhibition floated past. It quickly ascended the vertical side of the mountain and within a short time appeared to hover over the summit.

To me, climbing the Eiger was an impossibility, but ascending to the summit in a balloon would have been well within my capability! All that I would need to do would be to climb into the basket beneath the balloon, throw out the ballast, and start moving. In a remarkable way, the gravity-defying properties of the gas-filled balloon would have been imparted to me, and the mountain wall would have been ascended.

The God-defying principle of self and sin in the soul of a person can never be cajoled, challenged, or commanded to ascend the vertical wall of the fullness of Christ. But the person in whose life the sin-defying properties of the risen Christ are made real can constantly climb to new heights of spiritual experience. While certain spiritual laws demand our death through sin, we can scale the walls of that tomb because of God's forgiveness through Christ and the gift of eternal life.

Prayer

What wages we earn because we are sinners, Lord. But what gift is this of eternal life? What abounding mercy. Thank you. Amen.

October 19—Getting Along with Family

Scripture reading: Galatians 5:13-21

The petty squabbles, jealousies, and envyings of children usually disappear as quickly as they appear, but when the Lord's children engage in such things, untold harm is done, and the repercussions are extremely far-reaching. Many a missionary group has foundered on the rocks of incompatibility, and many a church has split on the same razor-edged barrier. Naturally, we must allow for differences of personality and recognize that incompatibility is the devil's masterpiece. As long as he can persuade the Lord's children to fight each other instead of fighting him, Satan is delighted.

According to Galatians 5:19-21, squabbles, jealousies, and envyings come from the identical source and are listed in the same category as murders, adulteries, and heresies. The attempted work and witness of the church of Jesus Christ is ludicrous in some instances because those who hold positions of mature authority engage in activities of juvenile stupidity!

Part of our training as Christ's disciples is to learn to get along—with people in general, but particularly with other believers. The body of Christ is the primary picture to others of God's kingdom.

Prayer

Help me to see Christ in my brothers and sisters, Lord. That will stop our fighting. After all, you might get hurt! Amen.

October 20—Our High Priest

Scripture reading: Hebrews 4:14-16

Knowing that we have such a great High Priest—and such a friend—helps us to tighten our spiritual grip around the tenets of our faith. We know Jesus did not stay aloof from troubles but came to endure them too. He has walked where we walk, cried our tears, gone to our funerals, and felt the betrayal and rejection of friends, disciples, and family. Yet he has given us the perfect example of responding rightly to suffering and thus learning "obedience from what he suffered" (Hebrews 5:8).

If the Lord Jesus could learn from his suffering, how much more can we learn from ours, especially when we know that he is in heaven—our advocate before God and the angels, and before the devil and all his accusations. Jesus prays for us. Even when we are pretty sure we do not have a friend in the world, we can know we have one in heaven. And what a friend!

Prayer

Thank you for praying for us, Lord Jesus. I know your prayers always get answered! Amen.

October 21—Balanced Self-Evaluation

Scripture reading: Luke 18:9-14

> There once was a nymph named Narcissus
> Who thought himself very delicious.
> So he stared like a fool
> At his face in a pool,
> And his folly today is still with us.

Jesus warned us about self-righteousness. And the apostle Paul stated, "Do not think of yourself more highly than you ought. But rather think of yourself with sober judgment, in accordance with the measure of faith God has given you" (Rom. 12:3).

If you are going to evaluate anything, you need criteria. What is the measure I use to arrive at a sober evaluation of myself? The answer to that is the measure of faith that God has given you.

Notice two things here: (1) we are to evaluate ourselves on the basis of faith; and (2) faith is something God has given us. God has granted us the ability to believe. So, we are not our own measuring rule like Narcissus. We do not measure ourselves by our own abilities and accomplishments, but by what we have done with what God has given us.

Prayer

It's so easy to put others down, Lord, in order to promote myself, and to feel better than others when I use my own measuring standards. Teach me to have a balanced evaluation of who I am because of you. Amen.

October 22—A Relic or the Body of Christ?

Scripture reading: Colossians 3:12-17

In his book *The Secular City,* Harvey Cox called the church "a patriarchal, agricultural, prescientific relic." Pierre Burton, the highly regarded Canadian commentator said, "In its desperate effort to preserve its established entity, the church has become fossilized." In some people's view, the church is a fossilized relic.

Other people regard the church as a respectable institution to be tolerated when it comes to celebrating births and weddings and performing funerals. Still others regard the church as a powerful enemy to be opposed. The long list of martyrs down through church history met their deaths because there were those who saw the church as a threat to the culture or the status quo.

What is our view? Do we see the church from a sociological or psychological standpoint? If so, our thinking has been molded to fit the world's thinking. If I see the church as it truly is, I see it as the body of Christ. It is not an institution, but a fellowship of believers, and these believers have a claim on me if I am a Christian.

Prayer

The church is your body, Lord; help me to respect it. The church is your bride, Lord; help me to delight in it. The church is your building, Lord; help me to build it. Amen.

October 23—Do-gooders or Doing Good?

Scripture reading: Romans 12:9-13, 21

If you talk about doing good, people get a little nervous, because in our culture as a whole, we do not like do-gooders. Do-gooders are the sort of people who interfere. Do-gooders suggest that things are not as they should be and say they know what should be done instead.

When doing what is good becomes part of the discussion, some people are afraid they are going to be judged. If, for instance, you are with some friends who want you to do something, and you say, "I would rather not do that," the friends want to know why. If you say, "Because I don't think that would be a good thing to do," the friends may not like that answer because they feel that you are being judgmental of them.

Our society has turned the meaning of *good* into something very strange. Feeling good and looking good are regarded as noble things, but being good and doing good are often looked down on. As believers, we need to do some straight thinking about this because the Bible is very clear. It says that we are to hate what is evil and cling to what is good. We are not to be overcome by evil, but to overcome evil with good. We need to make sure that we understand what is good and what is evil.

Prayer

Make me good and right and true, just as you, God, are good and right and true. Help me to see the absolute goodness, rightness, and truth in Jesus and mirror it. Amen.

October 24—Distinguishing Good

Scripture reading: Romans 14:1-8

Even when people disagree about what is good, it is often the application of a certain principle—not the principle itself—that they disagree on. For example, there is a furious debate going on regarding abortion on demand as a means of birth control. Some people would say that a woman has the absolute right to determine what happens to her own body, and government has no business interfering. Therefore, they conclude, the good is to make sure that the woman has the freedom of choice. Other people would say that the unborn child, the embryo, has the absolute right to be given a chance to be born and that, therefore, the good is to be pro-life and protect the unborn life.

Now, of course, these are totally opposing points of view. You will notice, however, that they have something in common. Both are appealing to what is "right." One is appealing to the rights of the woman, and the other is appealing to the rights of the child. So, even in a situation where people totally disagree about what is good, they are basing their arguments on a somewhat mutual understanding of something that is *good*—that there is something called human rights. But whose rights override whose?

People love to say that everything is relative, but sometimes they are much closer to agreement than they think they are.

Prayer

It's hard to choose between rights, Lord. I need your wisdom to discern your right thinking and then the courage to speak out for the absolutes you help me to understand. Amen.

October 25—Genuine Goodness

Scripture reading: Galatians 6:9-10

Years ago Jill and I did a tour of ministry in several countries across sub-Sahara Africa. One stop was a desolate place right on the edge of the Sahara Desert that seemed comprised of solid black cinders. The residents explained, "We're trying to grow greenery and flowers, but there's no soil. So we hack out a hole in this cinder and put in vegetable matter; whenever people fly in we ask them to bring a bag of soil." Layering soil and vegetable matter they eventually had compost. The one flower we saw blooming was the result of months of work and waiting.

On this trip Jill had been a walking museum of African diseases. As she rested in bed, our African friends appeared the next morning with a slender glass holding a beautiful rose. They had picked their only flower. They said, "We are so grateful that you came out to us here in the middle of nowhere, and we weren't sure how to say thank you. We felt that this just might brighten Jill's day."

I, being very British, gulped. And Jill, being very feminine, cried. There is nothing quite so touching as genuine, caring, self-sacrificing concern for other people. That is the essence of the good. This world of ours is full of junk and garbage and evil, and in the middle of it are God's people who are called to be good and to do good.

Prayer

Dear Lord, make me loving and giving, sacrificing my own comfort for the sake of others less comfortable. Grow in me maturity and self-forgetfulness so that others may grow. Amen.

October 26—Is Jesus All-American?

Scripture reading: Revelation 2:18-25

There is a very real possibility that God's people here in the United States are remaking God into their own image. We emerge with a God wrapped in stars and stripes, a God who endorses everything we endorse to make us comfortable. Increasingly we are removing ourselves from the reality of God and Christ.

Instead of the Christian church standing firm against the evils in American society, the Christian church becomes a cheerleader for American society. Even in American evangelicalism today, the Jesus who is being portrayed is very often not the Jesus Christ who overthrows the temple tables. He is not the One who speaks out against hypocrisy, the One who will have nothing to do with false piety and empty religion. The Jesus Christ who is portrayed in much of American evangelicalism today is a laissez-faire Christ, a champion of free enterprise.

Just like the church in Thyatira, we may be in danger of identifying too much with our culture. Jesus calls us back to our first love—pleasing him.

Prayer

Lord, you told us we needed to be in the world but not of the world. That's quite a task. But you can give me discernment. Give me the wisdom I need for your sake. Amen.

October 27—Hurry Up, God

Scripture reading: Philippians 2:12-13

One day about a hundred years ago, Phillips Brooks, the author of the Christmas carol "O Little Town of Bethlehem," was pacing fretfully in his office. A friend walked in and asked what troubled him. "The trouble is that I'm in a hurry and God isn't," Brooks replied.

That's often our trouble, too. We want immediate action when God seems content to move slowly—sometimes agonizingly so. Have you ever noticed this dynamic among people? You think Mrs. Brown should have mastered by now a problem that's plagued her for years. Mrs. Brown thinks Mr. Smith should be ashamed of making so little progress in some other area. And Mr. Smith thinks that any real Christian ought to be able to tame a quick temper (like the one you've got).

People want change to come quickly—especially when it's change in someone else. But Paul says believers are people in process. While there is a very real sense in which Christians have been redeemed as an accomplished fact, there is another sense in which being renewed is a process. In terms of forgiveness, your salvation is complete; but in terms of being changed, your salvation is an ongoing procedure.

Prayer

Thank you, Father, that not only are you patient with me, but you also constantly work on me to make me more and more like you want me to be. Amen.

October 28—God's Restoring Work

Scripture reading: 2 Corinthians 3:12-18

Scripture teaches that the Lord Jesus came into the world, died, and rose again, then sent his Spirit into the hearts of the redeemed. The objective of the indwelling Spirit is to work in the hearts of men and women so that ultimately they will be restored to the image of God. This process will come to its glorious consummation when we stand before the Lord. When we see Jesus, Scripture says we will be like him.

What will that mean? Since Jesus is the image of the invisible God, if we become like Jesus, we, too, will be the image of the invisible God. And this will occur when we finally see Jesus face to face, in all his glory. Any remaining confusion will flee, and we will understand clearly who we are as children of God. And we will be restored to our full humanity.

But Christ, through his Spirit, is changing us more and more into his image—even now, day by day, as we come to know him more intimately. What area of your life right now is God working in and transforming?

Prayer

When I look back to what I used to be, I give thanks to you, Lord. You have clearly been at work. Thank you for the promise of heaven where I will be fully restored, and see you face to face. Amen.

October 29—On Being Human

Scripture reading: Psalm 8

Many of our best scientific brains have contended that human beings are the chance product of circumstances in a universe that is itself the freak result of unknown occurrences. But the theories that lead them to believe that human beings "just happened" also logically lead them to believe that human beings are meaningless. And that is dehumanizing.

But there is nothing dehumanizing about the psalmist's view of humankind. "You have made him" is his great conviction. Despite the harsh attacks that have been made on the biblical view of man, it must be stated that nowhere else is such a high view of humanity taught. The Bible insists that we are the intelligent product of an intelligent Creator.

God delights in us as he delights in no other part of his creation. We are "fearfully and wonderfully made" (Ps. 139:14), and we are equipped for divine fellowship. It takes a mind that can understand something of the immensity of God, a heart that will respond to what the mind has grasped, and a will that can acknowledge in action what the mind and heart know.

Intellectually honored, emotionally glorious, and volitionally unique, human beings are truly "crowned with glory and honor."

Prayer

I praise you, God, for the glory of all your creation and especially for the unique way you have made me. May I honor you in my humanness and follow you with all my heart and mind. Amen.

October 30—Twice His

Scripture reading: Isaiah 43:1-7

A small boy made with great care a little boat and set it to sail down a river. Suddenly, he lost it down some rapids. Weeks later he couldn't believe his eyes when he saw his precious possession in a shop window. Running inside, he argued with the shopkeeper that he had made it, so it was his. The shopkeeper chose not to believe him, and nothing would do but for the boy to buy it back. As he walked out of the shop, he was heard to say to his little boat, "Now you are twice mine. I've made you and bought you back again!"

We are twice God's. Created and redeemed, we belong to him. This helps when difficult things happen in our lives. Then it is God's business to be sovereign; our business is to be loyal. We are his, and it is his business to take care of us.

Prayer

Whenever I feel overwhelmingly insignificant, you remind me that you created me. Whenever I need reassurance, you whisper, "I redeemed you. You are mine." Then I relax all over again and I rejoice in you. Thank you, Lord.

October 31—Walking a Narrow Road

Scripture reading: Matthew 7:13-14

It is not uncommon for people to accuse Christians of being narrow. In a sense, this is a compliment. If narrow means that I have a magnificent obsession, a total inflexible commitment to the person of Jesus Christ, then I plead guilty! I will not deviate from the way in which I am walking with him, no matter how narrow it is.

Actually, narrowness can be a virtue. Take the ground lights that tell the pilot where the airfield is. Only one angle of approach is right for each plane, and it is the pilot's business to bring his giant aircraft in on that very narrow and exact angle. It takes special discipline to produce this attention to detail, this narrowness of vision that assures a safe landing. Christians must be able to discriminate and discern God's way, and then have the discipline to follow it.

Jesus said, "I am the way and the truth and the life. No one comes to the Father except through me" (John 14:6). This is the small gate of discipleship. It doesn't take long to get through the gate by making an initial commitment to Jesus. But that is just the beginning. Walking the narrow way after entering it is done by daily saying yes to God's way and no to Satan.

Prayer

Lord, you claim to be the way to God, and I believe you. Help me grow in my resolve to follow you wherever you lead. Thank you that your path leads to life! Amen.

November

November 1—Running from Problems

Scripture reading: Genesis 16

All of us can remember times when we have tried to run away from our problems like Hagar did. However, when we looked over our shoulders, the problems were still there.

During the great plague in England, multitudes were dying, and a death cart would come around in the evenings to collect the corpses. One of the families living in this terrible situation decided to get out of town while they were still alive. They traveled to a town in the middle of the country that had not been touched by the disease. Unfortunately, what this family did not know was that the plague had contaminated their belongings. They brought the illness with them, and the whole town was infected.

This is a graphic example of how running away from difficult circumstances does not make the situation disappear. Everywhere we go, we will take our problems with us, and they may permeate our whole beings. Until we work the problems out, they will be with us. In fact, if we do not deal with them, we may end up infecting the people around us.

Prayer

Help me not to run away from my problems, Lord. Give me strength to face them. And, if you tell me there is no solution, enable me to accept that and live well in difficult circumstances by you and for you. Amen.

November 2—Help Right under Our Noses

After Hagar had left Ishmael under a tree so she would not have to watch him die, she sat down a little way off. Both mother and son were crying, alone with their own agonies. But apparently there was a difference! Hagar cried uncontrollably, while Ishmael managed to turn his tearstained face Godward. "God heard the boy crying." Tears talk, but we also should try to talk to God through our tears. God responded to Ishmael's prayer.

By now Ishmael was far too weak to help himself. His life was nearly spent, but God had heard his prayer and suggested that Hagar quit crying and open her eyes to the possibilities around her. She dried her tears then and saw that there was a well right under her very nose. She had not seen it because she had been crying so hard.

Does Hagar remind you of us? We get so self-absorbed when we are in the depths of despair that sometimes we miss God's marvelous provision. Prayer is a weapon we seldom use enough in our fight to survive. It is too often replaced by tears of trauma and terror which dim our sight so we cannot see God's answer to our dilemmas.

Prayer

My tears are not discounted by you, Lord, but teach me to see the well through my tears. You provide life for death, light for darkness, power for weakness. See my pain, Lord Jesus, and help me. Amen.

November 3—Hell Is Exclusion

Scripture reading: 2 Samuel 14:21-33

Our church youth group was in full swing. I was talking about the realities of hell to a bunch of lively junior high kids. "What do you think hell is really like?" I asked. They came up with some definitions for me.

"I think it's being allowed to take one good look at God and then never being allowed to look again," a thirteen-year-old boy announced seriously. I think he had one concept of hell right. It is the idea of exclusion from the very presence of God.

The word *hell* means to cover or to hide, and includes the idea of a turning away of the face of the Almighty in revulsion and rejection. Jesus talked about the eternal possibility of God saying, "I never knew you. Away from me, you evildoers!" (Matt. 7:23).

When King David's son Absalom rebelled against his father, his insurrection was put down. David allowed him to return and live in Jerusalem, but the Bible says he was not allowed to see the king's face. Absalom could not bear this. To be so close to his father, and yet never be allowed to see his face was an exclusion that he could not handle. Hell will be like that.

Prayer

Lord, I know hell is a reality because you said so. And you told us that whatever we think about hell, we need to know it is far worse than we can ever imagine. Yet you also promised us we can be saved from hell because of the Cross. I can never thank you enough. Amen.

November 4—Friendship with God

Scripture reading: James 4:4-6

If we are to be the friends of God, we need to bear something in mind: Anyone who chooses to be a friend of the world becomes an enemy of God. God says he would love to have a friendship with us; the Lord Jesus says he calls his servants his friends because of the intimacy of their relationship. But how can we regard God and his Christ as our friends if we are committed to a whole system that is so unfriendly toward him—what the Scriptures call "the world"?

It is worthwhile to look into our own hearts at this point and ask: Do I relate to God as my friend? Do I feel that there's heart-to-heart communication with him? Is there a two-way honesty and transparency between us? We can go even further: Do I relate to the Lord Jesus as my friend? Can I respond and honestly say that I regard him as my intimate friend? We ought to be able to identify our spiritual relationship at this level.

Prayer

Lord, you have assured me of your friendship over and over again. But my response has not always been what it ought to be. I have found myself all too often loving what you hate and resisting what you love. But I want to be your friend. Please continue to draw me closer. Amen.

November 5—I Believe the Church Is Catholic

Scripture reading: Matthew 16:13-20

The Apostles' Creed states, "I believe in the holy catholic church." Now what do we mean by "catholic church?" The word *catholic* comes from the Latin and from the Greek and in both cases means "universal." At the time of the Reformation, there were those who were less than enthusiastic about what the Catholic Church under the pope's leadership was doing, and so they seceded. They became Protestants; they protested what was happening. They also stopped using the word *catholic* in their creed and put in the word *Christian*—not because they didn't believe the church was universal, but just to differentiate.

Is the church catholic in the truer sense of the word? Absolutely yes! There's a universal need: All have sinned. There's a universal remedy: Christ died for all. There's a universal mandate: Go into all the world and preach the gospel and make disciples of all nations. And there will be a universal consummation in heaven: People from every kindred and tongue and tribe and nation will worship around the throne. The church didn't start in America. The church is found universally, catholic. And that's why I am very happy to affirm that I believe in the church, I believe it is holy, and I believe, in the true sense of the word, it is catholic. What do you believe?

Prayer

Give me a vision of the church for which you died, Lord. Expand my perceptions of it beyond the limitations of my own involvement and show me something of its universal scope and impact. Amen.

November 6—Help as Life Ends

Scripture reading: Romans 8:26-27; James 5:13-16

So often there is an eternal awareness of impending death borne upon a dying soul. When my father was dying, the doctors decided it was in his best interest to withhold that information from him. In fact, they believed he would only fight the disease if he were encouraged to believe he would recover. I was instructed not to tell him. And yet, he knew! So a few days before his death, my father put his affairs in order and put his business into his son-in-law's hands.

Never shortchange what the Holy Spirit does in answer to your prayers for a dying person. And do not be afraid to pray with the person and, as opportunity comes, share with him or her the Christian's hope of heaven. It is a hope—a glorious confidence that life there is far better than the best that earth can give.

Do not underestimate either the church's ability to demonstrate God's love to your friends whom you think do not know the Lord. His people are everywhere—on television and radio, in books and tracts, in spoken words of kindness, and in little deeds of love. When there are no human witnesses, God says the heavens tell his glory and the creation tells his story—he has not left himself speechless.

Prayer

Enable me, O Lord, to trust you to answer my prayers for dying friends or relatives. Whether I see the answers to those prayers or not, keep me trusting and praising you for my loved ones' salvation. Amen.

November 7—The End of the World

Scripture reading: 2 Peter 3:9-14

The end of the world as we know it is being delayed by grace. God is waiting because he does not want anyone to perish. The apostle says here that scoffers will scoff at the very idea of a climactic end to everything. Peter may have been talking to the early gnostics who resisted the idea of a time of judgment and moral accountability, but his words are as relevant today as then.

"Missing from most contemporary considerations of heaven is the notion of divine justice," a recent news article said. In fact, the very delay in the coming of these events causes such cynical comments as, "Where is the promise of his coming?" The believers' answer to that is, "It is delayed by God's goodness and grace. He is waiting for us to respond to his good news of salvation."

But when the end does come, it will come unexpectedly, "like a thief." We are not to try to fix a date—even Jesus said he did not know when all this would take place. This fact should keep us on our toes, watching our lives, and being busy with kingdom work.

Prayer

May I be busy preparing for your certain coming, Lord. Give me faith to keep watching despite all attempts to deride or distract me. Keep me faithful to my task, for your sake. Amen.

November 8—Developing a New Mindset

Scripture reading: Romans 12:1-2

How do we resist allowing our minds to be pressed into the mold of the present evil age? The answer is by developing a skepticism for much of what passes as the wisdom of this age. We must also make sure we have a deep distrust of the riches of this present age as an answer to our problems.

How do we retain this kind of mindset? The answer is found in the end of Romans 12:2. With the renewed mind, my mindset is now not to do what I want with my life; it is rather to pursue God's will and discover in it that which is good and acceptable and perfect. Relentlessly I commit myself to opening my mind up to what God has to say concerning the truth as it is in Christ; I put everything else through the filter of what Christ says that I might live wisely and well.

One of our culture's greatest needs is for men and women who can live in the midst of the culture and show what truth and reality and fullness of life are all about. The mind plays a critical role in that.

What do you need to do as far as the renewal of your mind is concerned? What things do you need to reject? What do you need to retain?

Prayer

Father, so often I know your will to be perfect and good, yet I struggle to accept it. Teach me to submit my will to your will and my mind to your truth in order to glorify you. Amen.

November 9—Letting Feelings Rule?

Scripture reading: 1 Corinthians 2:6-16

Notice the tremendous emphasis placed upon the mind and upon not allowing ourselves to be conformed to the wisdom of this world. We realize that it is imperative that we think straight in a messed up world.

Some people have the idea that thinking and faith are mutually exclusive. However, if you take a little time looking into Scripture, you will see that thinking is an intrinsic part of the spiritual life.

Serious problems develop if people insist on living purely in the realm of emotion, and divorce the mind and truths from their important place in human experience. David Wells, in *No Place For Truth*, says, "Descartes argued, 'I think, therefore I am.' And people after Freud translated that into the modern vernacular by saying, 'I feel, therefore I am.'. . . The search for the religious self then becomes the search for religious good feelings."

It is perfectly possible for us to live in the realm of the emotions, intent on feeling good, and to ignore the obvious with our minds—when we are clearly in the wrong. Scripture teaches that if we do not have our minds together, we will not have our lives together.

Prayer

It's hard, Lord, to do your will when I don't feel like it. But help me obey you whether I feel like it or not. May I be mature enough for this. Amen.

November 10—The Blind Can See

Scripture reading: Matthew 15:1-14

Jesus told the Pharisees that they were blind leaders of the blind. He, of course, was referring to their lack of spiritual understanding. He explained that we are born blind to God's will and purpose. Sin has robbed human beings of their spiritual sight. The apostle Paul stated it this way: "The god of this age has blinded the minds of unbelievers, so that they cannot see the light of the gospel of the glory of Christ" (2 Cor. 4:4).

The spiritually blind are lost. They grope about, looking for answers to life like blind men groping for something to hold on to. Jesus said he had come to seek and to save the lost. Because Jesus is the Light of the World, he can save us from our blindness. But the choice is ours. We can either choose to allow him to illuminate our lives with his truth, asking him to remove the cataracts of sin from our spiritual eyes, or we can reject his truth and remain spiritually blind.

Prayer

When you were on earth, Lord Jesus, you opened blind eyes. Yet the blind men had a choice. They had to ask you to heal them. I too have a daily choice to make. Open my eyes to the truth and empower my will to obey it. Amen.

November 11—Spiritual Vision Problems

Scripture reading: Luke 14:28-33

Even after people have "seen the light" and become Christians, they still at times suffer from spiritual eye disorders. Some believers, for instance, are thoroughly shortsighted. Physical shortsightedness can keep us from being effective and productive, and so can spiritual shortsightedness. If we see only the needs within our own church walls, then we are not likely to do anything about the need for a worldwide church missions program or an effective youth outreach in the community.

Another spiritual eye disorder is farsightedness. Who of us has not known folk who are busy having "visions" but who are not very good at working them out using common sense? When you are farsighted, it is often difficult to see what is going on right under your nose. In fact, you may be in danger of being so heavenly minded, you are no earthly good!

Some Christians also suffer from spiritual double vision. Jesus said that if our eye is single it will be full of light. Being single-minded in our purpose to follow the Lord is the way to correct double vision.

Prayer

You are the heavenly eye doctor, Lord Jesus. Give me heavenly vision and your wisdom to know what to do with it on earth. Amen.

November 12—Christ at Home in Us

Scripture reading: 1 Corinthians 6:19-20

When I was a little boy, I heard an old coal miner relate a moving story. He told about being summoned to Buckingham Palace by the late King George V to be decorated for extreme bravery in a coal mine explosion. He described the magnificent investiture room and said that he had just longed to escape, for he felt completely out of place in such luxurious surroundings. There was one young man in the palace, however, who seemed completely at home; he was the king's son. The old miner said he could not wait to get back to his little whitewashed cottage, and the king's son was quite happy to remain in the palace.

Have you ever, since the day you received Jesus, carefully searched your heart and life to discover if it is suitable for his presence and purpose? Perhaps you have never really discovered the majesty of his person and the immensity of his purpose. Perhaps you are still content to be a humble cottage with few hopes of bettering the situation.

Christ has come to make his home in us. Have we accepted what his majesty will do to our home for him?

Prayer

You are so holy, Lord, and I am so unholy. Forgive my sin, cleanse me from all unrighteousness. Help me keep your home fit for a king! Amen.

November 13—Fearing the Promised Land

Scripture reading: Numbers 13:26-33

Every Christian has ample opportunity to explore the Promised Land of freshness, fruitfulness, and fullness which is God's norm of Christian experience. It is impossible for a Christian to read the Word of God and fail to see that Christianity is a fulfilling way to live.

Yet many explore the land but never enter it. Why? I believe it is because many Christians are like Joshua and Caleb's colleagues. The half-hearted spies did not deny the wonderful qualities of the land, but having seen the giants, they immediately decided to abandon the whole project of moving there. One look at three giants convinced ten spies of two things. First, *These giants think we are grasshoppers;* and second, *We are inclined to agree!* These men of God felt like grasshoppers, and out of Canaan they hopped, leaving three delighted giants in control of God's chosen land.

Many people today, having tasted the possibilities, seen the potential, and believed the promises of God concerning the fullness of Christ, have been rudely reminded of the presence of the giant "flesh." Like grasshoppers they say, "Let's get out of here. This kind of Christianity is unrealistic and unattainable; we will settle for another kind not quite so ambitious. We will let the giants have the land, and we will manage without it." Evangelical grasshoppers!

Prayer

It's easy to be halfhearted, Lord. You don't like that. Keep me honest. Make me like Caleb and Joshua—fully following you. Amen.

November 14—Love Sees Our True Worth

Scripture reading: Psalm 139:14-18

Love delights to use ordinary people—
    to help people who don't
    realize how loved ordinary
    people are!

Teachers and friends, boyfriends, fiancés
    and even parents
    insist we discover we are special;
    after all, they tell us,

God thought we were worth
    dying for!

Prayer

When I realize that I am an ordinary person with a great big extraordinary God living inside of me—then I'll know I am special! Amen.

November 15—Committed Love Restores Us

Scripture reading: Hosea 3

In this passage, God still refers to Gomer as Hosea's wife. Even after what she has done, in spite of how low she has fallen, there is a covenant of marriage to be honored. And Hosea honors his commitment to Gomer. In spite of her sin, he continues to love this woman who has abused his trust and dishonored the marriage bed. When God speaks to him, he is willing to forgive Gomer and pay the redemption price to bring her back to himself. Notice that he goes for her at the place of her destitution. In all probability he brings her back home and lovingly cares for her. Their reconciliation allows her to receive strength, nourishment, and healing. She has a chance to think things through and come to repentance, rejecting her old life.

A definite sequence of events follows. Hosea tells Gomer that he will wait with her, and she will wait with him, for many days. During that period her prostitution and her adultery must not reoccur; she will have time to come to her senses, to repent.

When we consider that Hosea's story is a picture of God's love for his people, we cannot help but be amazed and humbled at the extent to which our God will meet us—even in our most disgusting, sin-affected state—in order to restore us to relationship with him.

Prayer

When someone has dishonored my trust, help me to look to the model of Hosea, Lord. Only you have power to help me reconcile. Thank you for your amazing love. Amen.

November 16—Hope in Judgment

Scripture reading: Joel 2:12-17

Looking at the nature of God through the eyes of the prophets, we discover that God always has a double strand in his message. On the one hand, God reminds his people that he is a God of justice, a holy God who will not tolerate sin. On the other hand, he reveals that he is a God of grace and of mercy, longing to forgive his erring people on the basis of their repentance.

Joel points out that if the people will come up with a serious response to God, if they will listen to the alarm, if they will come to the solemn assembly in repentance before God, their response will be the very basis of blessing. "'Even now,' declares the Lord, 'return to me with all your heart.'" There will be blessing and not judgment if they will return in their hearts to God.

Prayer

I need an internal revolution, Lord. Break my heart when people turn away from you. Then give me the breath I need to blow, not my own trumpet, but yours! Amen.

November 17—Our Refuge and Stronghold

Scripture reading: Joel 3:9-21

Even though Joel is speaking forcefully of the judgment of God, in the same breath he speaks of the grace and the mercy of God. God has made a covenant with his people. In effect, he says, "I am your God and you are my people. I commit myself at all times to be a refuge for you, a stronghold."

Who knows the form in which the judgment of God is going to come? Nobody knows; but that it will come, we do know. The covenant people of God will be preserved and protected at that time, we also know. Some say God will take his church out of this world before the great and terrible final judgment comes. Others say we will still be here. Still others say we will be here for part of it. One of these days we will find out who was right!

We do know certain things, however. We know that a final, cataclysmic judgment is coming. The judgment of God will be against those who have rejected him. They will be absolutely, meticulously, and relentlessly judged. Thank God we know this too: God's people (at all times and particularly at that time) will find in the Lord their refuge and stronghold.

Prayer

Lord, you are my "hiding place." Help me to invite everyone I know to hide in you too. Make me bold. Give me power in the face of disbelief. Amen.

November 18—Famine of the Spiritual Sort

Scripture reading: Amos 8:11-12

A divine principle emerges here. God will react to Israel's rejection. God will speak, his servants will echo his words, and the people will either hear or refuse to hear. But that is not the end of the matter. Jehovah has the final word. He will deal with the people's response, and we should never, ever forget that.

Let me bring this closer to home. Many people attend church services consistently where they hear the Word of God. But even though they are present in body, I wonder about their spirits. It is possible to become hardened to what God says, to go on blithely disobeying or ignoring what God says. Know this: The sovereign Lord Jehovah will respond in kind to our reaction to his Word.

Some who go on relentlessly hardening their hearts to what God is saying need to be alerted to the fact that God could respond by sending them a famine of hearing the Word of the Lord. Not a famine of the Word of God—a situation where the Word of God is not available—but as far as hearing it is concerned, an inability to even register its presence. Having resisted the Bible for so long, they no longer hear it. A famine of hearing the Word of God grips the soul, and it makes no impact at all.

Prayer

Lord, deliver me from a familiarity that breeds contempt. Keep me ever fresh and make me ever faithful. May I be feeding on your Word so that I in turn can feed others. Amen.

November 19—Theology or Politics?

Scripture reading: Obadiah 1-4, 15-18

I become alarmed sometimes at the political involvement of many believers today in matters totally unrelated to their theology. I am not suggesting that because we are spiritual people we have no time for politics or interest in international affairs. That attitude is quite regrettable. At the same time, however, it is out of order for Christians to take a political position more related to their tradition and economic status than to their theology. God judged the nation of Edom for similar political pride. It is absolutely imperative for us to recognize that theology comes first: We must understand who the Sovereign Lord is and recognize that he is building his kingdom.

Whatever our political persuasions might be, they must be in harmony with the principles of the kingdom of God. We must watch the events taking place in our world and be deeply concerned about them, but we must remember that as we see important events developing around us, the kingdom will be the Lord's. In all that is happening, the sovereign Lord is working out his purposes.

Prayer

Lord, make me aware that this world is not my home, I'm just "passing through." Help me work for your kingdom in the midst of an unstable world. Amen.

November 20—The Reign of the Lord

Scripture reading: Micah 5:1-5

God's plans are centered in One who will come to Bethlehem Ephrathah, whose origins are from of old. He will be Jehovah's representative, and he will ultimately rule over Israel. Micah is speaking of the King who shall come. This Messiah will come, and he will be uplifted in Jerusalem. He is the One to whom the eyes of the nations will look. He is the One on whom universal attention will be focused.

When he reigns, justice will prevail. When he is in control, righteousness will be the norm. When he is supreme, weapons will be made into plowshares and people will live in peace. They will be no longer afraid.

What is Micah saying? The day is coming when God must be allowed to be God. Christ must be allowed to be Lord. The One whom God the Father has sent, his glorious Son, will become King of kings and Lord of lords. As far as God is concerned, that day is coming. This is what we as Christians, children of God, can look forward to.

But we can also apply it to our immediate situations. For when Christ is Lord of our lives, no one can make us afraid. Justice will be what governs our heart and righteousness what we live for. From our very lives the Word of the Lord will go forth, and he will be our peace.

Prayer

Lord, my heart yearns for the time when the King will reign. May you be King in my heart now so you can use me to bring in the kingdom. Amen.

November 21—God's Jealous Love

Scripture reading: Nahum 1:1-8

If we can think in terms of God's being deeply moved, deeply committed—zealous for the object of his love and for the uniqueness and distinctiveness of his own nature and character—we will begin to understand what Scripture means when it says that the Lord is jealous. This zeal arises from his deep-felt love of his people and his deep-felt commitment to his own nature. This speaks positively of his love, the intensity of that love, and the activity of that love. God will brook no interference; he will let nothing get in his way. He is jealous of the object of his love.

When the Bible says that God is an avenging God, we sometimes have a problem because we usually think of vengeance in terms of retaliation. We do not want to know about such a God. We think he would be a relic of primitive Old Testament society, and we much prefer the New Testament God. At least that is how many people handle the problem.

But this will not do, because the exact words that describe the "Old Testament God" also describe the "New Testament God." In the New Testament, God is described as being jealous, as exercising vengeance, as displaying wrath. In fact, Jesus said more about these things than the Old Testament prophets ever did. It is nonsense to try to set the Old Testament against the New. It cannot be done.

Prayer

Lord, may the strong warnings of the prophets drive me to take you seriously. Deliver me from trivialities in my faith. Amen.

November 22—Justice for All

Scripture reading: Habakkuk 2

God is always right on time. Our job is to patiently wait for him to act—"for the revelation awaits an appointed time . . . though it linger . . . it will certainly come and will not delay."

Jehovah points out through Habakkuk that the offenders are going to be the means of bringing judgment. He is not suggesting for a moment that because they are to be the instruments of bringing judgment on Judah they themselves will not be judged. Rather, God says to Babylon, "I am going to deal with the Judeans, and then I will deal with you as well. I'm going to use you as an instrument first—then I will turn my attention to you."

God will deal with everyone in righteousness, holiness, and justice. This is the way he must work.

Prayer

Father, it's so hard to understand why you allow bad things to happen to good people. But I don't need to understand, I just need to trust you to do the right thing in the end. Amen.

November 23—Tough and Tender Love

Scripture reading: Zephaniah 3:14-20

A young fellow, busy stealing cars in California, was eventually caught and hauled before the judge. Wisely, the judge did not just send him to jail. He knew that there the boy would be introduced to all the advantages of a jailhouse education, and very probably this amateur car thief would become a professional. Yet, on the other hand, the judge knew that he could not just let the boy off. So he tried to blend some toughness with tenderness.

The judge sent the young fellow to a ski camp and told him to stay there in a grueling training program until he had mastered the sport of downhill skiing. Today, those who are interested in downhill skiing are glad that the judge dealt firmly with Bill Johnson—he became the gold medal winner in Alpine skiing at the 1984 Olympics. The judge was not so tough that he broke Bill, but he was not so tender that he let him get away lightly with his crime.

Tough and tender love is what is needed in our dealings with each other. When we think of God, we remember that he is a God of love, but we must remember that God's love is of the tough variety combined with quiet, loving tenderness.

Prayer

How can we be tough and tender with those we love who need discipline, Lord? You accomplish this all the time. Teach me to do so, too. Amen.

November 24—The Voice of the Lord

Scripture reading: Haggai 1

This passage gives us an excellent example of God's Word entering the picture and turning things around. The people recognized Haggai for what he claimed to be—God's messenger. They listened to what he had to say and they recognized it for what it was—God's message. They demonstrated tremendous reverence for the voice of the Lord, and they obeyed that voice.

One of the most exciting things we can do in our generation is to affirm that God has given us his Word. He has raised up people who will commit themselves to the study of that Word and, in the power of the Holy Spirit, proclaim it to be true. Those who do this are not any different from others. God has simply called and gifted them and appointed them for this particular task. As we hear God's Word through God's servants, we can either say that it is not God's Word—that it is just their bias—or we can say, "Let us hear the voice of the Lord."

Prayer

Lord, people are hungry for truth. So many have not rejected your truth; they haven't had a chance to receive it. Make me a messenger of truth—whatever it takes. Amen.

November 25—Covenant Marriage

Scripture reading: Malachi 2:10-16

The Israelites were far from perfect, which also meant they had less-than-perfect marriages. So Jehovah sent his prophets at regular intervals to remind them about the covenant he had made with them and the covenants they had made with each other before him.

When we make a marriage covenant before God, something is done to us *by* God. He takes two very different people, and in some remarkable way he makes them one. Remember Malachi's words in verse 15: "Has not the Lord made them one?" To make two people one "in spirit" is different from making them one "in flesh." Put in very simple terms, when two people are one "in spirit," it means something far beyond having sex. It means God is binding their two lives together so that over the years, through changing circumstances, they will discover a oneness of spirit that enables them to respond in ways that serve only to deepen their love and commitment to each other. They become more and more integrated into each other's personalities. They begin to see things through each other's eyes. They instinctively think each other's thoughts. Jill even finishes my sentences for me—not always the way I intended, but sometimes better than I could have done it!

Prayer

Thank you, Lord, that you put such a high premium on the covenant of marriage. Help me to remember that marriage is a creation ordinance—a precious eternal idea. Amen.

November 26—Praise Prepares Us

Scripture reading: Job 1:1-5; 2:7-10

Learning to receive the good gifts of God, praising him, and cultivating a thankful attitude in general, gets us into the right frame of mind to accept the problems of life. Job and his family had been the recipients of God's free blessings for seventy years. Their hands had been open wide, stretched out toward heaven to receive all the Lord gave them.

Job refused to take those same outstretched hands and clench them into fists to shake in the face of God when the gifts of grace, health, wealth, and happiness were withheld. After all, the Giver of gifts has a perfect right to give or to withhold. He is under no obligation to us whatsoever. Having been a truly thankful man all his life helped Job when he had nothing to be thankful about. Praise prepares us for problems. It does not keep trouble away, but it gets us ready for trouble when it comes.

Prayer

I praise you for the gift of praise, dear Lord. When I can't praise you for what you allow, help me to praise you for who you are in the midst of what you allow. Amen.

November 27—The Church to the Rescue

Scripture reading: Psalm 82:1-4

There is no shortage of criticism where the church is concerned. If a pastor falls, it is in the news; if a Christian fails, it is all over the grapevine. The very society that sidesteps its guilt before God by saying "Nobody's perfect" is quite perfectionistic when it comes to the church!

While the criticisms leveled at the church by society do have some validity, we must give consideration to another side of the issue. We are called to defend the poor and oppressed. The fact is, the church is making a positive impact on communities. In some segments of our society, the church is the only institution having any kind of effect on the subject of values. Recently I was told by a sociologist working in some of the most troubled major cities in America that, in his experience, the church was the only institution holding some dangerous areas together.

So, while it is unlikely that a lot of help will be coming from the educators, the media, or the politicians, perhaps we can be more hopeful about the church. Perhaps God's people can speak out winsomely and compellingly and cast some sweetness and light on the troubled nature of our culture's values. But what exactly does the church have to say? And is anybody listening?

Prayer

Jesus, I'm so tired of hearing people in the church called hypocrites. But I'm afraid some criticism is justified. Make us holy and blameless and active in helping the needy. Keep us true to our profession. Amen.

November 28—Learning to Teach

Scripture reading: James 3:1-2

Rosie, an elderly Christian woman, was once asked through whose preaching she had been saved. "Nobody's preaching," she replied. "Aunt Mary's practicing." I venture to suggest, however, that if Aunt Mary had not been able to articulate the hows and whys of her own good life and good works, Rosie would not have come to faith herself. We need teachers if we are to understand.

In the Western world, where Christian teachers and leaders are appreciated, affirmed, and even adored, there are tempting traps waiting to pollute their souls and ministries. Therefore, as leaders learn to lead, they must learn to lean—on the One who will teach them to teach, show them how to serve, and keep them thoroughly balanced. The same principle applies to every believer!

When people come to me and say, "I want to do what you do—teach in churches and large meetings," I think of James and his appropriate warnings about "presuming to be teachers." I first advise them to begin to teach in the Sunday school. "No, no," they say. "I don't want to teach Sunday school. I want to speak to large groups, like you do." So I try to tell them how I learned by teaching groups of five or six people sometimes for years. Usually, they are not impressed. Nevertheless, I have learned in all my speaking and teaching, that I need to balance whatever I am doing by meeting regularly with a small group of people and studying the Scriptures together.

Prayer

Lord, serving you takes submission and humility. Please humble me, teach me to lean on you, then use me to exalt you. Amen.

November 29—Spiritual Gold

Scripture reading: Luke 12:13-21

We tried to give our growing children exposure to others' needs. When David, our eldest, was fifteen, he went on a six-week assignment with members of his youth group to New Orleans. There they were "servants" to a mission in the French Quarter. It was hard work and quite a culture shock. They saw life in run-down tenements and ran children's clubs for the street kids. They learned what the other half of the world looks like and lives like. They were not paid, but they came back with spiritual gold, and that is what mattered.

As our children graduated from high school, Stuart arranged to take each one with him on a world missions tour. In Third and Fourth World countries, our children saw poverty, disease, and hopelessness firsthand. They met with missionaries serving God in posts where people lived without God and without hope. They watched missionary professionals laying up treasure in heaven instead of fortunes back home. None of our children returned the same, and it is no surprise to us that they are all in ministry today.

If we spend a lot of time building up spiritual riches with our families, instead of storing up things for ourselves, chances are that we will become "rich toward God."

Prayer

May our children have just enough trouble to drive them to you and just enough stress to turn them to prayer. And may they shed just as many tears as are needed to feel your pain for a lost world. Amen.

November 30—God Is with Us in Temptation

Scripture reading: 1 Corinthians 10:11-13

The Word of God not only records the good in people's characters, it also exposes the bad so that we can better learn to deal with our own shortcomings and temptations.

Temptation is universal. It confronts the best as well as the worst of us. Most of us know this to be true, and yet something inside us finds it hard to accept the reality that good people are tempted and that some of the best people succumb to temptation.

Temptation is not sin; otherwise Jesus could be called a sinner because he was tempted (Matt. 4:1-11). We may not be able to prevent evil thoughts from entering our minds, but we can stop them from settling in and setting up house in our thinking! God has promised to be with us in temptation and see us through it; "he will not let you be tempted beyond what you can bear. . . . he will also provide a way out so that you can stand up under it" (vs. 13). This verse does not promise to deliver us out of the fiery furnace of adversity without first having delivered us in it.

Prayer

You allow temptation, Lord Jesus. As I understand it, the purpose is to strengthen me not destroy me. My part is to resist it in the power of your Holy Spirit. You promised that sin would not have dominion over me. Help me do my part. Amen.

December

December 1—God's Authentic Presence

Scripture reading: Ezekiel 2:1-5

It is a tragic day for any individual or institution when the reality of the Lord's presence is lost and the tangible evidences of his abiding are withdrawn. I am convinced that this is what has happened in innumerable lives and countless institutions.

Many Christians are so wrapped up in themselves that they have lost any real sense of God himself. Many churches are so oriented to catering to the improvement of people's circumstances that they tend to overlook the One whom the psalmist said was "the strength of my heart and my portion forever" (Ps. 73:26). Some countries are proud of God in their heritage and of Christian principles in their roots, yet they so abuse the Lord by chronically neglecting or blatantly disobeying him, that they are hardly recognizable as anything other than pagan cultures.

We must join Ezekiel in the desert dust before God's revelation of himself in order for our fantasies to be replaced by a true perspective and the truth of God.

Prayer

Lord, may my life be distinctive, my service Christlike, and my example a light for those in darkness to follow. Amen.

December 2—Hard Work for the Messenger

Scripture reading: Ezekiel 2:6-10

The Lord told Ezekiel what to expect, as was his custom when sending his servants. He told Ezekiel the way people would look at him, the things they would say to him, and the actions they would take against him. Their faces would be hard, their gaze unflinching, their demeanor unyielding, their attitude unrelenting. Their words would be harsh and bitter, their attacks vicious. It would be like someone running through briars and thorns, being ripped to shreds, and falling exhausted to the ground bleeding and hurting, only to land on a scorpion and be stung.

Ezekiel could anticipate being bitten and ripped, abused and rejected, but he was to go anyway. God's truth must be released and God's people must be exposed to their own condition. God had to do this to be consistent with his own nature. He had to do it to be faithful to his own people. He had to deal with his people so that the nations around would know the truth of God.

Prayer

It's hard, Lord, to tell people what they need to hear when they don't want to hear it. Give me courage. Make me an Ezekiel. Amen.

December 3—The Necessity of the Word

Scripture reading: Ezekiel 3:1-9

There is no doubt that many Christian believers seek fresh experiences with God. More and more people are demonstrating a hunger and thirst for fuller and deeper knowledge of God, yet some of the seeking and much of the desiring is off-center. This is understandable. If the way to spiritual power is through the study and assiduous application of God's Word to our lives, it is obviously going to take a considerable amount of time, effort, and discipline.

On the other hand, our contemporary society is so programmed to expect and demand the instant solution, the immediate answer, and the ready-made maturity that believers have become infected with the same plague. There is a great interest in anything that offers or implies a quick, easy way to success. We are producing many earnest believers who have gone through numerous exciting spiritual experiences but who are still biblically illiterate. They have been led to expect spiritual power and effectiveness without taking the yoke of the Lord Jesus upon them and learning of him.

It was God's Word that made Ezekiel harder than flint against the rebellious hearts of the Israelites. We must be wary of the means to spiritual growth that appear to do away with the necessity for the Word of God.

Prayer

Lord, your Word is a lamp, a light, a seed, a force, honey to my taste, truth for my mind, and a hammer for my hard heart. How could I live without it? Thank you. Amen.

December 4—God Makes Obedience Possible

Scripture reading: Ezekiel 3:10-15

This passage shows another of those important, strange ways of God. When the Lord commands his children to do things, the only valid response is obedience. This requires an act of the will, and nothing ever takes away the necessity for human beings to act in obedience by exercising their wills in line with God's mandates

That necessity for obedience is always present, but the capacity for obedience is often lacking. Many people have assumed that because they do not have the capacity, they are released from the necessity. They say to themselves, *God knows I can't do that, so I will ignore the fact that he told me to do it.* Such an attitude makes it easy to live a life of disobedience and still feel comfortable.

But disobedience is never right, even if we have persuaded ourselves that we cannot obey. If God commands, he demands obedience, but only because he supplies the ability to obey whenever he commands. Ezekiel was commanded to stand when he could not, but as he obeyed the command, he found the strength available.

Prayer

Who can stand, Lord, unless you give the strength? Who can obey unless you motivate the spirit? I am helpless without your help, loveless without your love, and hopeless without your hope. What a Savior you are! Amen.

December 5—Poor and Happy

Scripture reading: Matthew 5:3-5

These three verses are a paradox to the modern mind. They fly right in the face of general opinion. "Blessed are the poor in spirit? Baloney!" says the secular person. "You have to get out there and hack out your own little niche in the wilderness of the world." Though this is a rather simplified translation of society's philosophy, with all due respect, I label this philosophy "baloney."

The United States is filled with people who have lived by this erroneous belief, and they've worked and worked and hacked out their own pieces of the world. They stand on it firmly planted, hands on their hips—and they're still miserable. Happiness does not come from centering one's life around oneself. Blessed happiness comes only to the poor in spirit.

Look at it from God's perspective. When we recognize what we are—sinners—then we are ready to look at God realistically too. When we know our need, then we're interested in what God gives. And what God gives is blessedness and comfort and heaven.

Prayer

Lord, when I forget my poverty of spirit, bring me back to the true picture of who I am and who you are. Help me admit my need and find your blessing. Amen.

December 6—Can We Be Self-Sufficient?

Scripture reading: 2 Chronicles 26:16-23

King Uzziah was a singularly gifted king who did a wonderful job. But then something very subtle began to happen. The more he was successful (because God was enabling him, we are told that quite definitely), the more he began to become convinced of his own ability. In the end he became so self-sufficient that he decided to dispense with God. He did things his own way, in flat contradiction to what God had said.

I would suggest that when any human being arrives at this position of self-sufficiency, he or she has got an overly exalted view of the self. How self-sufficient can a person be who cannot keep himself alive? Think about it. Do you know how to keep yourself alive? One of my favorite verses of Scripture tells me that God is one in "whose hand my breath is" (Dan. 5:23, KJV). I do not wake up in the morning and say, "God, got any breath in your hand for me today?" Because, quite frankly, if he does not, I am through.

Our self-sufficiency is therefore self-delusion. Yet, in how many ways do we act as though we are taking care of ourselves and determining our own destiny?

Prayer

Teach me the dependence that is necessary to live for you. May others see my neediness and recognize that however successful I may be, you are the source of my help. Hold me up, Lord. Amen.

December 7—Seeking Sinners

Scripture reading: Luke 18:9-14

Two men are praying to God, one a "righteous" Pharisee, the other a "sinner"—a tax collector. In New Testament language, a sinner was a person who was openly, blatantly immoral. A sinner was one who flatly ignored God's laws and did not really care that he was doing so. Because Rome turned a blind eye to any extra money taken in by tax collectors for themselves, such people were known as traitors and cheats. To the Jewish community, a tax collector was certainly a sinner.

But Jesus came looking for such people as these. And today God is still looking for sinners of all varieties—those people we know who thumb their noses at authority and morality, those who sell out to the highest bidder, those who do as they like and do not care what others think of them.

Whether we are hardhearted sinners, self-deluded religious folk, or disoriented people whose spirits have deteriorated, God, in Christ, comes looking for all of us.

Prayer

You are the seeking God. I am the lost one—the one who desperately needs finding. Help me to allow you to draw me to yourself. Amen.

December 8—We Are Not Perfect

Scripture reading: James 1:12-18

The evil one wants us to stay in our guilt and sin. He taunts, "Who are you to teach others, or say you're a Christian? Look what you did yesterday!"

Years ago, the youth group at our church put on a play in which the lead actor was a young person straight out of the Jesus Movement. He was very talented. Two days before the play, however, he came to me and said, "I can't do this because I'm out of touch with God and have sinned." Indeed, the problem he shared needed attention. He had stumbled badly. "How can I be in this play and teach others through this drama when I have been such a fool?"

"Go over there," I told him, "and get into touch with God again! Then, after you have repented before God, put right what you can. Make your phone calls and do whatever else you need to do." I reminded him, "Nobody's perfect. However, your responsibility is to show others the devil's trap of telling us that until we are perfect, we can't perform!"

Fortunately, he took my advice and let God cleanse him. Humbled and renewed, this young man was ready to fulfill his assignment, and he did it very well.

Prayer

Keep me in touch, Father, so I can help others to stay in touch too. Harness my renegade spirit. Chain it to your cross. Bring me to my knees in submission. Amen.

December 9—The Power of the Tongue

Scripture reading: James 3:1-12

The tongue is compared to the rudder of a large ship. It has the power to change the direction of our conversation, even our lives and the lives of others. How does this work?

Imagine chatting with a group of people in the church foyer. Somebody says, "Did you know that Mrs. Adam has been appointed head of the Christian education department?" So far so good. There we are, sailing along like a little ship on Lake Placid.

The tongue, however, can steer the conversation any way it wants to go. It could say, for instance, "It's such a pity that her kids are in such trouble. Have you heard?" Suddenly Lake Placid has turned into a whirlpool—and Mrs. Adam is in big trouble. On the other hand, we could say, "Mrs. Adam is a great choice. She can really identify with all of us who have had some bad moments with our kids. She'll be able to help us all a great deal."

If we do not want our words to cause someone a shipwreck, we need to give Jesus the rudder. Have you ever done that? If not, kneel down and yield all of yourself to him, your hands, your feet, your heart, your mind, and your tongue.

Prayer

Lord, here is my tongue. So small an instrument with such power. Control it for me so it is a blessing and not a curse. Amen.

December 10—Not Too Much or Too Little

Scripture reading: Proverbs 30:7-9

The attitude displayed in these verses is incredibly mature. It recognizes the temptations that either a shortage or an excess of money can bring. It sees honoring the Lord as more significant than making money. It admits to inherent weaknesses of character that need to be disciplined. It testifies to a willingness to be content with life's basics rather than chase after life's luxuries.

John D. Rockefeller, the multimillionaire, was at least honest when asked, "What do you want most in life?" His reply: "Just a little more." Most people are critical of this kind of attitude, as many were when professional baseball players in the U.S., who earn an average salary of $1.2 million, went on strike in 1994. The players were accused of greed, and the owners of being just as bad. But given the chance to get "just a little more," how many of their critics would have acted any differently?

Prayer

Help me to want a little more of you, Lord. That will stop me wanting a little bit more of anyone or anything else. Amen.

December 11—Escape from "Me-ness"

Erma Bombeck wrote the following in a newspaper column I clipped years ago:

> During the last year I have dissected my marriage, examined my motives for buying, come to grips with midlife, found inner peace, outer flab, become my best and only friend. I have brought order to my life, meditated, given up guilt, adjusted to the new morality, and spent every living hour understanding me, interpreting me, and loving me. And you know what? I am bored to death of me.

The results of being egocentric are boredom, nonfulfillment, and a bad self-image. It stands to reason that God's creatures—living in God's world, sustained by God, intended by God to live for God—will be pretty miserable divorced from God.

The church at Ephesus had become self-centered and lost their first love. Some Christians seem to flirt with the world for the rest of their lives—thus falling into the "me" trap and putting their relationship with God on hold.

Prayer

Teach me, Lord, to want more "you-ness" and less "me-ness." Meet me at the Cross. That will do it! Amen.

December 12—Keeping a Secret

Scripture reading: Matthew 6:1-4

Every one of us has a tendency to revel in our own self-righteousness. We are quick to justify ourselves by what we do for the Lord and announce our acts of charity. But the Bible says that our righteous acts are like filthy rags at best. God's way is different.

Once we have rejected our self-righteousness and repented, God is then prepared to give us his righteousness in Christ. He is ready to forgive us, restore us, and reconcile us to himself. Then true charity is a product of that divine righteousness.

Jesus is not condemning any public act of piety. He is simply saying our motives must be right. If we do it to be noticed, to bring glory to ourselves, then our motivation is wrong. This is not an excuse to show our humility by doing absolutely nothing, as some people do. Rather, it's a challenge to do it all for God.

Prayer

Keep me from hypocrisy and showiness in my service, Lord. Give me a heart for honoring you whether in private or public acts of giving. Amen.

December 13—God Seeks the Lost

Scripture reading: Luke 19:1-10

I like the story of the young man in England who was driving through the countryside in his spiffy sports car. Seeing an old gentleman at a crossroads, he screeched to a halt and shouted, "I say, do you know how far it is to London?"

"No," said the old gentleman.

"Well, do you know which direction to London?"

"No."

"Can you tell me what time it is?"

"Can't say that I can, young man."

"I say, you don't know much, do you?"

"No, but I'm not lost."

We have all come across people who may know an awful lot, but who still are very lost. All of us have been in the "lost" category at some time. People are made for God, but they have lost God. They may be driving around looking good and sounding intelligent, but they are totally disoriented. They make a wrong decision or base actions on wrong premises and suddenly their lives are in shambles. Sometimes we take stock of our lives and are horrified at how far we have strayed from where we intended to be.

The good news, though, is that people who are lost and wandering and disoriented are just the ones God came to find.

Prayer

O Lord, make me honest enough to look at the journey of life I am taking and admit the wrong turns I've taken. Unravel the mess I make. Show me the way home. Amen.

December 14—Dawn in Our Disobedience

Scripture reading: 2 Peter 1:19-21

I have often talked with people who argue against the Christian gospel on supposedly intellectual grounds. I do not do very well in those situations. I get impatient and tongue-tied. Sometimes such people tie me up in knots. But I often say to them, not *"Do* you believe?" but *"Will* you believe?"

Most of us have reasons for not believing. A part of us just does not want to be good. What we need to say is, "God, I really don't want to be good. Make me want to want to. Dawn in my heart. Forgive me for not wanting to be good." That is where it all begins.

Light transforms everything it touches. Take time to watch the sunrise some morning. Notice how radically the light changes absolutely everything it touches. The dawn of Christ is just like that. Even in all the dark corners of our disobedience, the rising of the Morning Star can transform us.

Prayer

St. Augustine once prayed, "Make me holy—but not just yet," and so often I find myself saying the same thing. Lord, please shine into my darkness and illuminate my mind. Then strengthen me to be good and do good for your sake. Amen.

December 15—Dawn in Our Disappointments

Scripture reading: Luke 1:5-20

The priest Zechariah needed a light to dawn in the midst of disappointment. All his life he had prayed for a child, but now he and his wife, Elizabeth, were old and childless. In his old age he finally got the opportunity to enter the Holy of Holies and present the daily offering. In Zechariah's day, this was a once-in-a-lifetime opportunity.

As Zechariah carefully followed the prescribed temple rituals, an angel appeared to him, frightening him out of his wits. The angel said, "Zechariah, I've come because of your prayer . . . about the baby." And Zechariah probably thought, *Huh? Oh . . . that prayer.* I wonder when he had stopped praying that prayer—undoubtedly years before.

But you see, God never lets your prayers fall to the ground. Years after we have stopped praying, God answers our prayers. Sometimes we do not even recognize when God answers because we have forgotten all about it. But God in his grace answers anyway. So the baby came, and the dawn rose on Zechariah's disappointment.

Are you like Zechariah? Have you been sitting in darkness because of a lifetime of disappointments? Zechariah was not what we would call a bad person; he was quite devout, probably a righteous man in human terms. Yet disappointment had set its shadow over his life. And then the light dawned.

Prayer

When we are living in the darkness engendered by our disappointments, O Lord, teach us to persevere in prayer, believing that one day you will answer us, in your time and in your way. Amen.

December 16—A Time for Giving

Scripture reading: Luke 1:26-38

There could not have been a Christmas without Mary. God needed more than just a devout person, someone who attended synagogue and said her prayers. The Christ child needed a body to live in!

> When God became a baby, he knew he would
>   compress,
> His vastness, glory, all that power, into littleness.
> A baby was the answer, but where to find the one,
> The one who'd say, "Be born in me—
> Oh, let me bear your son"?

Would Mary be the earthly vehicle for God's divine action? "Now wait a minute," the devil must have whispered to her. "You've got everything going for you—you're engaged to be married; what will people say, when you say that your baby is conceived a new way?" But Mary offered the gift of her body. She whispered to the angel Gabriel, "I am the Lord's servant. May it be to me as you have said."

Christmas is a time for giving. The prophets gave their promises. Elizabeth gave her praise. Mary gave her body. Joseph gave his reputation. The innkeeper gave his stable, the shepherds, their time. And God, his Son. Tell me, do you see *your* present there?

Prayer

Lord, our Christianity must be lived out in our bodies. Mary showed us how. Help us to follow her example. Amen.

December 17—Spirit of Christmas or of Christ?

Scripture reading: Luke 2:8-14

I once heard an elderly German man talk about his experiences in World War I. The combat was hand-to-hand in the fields of France, dug into trenches so close to each other that enemies could actually hear each other talking.

One cold Christmas Eve, during the annual Christmas truce, the men were huddled in the bottom of their trenches. Suddenly, from the British trenches, a clear tenor voice began to sing "The Lord Is My Shepherd." Then, from the German side, a rich baritone joined him in German. For a few moments everybody concentrated on the two singing praise to the Shepherd. Early Christmas morning some of the British soldiers climbed out and started kicking a soccer ball around in the no-man's land between the sides. Then some of the German soldiers joined them. England played Germany on Christmas Day in the middle of a French battlefield during a war! But the next morning, the fighting and carnage resumed.

That is how it is with us. The spirit of Christmas will produce a truce, but it does not produce peace. It makes people think of peace and goodwill, but the strain of keeping it up is too great. We need something more. The annual spirit of Christmas must be superseded by the eternal Spirit of Christ. The spirit of Christmas is sentimental; the Spirit of Christ is supernatural. The spirit of Christmas is a human product; the Spirit of Christ is a divine person. That makes all the difference in the world.

Prayer

Lord, your Spirit brings peace in conflict, joy in sorrow. Christmas in our hearts means reconciliation. Teach me my part and make me diligent to follow through. Amen.

December 18—Giving Time, Not Things

Scripture reading: 2 Corinthians 8:1-7

Years ago as Christmas approached, my daughter and I sat down to figure out the family gift list. We came to the conclusion that none of us had everything we wanted, but all of us had everything we needed. The one thing we were all short on was time with each other. That year we decided to try an experiment and give time, not things. This necessitated some creative brainstorming and asking God for good ideas.

"Maybe the boys would enjoy tickets to the basketball game together," Judy suggested. "Perhaps you and I could go to a pretty Victorian tea shop and have English tea and a good talk together," I proposed. We also came up with ideas that cost no money. One way or another that Christmas we managed to give each other the priceless gift of time. After all, Jesus came that first Christmas night to give us his time—thirty-three years of it, to be precise. What a gift!

This Christmas we may not have a lot of riches as the world sees it, but, we can excel in the grace of giving. In giving of ourselves to each other without reservation, as Jesus did when he came to earth, we can all know wealth beyond anything this poor world might have to offer.

Prayer

Father, teach me that my friends and family want *me*, not the things I give them. May I invest in my relationships by giving of myself. Amen.

December 19—The Quest for Truth

Scripture reading: Matthew 2:1-2

These wise men were probably astrologers or astronomers—men highly respected for their wisdom. Astrology is based on the idea that the movement of the stars powerfully influences the affairs of humanity. These men studied the stars to discover truth. They wanted to know something of the hidden, inner workings of the universe.

Beyond their curiosity, however, these men already had some knowledge of the truth. In part, that knowledge probably came through Jews who, in their historic captivities in Egypt, Assyria, and Babylon, had left many pieces of information concerning the Scriptures. So these men had access not only to the insights of astronomy and philosophy, but to the vast riches of the Old Testament as well.

These Magi, presumably from Babylon, went to considerable trouble to find the One to be born king of the Jews. What could possibly have motivated this interest? They seemed to be driven by more than political concerns. Something more significant was motivating their inquiry. And even though they engaged in astrology—which God had specifically forbidden his people to be involved in—the Lord used their faulty understanding to lead them to the truth.

Prayer

Wisdom comes from you, Lord, wisdom that helps me follow the right stars in my search for the Christ. So many people are searching—help them find you. Lead them to Bethlehem. Amen.

December 20—A Diligent Search

Scripture reading: Matthew 2:3-12

When the Magi got to Jerusalem, everything disintegrated. Imagine arriving at your destination after two long years of travel, only to have things fall apart. When the Magi came to King Herod asking about the "one who has been born king of the Jews," the frightened Herod called together the wise men of Jerusalem to find out where the Messiah was to be born. He then secretly met with the Magi, pretending concern for the search, and sent them to Bethlehem. A paranoid, power-hungry murderer, Herod really wanted to exterminate the possibility of this new king.

The wise men had gone to the right place and asked the right questions, but they received the disappointing answer, "He's not here." They might have been discouraged, but they had come this far, and they were not giving up now.

It is interesting to hear people's reasons for putting off their search. One person says she went to church but could not understand the sermon, so she did not go back again. Another person says he heard about someone's uncle who ran off with the church organist, and that is reason enough not to go to any church anywhere. A genuine quest for God involves a lot of looking, reading, listening, and praying. If we are diligent in our search and ask honest questions, God will reveal himself to us, regardless of where we are coming from.

Prayer

O God, you said I would find you when I searched for you with *all* of my heart. Keep me diligent, Lord. Amen.

December 21—The Crossless Crib

Scripture reading: Luke 2:1-7

There is something beautiful and delightful about the birth of the Christ child. In our cynical world we have become accustomed to seeing bloodshed, violence, hatred, and suffering. One of the wonderful things about the Christmas season is that for a few short hours we concentrate not on violence, but on something unbelievably innocent and beautiful—the baby in the crib. The beauty of this baby's birth led to the wonder of the Savior's life.

However, if we concentrate only on the innocent baby's birth, leading to the sinless Savior's life, we arrive at a very unpleasant conclusion: The life Jesus lived ultimately condemns the life *we* live. When we evaluate our lives against that one life, we can only admit the hopelessness and helplessness of our condition. We cannot live as he lived, and we cannot undo the consequences of our own shortcomings.

If we only look at the crib, we arrive at a point of despair. The beautiful crib led to Jesus' majestic and superb example, which leads us to a sense of helpless inadequacy. A crossless crib leads to hopelessness.

Prayer

Thank you, Lord Jesus, that you knew all about the cross when you came to the crib, yet you still came because you loved us. What amazing grace! Amen.

December 22—The Cribless Cross

Scripture reading: John 1:10-14; Hebrews 4:14-16

I suppose that Jesus could have just stepped off his heavenly throne for a moment, come to earth and died for us, and gone straight back to the throne again. He could have bypassed the crib and gone straight to the cross. But God, in Christ, chose to become one of us. The babe was born, went through childhood and adolescence, and grew into young adulthood, managing the same routines and crises that all humans do.

We must never downplay the humanity of our Savior, underscored by his birth in the stable. We can be confident that he understands us and our world. We can pray to him, knowing that he truly knows us and all our needs.

Prayer

Lord, the mystery of the Incarnation leaves me breathless. May I never get over the wonder of it all. Amen.

December 23—The Crownless Crib

Scripture reading: John 17:1-5; Philippians 2:6-8

If we read Scripture very carefully, we will recognize that before the crib there was the "crown" of Jesus. And after the crib, that crown will be placed once more on his head. In other words, the life, ministry, death, and resurrection of our Lord Jesus on earth served as a glorious interlude in the eternal reign of the Lord of all glory.

This baby who was born came from eternity. While he was on earth, he prayed, "Father, glorify me in your presence with the glory I had with you before the world began" (John 17:5). We cannot really consider the Son of God in the crib apart from the Son seated on the throne of heaven. We should always beware of the doctrine of the crownless crib. For if we forget the crown, we will lose our sense of who Jesus really is.

Prayer

Jesus, you are King! May Christmas fill me with the wonder of that truth. Amen.

December 24—The Crib, Cross, and Crown

Scripture reading: Romans 6:1-11

The Lord Jesus explained that membership in God's kingdom involved being born from above. The apostle Peter says that we must be born anew, have a new seed in us, and become partakers of the divine nature. In short, Christians need to be clear that there is a crib in our lives—the miracle of regeneration. Just as the eternal Son of God was born in a stable, so the risen Christ is born in us.

But the crib is not enough. If Christ has been born in us, we must grow and mature as his disciples. Jesus said, "If anyone would come after me, he must deny himself and take up his cross daily and follow me" (Luke 9:23). "Taking up our cross" means submitting our wills to God's will. We must identify with the will of God as surely as Christ identified himself with the eternal purposes of the Father.

For believers there is not only a crib and a cross, but the sure promise of a crown. We will live through all eternity with the risen, ascended King of kings, who will wear a glorious crown. And we too will receive crowns for faithful service to him.

Those without a crib have yet to experience new life in Christ. Those without a cross have not given over their self-centered lives in exchange for the abundant God-centered life. And those without a crown have no depth or sense of hope. Crib, cross, and crown—are all three present in your life?

Prayer

Lord, I welcome the crib and the crown into my life. It's the cross I balk at. May I gladly pay the price necessary in order to honor you. Amen.

December 25—Responding to the Christ Child

Scripture reading: John 1:11-14

We have come to the manger and we have met God there. We have begun to understand what it means that he came to visit us. The man Jesus said, and continues to say, "Open your life to me. Allow me to come in and bring light into your darkness, life to your deadness, and truth to your confusion. Repent of your old way of life. Commit yourself, your life, your future, to me." The coming of that Christ child ultimately means that we have a decision to make.

And, while we talk sentimentally about peace on earth and goodwill toward all, the Bible tells us that peace and goodwill can happen only from the inside out. The Christ child must be born within each one of us. And only the Holy Spirit can release us from the power of our sin, self-delusion, and lostness. Only as his light dawns within us and begins to transform every aspect of our lives can we become all that we were meant to be.

Prayer

Transform me from the inside out, Lord. May others see your face stamped on my spiritual features. May there be no mistaking the image of Christ. Amen.

December 26—A Glorious Epiphany

Scripture reading: Matthew 24:30–31

Christ's initial epiphany was an unbelievable demonstration of grace and the means of our salvation. We cannot save ourselves from the past or the unknown consequences of the future. We cannot make ourselves fit for heaven without this initial appearing of God in our midst. Christ was the ambassador from heaven, holding within himself the means of getting us there.

How shall we live then in light of this first appearing? With gratefulness for salvation, a desire to live holy lives, and with a new ability to say no to the things that drag us away from God's will.

How shall we live then in light of Christ's appearing yet to come? With greater passion to live pure lives in anticipation of his coming. We must give an account for the salvation purchased for us at such a great price. We will live with hope and joy, confident that the God-man, whose first appearance radically transformed the very fabric of our lives, is coming again in power and glory.

The babe who came to us in a lowly manger will appear again in awesome glory. This, indeed, is the glorious epiphany.

Prayer

I praise you, Lord Jesus, that your first coming was as a baby to bring salvation. May I now live in the light of your coming again in glory. Amen.

December 27—Steps to True Wisdom

Scripture reading: Proverbs 2:1-6

Wisdom does not grow on trees; neither does the fear of the Lord just happen. There are steps to be taken, as outlined in these verses. Wisdom is the result of not only desire but active seeking. Fools despise wisdom—they do not want to be told anything. Each of us must decide whether or not we want to be bothered with what God says. There is resistance in our hearts—a naturally rebellious streak that never really wants to be told what to do.

Sometimes it takes a mammoth step for us to start looking at things God's way after a lifetime of doing it our own way. For many people it takes a monumental crisis for them to begin to look at where society's values have taken them and likewise to take a hard look at what God has said. A friend of mine who had lived a number of years in a rebellious, independently minded attitude, said that it was only when he "became sick and tired of being sick and tired" that he returned to the principles he had rejected in adolescence after learning them in childhood.

Prayer

Father, I know what's right, and I know what's wrong. I thank you for a spiritual heritage that taught me these things. Help me resist the temptation to reject what I know is truth. Amen.

December 28—Hanging Up Your Harp?

Scripture reading: Psalm 137

Have you ever hung your harp on a weeping willow tree? In other words, have you ever lost your joy? God's people had forgotten what it was like to sing. They mourned their captivity by the rivers of Babylon. The Babylonians taunted them, saying, "Sing us one of the songs of Zion!" The people of Israel replied bitterly, "How can we sing the songs of the Lord while in a foreign land?" Their response reminds me of the bitter comment of a lady who was in the midst of a sticky divorce: "Don't tell me to praise the Lord. He let my husband walk out on me!"

It is hard to sing the Lord's song in a foreign land. How many of us have been carried into situations we would never have chosen for ourselves? People who do not share our faith in Jesus Christ are always eager to see how we do in such circumstances. They expect us to handle it with Christian fortitude and serenity, and some will even be so bold as to tell us that. Somehow, I think they have the right to ask us for a song. After all, if the people of God cannot make music in their misery, who can? But we will not find that song on our own. The Music Maker will have to compose it for us.

Prayer

Lord, there are so many places where I lose our joy, yet these very places can be the music room where I practice songs of praise. Teach me to sing a song of Zion when you allow me to be carried into a "foreign" land. Amen.

December 29—Peace Like a River

Scripture reading: Isaiah 48:17-22

"Peace like a river" enables us to know wellness of soul. This wellness is not a feeling that suddenly envelopes us, but rather the sense of well-being that comes from knowing everything is under control. This control is related to the Lord in his capacity as the One who "teaches you what is best" and "directs you in the way you should go." But, of course, this teaching, directing, and commanding requires a willing spirit and a glad submission to his benevolent direction.

It should never be forgotten that Isaiah immediately goes on to state that there is "no peace . . . for the wicked." Those who reject what is best and go where they should not go, disregarding the principles of God, will understandably know nothing of peace.

It is rather like getting a new car. When the oil is changed regularly, the tires kept at the correct pressure, and the moving parts properly lubricated, there will be a sense of well-run order. But if the old oil is left to clog up the works and underinflated tires are run for miles, soon things will begin to fall apart, and the car will not move smoothly like a river, but more like a capsized canoe in a cataract. The tranquility of order is only for those who carefully order their lives according to the principles of the God of order.

Prayer

Father, you have given me a manual of behavior to follow. I have all the direction that I need in your Word. Give me determination to walk in your statutes and so find your peace. Amen.

December 30—Into God's Arms

Scripture reading: Psalm 17:5-9

A train was rattling along the track from one city to another. It carried a full load, and the journey was a long one. In one car the passengers' boredom was alleviated slightly by the entertainment afforded by a small child who flitted from one person to another, smiling and chattering away. She was a personable and sociable little girl, and the passengers began to wonder who her parents were. It was hard to tell, as she gave her attention to each and every one in turn. The passengers, however, were not left wondering for long. Suddenly the train whistled and entered a long, dark tunnel. The little girl flew across the car, straight into the arms of her father!

When trouble comes, the world needs to see us flying into our Father's arms. People are desperate for that example. We need to show them there is a place to hide when we suddenly enter the long, dark tunnel, and they need to hear from us that the arms we run to are loving ones. In our refusal to charge God with a spiteful spirit, we publicly profess our belief that God is good.

Prayer

When trouble comes calling, may I be found flying out of myself and into your arms, Lord. This way those who watch will see my source of strength and give you glory. Amen.

December 31—Trusting through Trouble

Scripture reading: 1 Peter 5:8-11

When I was a child during the Second World War, a particularly vicious air raid resulted in our piling into the car and moving as far away from the bombs as we could. Seeing that everyone was doing the same thing, my father moved us to a sturdy little cabin cruiser until he could find suitable housing on land in our new environment. We loved living on the lake and the early morning swims.

I will never forget breaking the thin film of ice on the lake as winter came. It made us gasp and splutter, and Mother would cook extra bacon and eggs, knowing what the experience would do to our appetites. No matter that we knew how cold that water was and no matter how equipped we believed we were to face it, no amount of mental preparation could help us with the actual experience of jumping into that cold water.

In the same way, no matter how well we think we have prepared ourselves for the troubles we know will be our lot, no matter how much we have rehearsed our part, the actual experience takes our breath away. We are never fully equipped, outside of the grace of God, which comes to us moment by moment, just when we need it.

Prayer

Lord, sometimes life takes our breath away. May we always have enough left to praise you with. Give us the grace to sing songs in the night. Amen.

Other books available from Shaw Publishers:

Stuart Briscoe

The Apostles' Creed
Discipleship for Ordinary People
The Fruit of the Spirit
The Fruit of the Spirit (Fisherman Bible Studyguide)
Genuine People
Men of Honor and Influence
Nine Attitudes That Keep a Christian Going and Growing
Philippians
Secrets of Spiritual Stamina
The Sermon on the Mount
The Ten Commandments
The Ten Commandments (Fisherman Bible Studyguide)
Titus
Transforming the Daily Grind

Jill Briscoe

Renewal on the Run
Running on Empty
There's a Snake in My Garden

Stuart and Jill Briscoe

Living Love
Marriage Matters!
Meet Him at the Manger